Wollaton Hall

An Archaeological Survey

WOLLATON HALL

An Archaeological Survey

by

Pamela Marshall

with drawings by

D. Taylor

Nottingham Civic Society

1996

For Maurice

ISBN: 0 9504861 8 3

Designed and Typeset by Philip Dixon
in 12/16 and 10/12.5 Times New Roman bodytext
Using Aldus PageMaker 5.0

Front cover: *The south facade of Wollaton Hall. (Photo by Pamela Marshall.)*

Printed by Technical Print Services Ltd, Nottingham, England

Contents

Introduction	1
1 History of the house	5
2 Description of the house	9
3 An analysis, floor by floor	18
4 Survey of the house	48
1 structure and fabric	48
2 room by room survey	50
3 underground works	81
Appendix I: The Household Inventories	94
Inventory table	110
Appendix II: Geophysical Survey of the Gatehouse Area *by Dr Patrick Strange*	112
Appendix III: A Note on the Wollaton Bricks *by Dr Ron Firman*	114
Bibliography	115

List of Illustrations

Key Plan I (fold out from back page)
Key Plan II: Inventory of October 1601 . . . . **95**
Key Plan III: Inventory of October 1596 . . . . **100**
Key Plan IV: Inventory of December 1596 . . . . **104**
Key Plan V: Inventory of October 1599 . . . . **106**
Key Plan VI: Inventory of September 1609 . . . .**108**

Colour Plates, between pages 10 and 11
Front cover: The south facade of Wollaton Hall
plate 1: Wollaton Hall from the north-west
plate 2: A bird's eye view of Wollaton Hall from a painting by Jan Siberechts, 1697
plate 3: A turret pavilion seen from the roof of the central tower
plate 4: The High Hall or Prospect Room, looking west
plate 5: The Great Hall and Screen
plate 6: A cutaway drawing of Wollaton Hall c.1590
plate 7: The Screen
plate 8: The Regency Saloon
plate 9: The hammer beam roof in the Great Hall
plate 10: Hammer beam roof: detail
plate 11: Hammer beam roof: detail
plate 12: Wyatville's entrance hall
plate 13: The north state staircase

Illustrations
Ill. 1. Location Plan of Wollaton Hall **3**
Ill. 2. Sir Francis Willoughby, builder of Wollaton Hall **4**
Ill. 3. Cassandra Willoughby. **8**
Ill. 4. Perspective elevation drawing of a corner of Wollaton Hall by Smythson **10**
Ill. 5. Design drawing of Wollaton Hall by Smythson. **11**
Ill. 6. The south wall of room 4/14, incorporating robbed Romanesque masonry. **12**
Ill. 7. Axonometric drawing of the leads (level 1). **13**
Ill. 8. Plan of the High Hall or Prospect Room. **14**
Ill. 9. A buttress on the central tower. **14**
Ill. 10. An elevation drawing by Wyatville c.1823 showing the proposal for a servants' wing **15**
Ill. 11. The corridor to a mezzanine level suite of rooms built over the Long Gallery c.1809 . . . . . **16**
Ill. 12. Reconstructed plan of the Tudor ground floor (level 3). **18**
Ill. 13. Axonometric drawing of the Tudor ground floor. **19**
Ill. 14. Smythson's design drawing for the screen. **20**
Ill. 15. Phased plan of the ground floor (level 3). **22**
Ill. 16. Plan of Wollaton Hall from Britton's *Architectural Antiquities* **23**
Ill. 17. The service staircase. **24**
Ill. 18. A design drawing by Wyatville for wainscotting in the Great Hall, 1832. . . . . **25**
Ill. 19. Reconstructed plan of the Tudor first floor (level 2) **26**
Ill. 20. Axonometric drawing of the Tudor first floor. **27**
Ill. 21. Phased plan of the first floor (level 2). **28**
Ill. 22. The central Tower and half roof viewed from the leads. **29**
Ill. 23. Timber staircase built during Phase 2 to link the first floor with the leads. **30**
Ill. 24. Reconstructed plan of the Tudor basement (level 4). **32**
Ill. 25. Axonometric drawing of the basement. **33**
Ill. 26. Corridor in the 'Yeomens' Lodgings'. **34**

Ill. 27. Doorway from the western courtyard into the Lobby/Servery (4/1). 35
Ill. 28: The 'inner kitchen' (4/4). 35
Ill. 29. External door to the Tudor wine cellar. 36
Ill. 30. Blocked external doorway to the Tudor ale cellar (4/9). 36
Ill. 31. Phased plan of the basement (level 4). 37
Ill. 32. Chimney disguised in a baluster on the leads. 38
Ill. 33. Mezzanine level dormitory under the vault of the Tudor ale cellar. 38
Ill. 34. Wyatville's roughly drawn plan for the service extension c.1823. 38
Ill. 35. The main passage in the eastern sewer system. 39
Ill. 36. Culvert linking a garderobe in the south-east tower with the main sewer. 39
Ill. 37. Location plan of the underground works. 40
Ill. 38. Perspective elevation of the east side of the house, showing underground works. 42
Ill. 39. Perspective elevation of the west side of the house, showing underground works. 43
Ill. 40. Subterranean Ale Cellar. 44
Ill. 41. Staircase leading to the 'caves' system from the Tudor ale cellar. 45
Ill. 42. Rock-cut cistern known as the 'Admiral's Bath'. 45
Ill. 43. View of the main passage in the 'caves' system. 45
Ill. 44. Plan and sections of the 'Caves' system. 46
Ill. 45. Spring fed well in the 'caves' system. 47
Ill. 46. Niche with shell motif in the High Hall. 52
Ill. 47. Joint types used in the High Hall floor. 52
Ill. 48. Plan of mezzanine level suite over the north end of the Long Gallery and north chamber. . . 54
Ill. 49. Plan of mezzanine level suite over the south end of the Long Gallery and south chamber. . . 55
Ill. 50. Original joist arrangement in the south Great Chamber. 57
Ill. 51. Joint type used in the south Great Chamber. 58
Ill. 52. Plan of mezzanine level suite over the north-east corner chamber 64
Ill. 53. Plan of mezzanine level suite over the Buttery and Pantry. 66
Ill. 54. An abortive plan by Wyatville for the western service extension c.1823. 73
Ill. 55. Plan of mezzanine level floor inserted into the Tudor Ale Cellar (4/9). 74
Ill. 56. Plan and sections of the eastern sewer system. 80
Ill. 57. Plan and sections of the western sewer system. 82
Ill. 58. Plan and sections of the western sewer system beneath the subterranean Ale Cellar. 84
Ill. 59. Plan of the subterranean Ale Cellar. 89
Ill. 60. Sections and elevations of the subterranean Ale Cellar. 90
Ill. 61. Sections and elevations of the subterranean Ale Cellar. 91
Ill. 62. Elevation of the east wall of the subterranean Ale Cellar. 92
Ill. 63. General plan showing the location of the geophysical survey. 114
Ill. 64. Processed results of the geophysical survey. 115
Ill. 65. Interpretative sketch of the geophysical survey. 115

Preface

Until this publication Wollaton Hall had no definitive history and no proper archaeological survey of its structure, detailed construction and services. The late Professor Maurice Barley had a long lasting ambition to complete a proper archaeological survey and was responsible for initiating the work so ably completed by Pamela Marshall working together with Nottingham University.

The Nottingham Civic Society have financed the survey and the publication and have dedicated it to the memory of Maurice, who was a founder member of the Society. Maurice became Chairman for many years and then continued to guide the work of the Society as President. His inspiration and tenacity - he was known as indefatigable - has enabled his successors to continue the struggle for a better and more beautiful City of Nottingham.

Creating a more beautiful Nottingham involves promoting better modern architecture, as well as retaining that essential respect for the past. Maurice believed in gradual change and in his lecture 'The End of an Era' condemned massive comprehensive developments and consigned them to the past. It is our wonderful legacy of historical buildings which makes Nottingham, Nottingham.

Above ground archaeology was Maurice Barley's passion - buildings, particularly domestic architecture. When he rescued Severns, a medieval house on Middle Pavement and moved it to its present site by the Castle Gatehouse, he did so not for himself but for future generations of students.

Our heritage of buildings becomes more and more valuable and provides that essential link with the past which gives us a real sense of identity with our City.

Robert Cullen

Acknowledgements

Many people have contributed to this work by their co-operation, encouragement and advice. Particular thanks are due to G.Walley, D.Biggs and all the staff of the Wollaton Hall Natural History Museum, who have not merely tolerated the disturbance caused to them during the course of the survey, but have always shown the utmost interest in its progress and findings.

I am grateful to Dr P.Dixon, Mr D.Durant, and Dr M.Girouard for their willingness to discuss the work and for their helpful comments. Thanks are also due to Dr D.Johnston and the staff of the Department of Manuscripts and Special Collections at the Hallward Library, University of Nottingham. Conversations with J.Key, Nottingham City Mason, and P.Coveney of Nottingham City Engineers Department have been invaluable. Lord Middleton and Mr Middleton have graciously allowed the reproduction of paintings and manuscripts, as has the Royal Architectural Library, R.I.B.A., London. The photographic skills of P.Dixon and C.Salisbury contributed further to the illustrations. D.Wain and M.Mahoney braved less than salubrious conditions to assist with the survey of the drains and underground works not only without a murmur, but with enthusiasm.

The survey was made possible by the Civic Society of Nottingham, whose committee and members should all receive credit. Special acknowledgement, however, is due to Ken Brand who has stalwartly read and re-read the drafts and who has seen the work through to publication. My final acknowledgement is to the instigator of the project, Professor Maurice Barley who was an inspiration to me and who is sadly missed.

INTRODUCTION

Wollaton Hall, set dramatically on the crest of a hill amid extensive parkland (plate 1, ill. 1), has remained a Nottinghamshire landmark since its completion in 1588. Commissioned by Francis Willoughby and designed by Robert Smythson, it has been both praised and criticised for its flamboyant and innovative style, and has attracted the attention of travellers, antiquarians and scholars from the 17th century to the present day. This great house has been the object of considerable research. Historians have studied the archives while architectural and art historians have placed the house in context on the basis of both style and plan. The purpose of the present study was not to repeat this work, but to adopt a different approach. By using detailed archaeological survey, it was hoped to investigate the original form and function of the house and to arrive at a better understanding of the changes which were introduced from the late 17th century onwards. This work was sponsored by the Nottingham Civic Society, under the direction of a working party called together by the late Professor M.W.Barley[1] and was carried out by members of the Department of Archaeology, University of Nottingham.

[1] The members of the working party were Professor Barley, Dr Rosalys Coope, Dr Philip Dixon, Mr David Durant, Mr Alan McCormick, and Dr Peter Tregenza.

The Scope of the Survey

The main building was surveyed in detail by the author. Floor plans (**illustrations 12,19,24**) and axonometric views (**ills 7, 13, 20, 25**) of the reconstructed Elizabethan house were drawn, as well as phased plans of the house as it now stands (**ills 15, 21, 31**). From this reconstruction an analysis of the original function of most rooms was possible with the help of some surviving household inventories. These not only list the contents of the rooms, but occasionally indicate the existence of features now lost.

At this time a cursory survey of extensive underground works ancillary to the house revealed the need for further investigation, for these had never received any attention. A second phase of work was therefore carried out assisted by David Taylor, the project draughtsman. The general location of these structures is shown on **Ill. 37** and they comprise the following:-

• Two independent sewer systems, one on the east and the other on the west side of the house. These belong to the original build, although there are some secondary features attached to them.

• A large subterranean ale cellar built by the north-west corner of the building during Phase 2 (late 17th to early 18th century). This also has some later additions.

• A cellar system which was tunnelled through the natural rock on the east side of the house and partially lined with brick. The dating of this is more problematical

Additional contributions were made to the survey by Dr Patrick Strange of the Department of Electrical Engineering and Dr R.Firman of the Department of Archaeology, both of the University of Nottingham. Dr Strange carried out a geophysical resistivity survey on the north side of the house in an attempt to verify the position of a gatehouse and arcaded walkway which are clearly shown on Smythson's surviving design plan. A demolition layer was indicated and the full results are given in Appendix II. Dr Firman examined the fabric of the bricks used in the Hall and ancillary structures, and his note is given in Appendix III.

Other Sources

Documentary evidence used in conjunction with survey findings included various plans, letters, drawings and pictures, which are mentioned in the text where relevant. Building accounts have survived for the years 1582 - 1588, but those of 1580-82, the first two years of construction, are missing. There are also some accounts of extraordinary expenditure. Five Tudor and Stuart household inventories were of particular value in attempting a functional analysis of the rooms and in reconstructing parts of the original house where less archaeological evidence has survived.[2] These documents are housed in the Middleton Collection in the Documents Division of Nottingham University Library. Information from the household inventories is included in Appendix I. Further 16th and 17th century documents have survived only at second hand in a family history compiled by Cassandra Willoughby between about 1690 and 1720, based on 'the Pedigree, old Letters, and old Books of Accounts in my Brother Sir Thomas Willoughby's study'.[3]

Using the Survey: Labelling of Rooms

Wollaton Hall is a complex building, both because of its size and also because its largely symmetrical plan has given rise to the repetition of similar chambers, staircases and service rooms. Some rooms have easily identifiable names, (e.g. Prospect Room, Great Hall), but this does not apply to many and some names have changed over the centuries. Other chambers appear in the inventories bearing the personal names of their then current occupants. Although the names of rooms are given where known, to ensure that identification is quite unambiguous each room has a survey reference number. This is used throughout the text, on plans or in the Inventory Table.

The key to this numbering system is as follows:-

The first digit identifies the floor, according to the following scheme:

- Level 1 = Above the leads or half roof. This includes the central tower and turret chambers standing on the leads.
- Level 2 = The first floor, where the state rooms were located.
- Level 3 = The ground floor (that is main entrance level).
- Level 4 = The basement, where the services were housed.

The next digit identifies a particular room on that floor: for example, room 4/2 is number 2 on floor 4 (the basement).

Corridors and stairs are separately treated: the letter S refers to a staircase. The state staircases are identified as NS (North staircase) and SS (South staircase) The main service stair is referred to as WS (West staircase).

Where additional Roman numerals are appended, these refer to adjacent spaces or to mezzanine floors. Thus the number '4/WSi' would refer to a short stretch of corridor (i) attached to the Western staircase (WS) in the basement (4). Mezzanine floors are numbered with reference to the chamber **above** which they lie, so that '4/3i' refers to a mezzanine level chamber (i) over room 3 in the basement (4).

Using the Household Inventories

The complexity of Wollaton makes it a difficult building in which to follow a description even for those who are very familiar with it. The household inventories have been presented in Appendix I in the form of a table and as room lists transcribed from the original documents. Because they are so important to understanding the function of the house, they have been related to the survey in the following ways so that the reader might be able to refer to them as she/he follows the text.

---

[2] A further inventory of 1599 (Mi I 8ii) has not been included as it deals only with the kitchen. Another, of September 1599, has been omitted as it gives only a list of goods without mentioning rooms. In any case it is likely that these were compiled in relation to the October 1599 inventory, which has been included.

[3] Volume 1 of this work (Mi LM 26) was published in part by H.M.C. Historic Documents, 1911. Volume 2 (Mi LM 27) was published by A.C.Wood, 1958.

Ill. 1 (opposite): The Location of Wollaton Hall

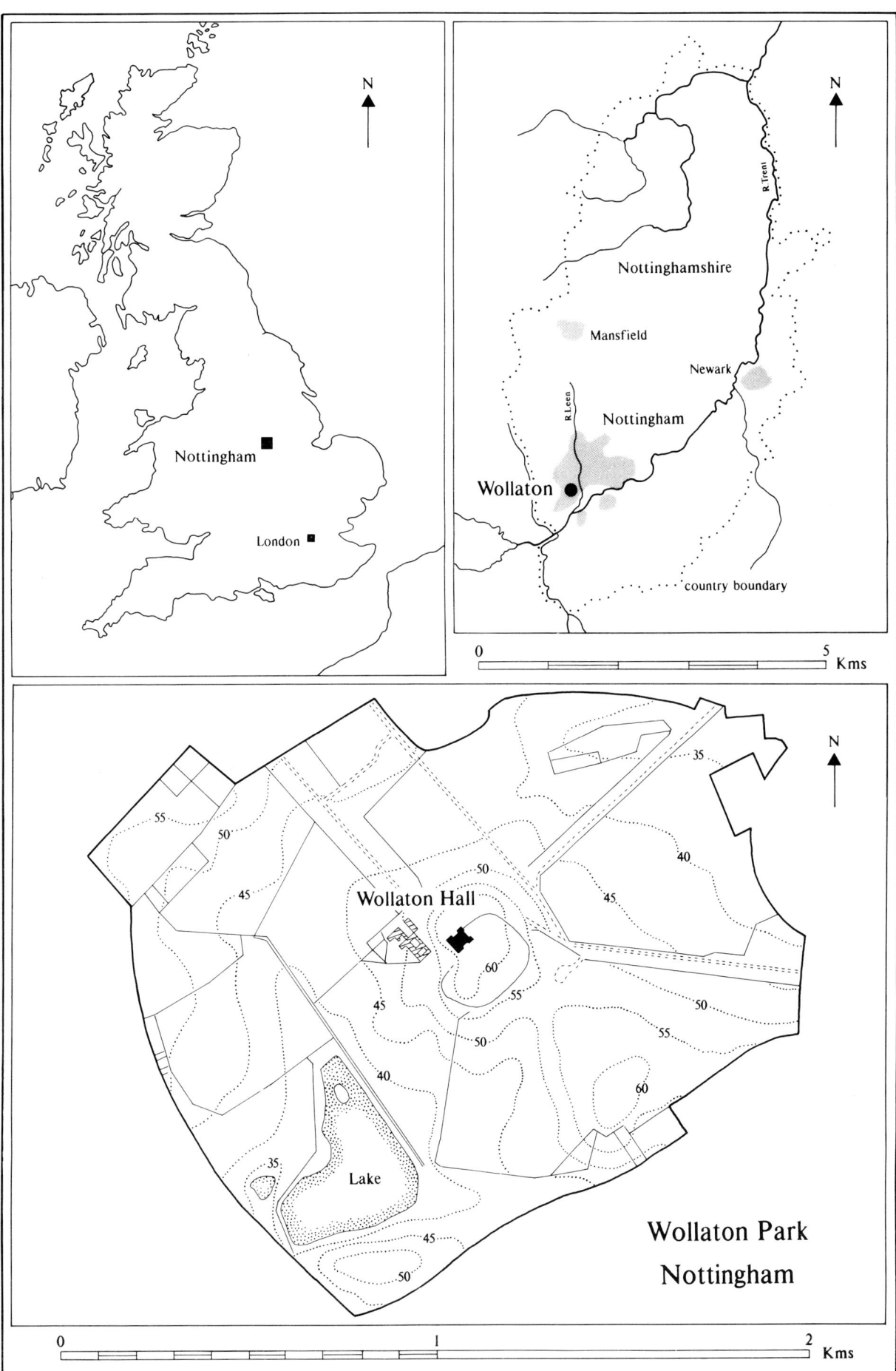

1. Inventory Table (pages 110-111)

The Inventory Table includes all rooms which are mentioned in the inventories. If a room is included this is indicated by the words **Inventory Table** in brackets after its heading in the Room by Room Survey (Chapter 4). Quick reference can then be made to the **key plan**, which folds out from the back page, to find out where the room was, then to the table itself to find out which of the inventories included that particular room and by what name(s). The Inventory Table works in the following way:-

- The vertical columns each represent a single inventory and the horizontal rows represent individual rooms.

- Some rooms do not figure in every inventory, so there are some blank spaces.

- The rooms are identified in the first column by their survey numbers.

- The number in the bottom right-hand corner of each entry indicates the **order** in which the room was listed in that particular inventory, since this often has some bearing on the identification of an individual room.

- A key diagram shows quickly where a room was located in the house without referring to the main plans. This folds out from the back page.

2. Inventory Room Lists (Appendix I)

The rooms in each inventory are listed in the order in which they appear in the relevant document. They are named as in the documents, although most have also been identified by their survey number and have a short commentary. A key plan accompanies each list to make it easier to follow an individual inventory. The numbers here correspond with the **order of appearance** in the original document, so they match the **subscript** numbers in the Inventory Table.

The inventories have been fully transcribed, excepting that of September 1609, which is presented as a room list only.[4] The original spelling of the manuscripts has been used. As the interpretation of some rooms in the earlier inventories relies on clearer information from the inventory of October 1601, this has been listed first and the other documents have then been listed in chronological order.

[4] *A full transcription of this inventory can be found in HMC (1911), 485-91*

Ill.2: Sir Francis Willoughby, builder of Wollaton Hall; prtrait by George Gower, by courtesy of Lord Middleton

1: HISTORY OF THE HOUSE

[1] *The following short account is intended merely to summarize the fuller treatment in works referred to in the footnotes, with greater emphasis on the structural development of the building than was appropriate there.*

The present Wollaton Hall is at least the second great house to have been built in the manor which the Willoughby family had owned since the early fourteenth century.[2] The old hall was situated on the edge of the village near the parish church of St. Leonard and had been built by earlier landlords, the Morteyns. It is likely that the Willoughbys would have added to and altered the building, if indeed it was not rebuilt by them. The family retained its use for some forty years after the completion of the new Hall;[3] it was then converted to estate workers' cottages and was not finally demolished until 1671. Unfortunately no record of its form remains, but it was probably a fairly typical example of a late Medieval vernacular manor house. A substantial timber-framed building is shown in the far distance in Siberechts' painting of Wollaton Hall (plate 2), which might be a representation of the old family home, although the painting was executed over twenty years after its demolition.

[2] Smith (1988) 1.
[3] Strauss (1978) 11.

[4] *Mark Girouard has written a definitive account of Smythson's career (1983).*
[5] *ibid, 40.*
[6] *ibid, 82.*
[7] *ibid, 108.*
[8] *Smith (1988) 19.*

[9] *Detailed analyses of these on both the plan and ornament at Wollaton have already been published and lie outside the scope of this work. The reader is referred to Girouard (1983), 88-107; Durant (1972) 13-16; Friedman (1989) 72-102 and 108-134.*

The new Hall (plate 1) was built for Sir Francis Willoughby between 1580 and 1588, at a distance of about one mile from the village on an elevated site within parkland created by enclosure by Sir Henry Willoughby half a century earlier (ill. 1). The house commanded views of distant Nottingham and the surrounding countryside and was itself supremely visible for miles. The intention was clearly not only to replace a rather outdated family home, but to produce a building in a class of its own. The architect was Robert Smythson,[4] who already possessed some reputation as a master mason in 1568 when he went to work at Longleat House in Wiltshire with good references from Humphrey Lovell, Master Mason to the Queen. At this date Smythson had his own gang of five skilled workmen.[5] Later he carried out renovations at Wardour Castle, the seat of Willoughby's brother-in-law, Sir Matthew Arundell, and it was doubtless through this family connection that he came to work at Wollaton. Smythson later went on to design and build many more country houses, including Hardwick Hall for Elizabeth, Countess of Shrewsbury, and Worksop Manor, a hunting lodge, also for the Shrewsbury family. Despite his advancing age, he might have had some influence on the plan of Bolsover Castle which his son John designed for the Cavendish family. At Wollaton he probably enjoyed greater independence as a designer than he had hitherto experienced,[6] but his full expression had to wait for these later buildings, for there is no doubt that his patron's tastes were brought strongly to bear on the style of Wollaton Hall.[7] This is also true of the working plan. The whole building must be seen as a collusion between patron and architect, the former dictating the criteria of accommodation and taste which the latter strove to incorporate into a workable whole. The result is a house which combines innovation with conservatism to a remarkable degree. In late 16th century Nottinghamshire Wollaton Hall must have stunned its beholders, few of whom could have seen anything remotely comparable, yet internally the house was designed to work according to the strict conventions of late medieval domestic planning.

Sir Francis Willoughby (ill. 2) was the owner of an extensive library, including many volumes on architecture from different parts of Europe.[8] The new hall embraced many of the new influences which were to revolutionise architectural taste in England.[9] It can be argued that it embraced too many. Pilasters, friezes, niches, cartouches, elaborate Dutch gables and bartizans all vie with each other for attention, while the Renaissance lines of the fenestration employed on most of the house revert to late Gothic on the central tower.[10] The overall impression resembles a piece of confectionery, perhaps an over-elaborate wedding cake. Queen Adelaide liked it very much and is reported to have said that the house was so beautiful it should be kept under a glass case to protect it from the elements.[11] Nevertheless, many critics have found the eclecticism displayed in the treatment of the external elevations too overpowering. Girouard attributed this excess partially to Smythson's inexperience, but also in some measure to the character of the patron, summing up the building as an unbalanced house built by an unbalanced man, with something of the quality of a nightmare.[12]

Naturally the new Hall excited admiration and attracted comment, some censorious of Willoughby's extravagance. In 1600 William Camden wrote of Wollaton, 'Sir Francis Willoughby, knight, out of ostentation to show his riches, built at vast charges a very stately house, both for the splendid appearance and curious workmanship of it.'[13] By the time the Hall was completed Sir Francis' riches had been converted to debt amounting to almost £12,000 on which he was paying 10% compound interest yearly.[14] Immediately after the knight's death, his chaplain wrote of his fear that the family would be made a laughing-stock if his daughter and her husband, heirs to the estate, did not take up residence at the Hall, which, 'now called Willoughby's Glory, would, if not dwelt in, soon be termed Willoughby's Folly.'[15]

Sir Francis Willoughby's family was not *nouveau riche*. It descended from a successful Nottingham merchant, Ralph Bugge, who invested in land at Willoughby-on-the-Wolds during the thirteenth century.[16] The manors of Wollaton and Cossall were acquired by judicious marriages during the early 14th century and further lands were accumulated in Warwickshire, Herefordshire and Lincolnshire. By now well established amongst the gentry, the family maintained a second seat at Middleton in Warwickshire but, as the influence of Sir Henry Willoughby (c.1451-1528) became paramount in the county of Nottinghamshire, Wollaton became their chief residence. As early as the 1490s he was exploiting coal reserves on his estates, in the vanguard of 16th century industrial expansion.[17] His career raised the standing of the family to courtly level, although his ambition was apparently contented with local rather than national prominance. A. Cameron commented that he raised the family to 'something more than gentry and less than nobility'.[18] For the rest of the 16th century the Willoughbys maintained this position, apparently with little effort and without entering into the political intrigues of the age.[19] Despite some fall in land revenues and the exhaustion of the early surface pits, Francis Willoughby inherited a considerable fortune in 1559.[20] He was a younger son, unexpectedly inheriting on his brother's premature death, and the magnificent Hall he built at Wollaton cannot be truly understood without some reference to his strong willed and somewhat eccentric character.

Much of Willoughby's life proved unhappy. Orphaned at two years, he was brought up with his sister in the household of George Medley, his mother's step-brother. Although his guardian maintained a well-appointed household and gave the children a good education, his elder brother Thomas, who stood to inherit the family fortune, was placed with the Marquis of Dorset, later to become Duke of Suffolk. Throughout his life Francis appears to have been jealous of status and was anxious not to be outdone. When he was seven years old his guardian was imprisoned in the Tower for his implication in the plot to make Lady Jane Grey queen. His brother's guardian, the instigator of the plot, was beheaded. For a time the children's future must have seemed very uncertain and the effect of this crisis might help to explain the suspicion which clouded Francis's relationships for the remainder of his life.

At fourteen Francis became heir to the Willoughby estate and his wardship was purchased by Sir Francis Knollys. Four years later it was bought back by the executors for £1,500 when Francis refused to marry his guardian's daughter. It was common practice for eligible minors to be bought and sold as valuable assets, but one can detect an unwillingness in the young Francis to co-operate. His early life displays the quite wayward behaviour which characterised the remainder of his career. Having refused an arranged marriage, he enraged his sister by choosing a wife against the advice of his family. Although apparently a love match at the start, his relationship with Elizabeth Littleton proved stormy. Their quarrels became more frequent and more public, exacerbated by her failing health which might have been attributable to her frequent pregnancies, but was probably at least tinged with some hypochondria. Willoughby was disappointed by their failure to produce a surviving heir, although they brought six healthy daughters to maturity.

[10] Although these windows were probably reglazed by Wyatville, a print by Hollar published in 1677 shows that Smythson's original tracery design remains unaltered. A similar design is found on the lantern of the Little Castle at Bolsover.

[11] Strauss (1978) 20.
[12] Girouard (1983) 108.
[13] Camden (ed.1695) 482.
[14] Smith (1989) 25.
[15] Wood (1958), 29.
[16] For a more detailed account of the family history see Smith (1988) 1-4 and Friedman (1989) 14-15.
[17] For a full account of Sir Henry Willoughby's career see Cameron (1970), 10-80.
[18] ibid, 19.
[19] In 1588 they were included by lord Burghley in a list of families considered suitable for elevation to the peerage, although this was not acted upon. Stone (1965) 196-7.
[20] Strauss (1978) 25.

To judge by his library list, he was a cultured man, something of an intellectual, who probably studied at Jesus College, Cambridge.[21] He was certainly conservative and preoccupied with form and protocol. A household order of 1572, relating to the Old Hall, lays down the duties of the staff. It is concerned in minute detail with the attention due to different ranks of occupant, including the treatment of varying categories of guest. Willoughby was difficult to get on with, falling out in turn with his sister, wife, daughters, business associates and even servants, who seem to have exploited his suspicious nature by deliberately fostering factions and intrigue within the household. He became convinced by them that his son-in-law had plotted his death and was never properly reconciled with him.[22] Meanwhile inflation was eating into the revenues of his estates and he was borrowing more money. Some precarious business ventures, designed to alleviate his financial problems, only made his situation worse. By 1582 his marital relationship had deteriorated to such a degree that his wife sought a separation sanctioned by the Queen and Willoughby was forced to pay £200 per annum for her separate maintenance.[23] After Elizabeth Littleton's death in 1595 his second marriage caused further dissent in the family and there are some grounds to suspect that he died of poison.[24] His posthumous child by this second marriage was, to the infinite relief of his first family, also a daughter and they had gone to some lengths to ensure a male changeling was not substituted for the girl.[25]

The sole clear achievement in the course of this turbulent, dissatisfied life was the creation at Wollaton of a palace. Its cost, estimated at £8000,[26] contributed significantly to the substantial debts left at his death in 1596, but the project may have come to represent his only claim to recognition. The germ of the plan might be dated to the mid 1570s. Willoughby expected to be presented to the Queen while she stayed at Kenilworth in 1575. His uncle, George Willoughby, gave advice about how he should present himself on this occasion: 'Sir Francis's number of servants should in no wise be less than 50, as well because heretofore he had not shewed himself to the Queen, as also that his estate was very well known both to Her Majesty and the whole Counsel to be nothing inferior to the best'.[27] While the Queen was at Kenilworth she received three invitations, including one from Willoughby to visit Middleton. She certainly went to the other two (Lichfield and Worcester), but not apparently to Middleton, perhaps because the old manor house there was not considered sufficient for a royal visit. If so, the experience would have been a factor in Sir Francis's decision to build a showpiece new hall at Wollaton.[28]

As in so many other personal ambitions, Sir Francis was to be disappointed: the Queen never visited him. A royal visit did take place in the next reign, however, when Queen Anne of Denmark and Prince Henry stayed at Wollaton in 1603.[29] Ironically the honour fell to Sir Francis's daughter Bridget and to Percival, the son-in-law with whom he had quarrelled so bitterly.[30] The royal visit was followed by another in 1604 by the Duke of York, who later became Charles I.[31]

At Francis's death in 1596 Percival and Bridget Willoughby inherited not only the house, but debts of £7,000 and a host of legal wrangles with other members of the family.[32] Despite this, they were living 'in a very plentifull manner' in 1599, according to an account book quoted by Cassandra Willoughby.[33] Nothing at present in the house can be dated to their period of occupancy save possibly some of the sculpture on the exterior, for example a bust of Charles I on the south facade. Lady Bridget died in the mid-1620s, and Sir Percival lived on in increasing ill-health, alone except for his servants. We learn from Cassandra's *Account* that a fire occurred in 1642,[34] but only essential repairs costing £322 7s. 8d were undertaken.[35] Percival died in 1643, almost 90 years old, and the house was not to be properly occupied again for 44 years. Some parliamentary troops were garrisoned in the Hall, but apart from one Royalist raid, the house had a quiet war.[36]

Sir Percival's heir, Francis, chose to live at Middleton, concentrating his energies on restoring the family's wrecked economy.[37] His son Francis became an eminent scholar and naturalist who visited Wollaton only occasionally, and who died young. It was his son, also called Francis, who chose to return to Wollaton at the age of 19, and take over the estate which he considered had been mismanaged by his stepfather. In 1687 he re-opened the house, bringing his sister Cassandra, then 17 years old, to act as housekeeper (**ill. 3**). In her *Account* she describes the state of neglect in which the house had been left, with 'heaps of rubbish' still remaining from the fire of 1642.[38] Francis died the next year, but his brother Thomas, aged only 16, inherited the house. He became MP for Nottinghamshire and was raised to the peerage as Baron Middleton in 1712.[39] Cassandra Willoughby remained mistress of

---

[21] *Smith (1988) 8.*
[22] *ibid 23.*
[23] *Friedman (1989) 63.*
[24] *Smith (1988) 33-4; Smith (1961) 27-46*
[25] *Smith (1988) 37.*
[26] *ibid, 20.*
[27] *Quoted in Smith (1988) 17.*
[28] *ibid. 18.*
[29] *A book of extraordinary expenditure was compiled as a result of this visit: Nottingham University Library Documents Division Ms Mi A 80 (205).*
[30] *Smith (1988) 23.*
[31] *The household inventory of 1609 records that three chambers had become known as 'the Queen's chamber', 'the Prince's chamber' and 'the Duke's chamber' respectively after these visits.*
[32] *Smith (1988) 40.*
[33] *Wood (1958), 33.*
[34] *Wood (1958) 66-7.*
[35] *Building accounts for these repairs start in December 1641 and end in November of the following year, although little work was done at harvest time (August) and none in September: Mi A 90a (205).*
[36] *Hodson (1962) 3-15; Smith (1988) 49.*
[37] *Smith (1988) 49.*
[38] *Nottingham University Ms Mi 90(a).*
[39] *Strauss (1978) 24.*

Wollaton in all but name, even after her brother's marriage, until she married late in life in 1713. She threw herself into the double task of writing the family history and restoring the house to its former glory. Her brother's descendants lived at Wollaton until the fifth Baron made Birdsall in Yorkshire his principal residence, a property acquired on his marrying Elizabeth Southeby. Shortly after the turn of the nineteenth century the sixth baron commissioned Jeffry Wyatt to carry out a major restoration of the house, although the family was already spending more time in Yorkshire.[40] This architect made a reputation in the field of restoring and modernising historic houses, culminating in his commission for work on Windsor castle for George IV. He changed his name to Wyatville in 1824 and was knighted in 1828. Extensive alterations to the interior effectively destroyed Wollaton's Tudor plan and a service extension was added to the west side. Despite these works the Middleton family used the house less and less in the later part of the 19th century.

In 1921 the 9th lord Middleton refused an offer for the house from Sir Jesse Boot, who wished to found a new university on the site. Four years later his successor, the 10th baron, sold it to Nottingham Corporation to raise death duties.[41] It was opened in 1926 as a Natural History Museum, a function which it still fulfills, and some adaptations have been made to the building as a result.

Four significant phases in the architectural history of the house can thus be identified:-

Phase 1 (1588-1687) comprised the original house designed by Smythson which probably remained little altered, though slightly damaged, for a century after its completion.

Phase 2 (1687-early 18th century) is represented by renovations largely carried out by Cassandra, Francis and Thomas Willoughby. Their improvements were concentrated on the grounds and on building a subterranean Ale Cellar, while internal changes to the house were not fundamental.

Phase 3 (1801-32) 1801-1832 saw three major campaigns of renovation under Sir Jeffry Wyatville, when radical changes were made to the interior. After this changes were superficial.

Phase 4 (1926 onwards) comprises the period of ownership by the City and occupancy by the Museum. Although some changes have been made in connection with the new use of the building, these have been relatively superficial.

Ill.3: Cassandra Willoughby, whose History, written in the early 18th century, has preserved much information on original documents, now lost, about the house and family. Portrait by courtesy of Lord Middleton.

[40] *The exact date when Wyatt began work is not known. The Builder states "about 1801", but is not clear on what authority. In 1804 Wyatt submitted an engraving of the Great Hall to the Royal Academy and in 1809 Britton wrote of recent alterations having been made at the hall. Linstrum (1972) 255.*

[41] *Strauss (1978) 47.*

2: DESCRIPTION OF THE HOUSE

Wollaton Hall essentially consists of two storeys above a semi-subterranean basement (plates 1 and 6). The Great Hall, which occupies the central space on the ground floor, was built upon solid Bunter Sandstone, the levelled summit of a hill. At basement level this core of rock was cut back to form four vertical faces and the basement rooms were built around the central block thus formed. Here the floor level rises and falls considerably as the natural topography of the site was exploited. The ground floor is in reality slightly above ground level. The Great Hall, placed on its rock foundation, is totally encircled to a height of two storeys by other rooms which overlie the basement rooms. The flat roofs of these encircling wings, called the 'half-roof' or 'leads', provided walkways from which views of the surrounding countryside could be enjoyed. The Great Hall is lit by a clerestory which rises above the flanking wings, so that on the exterior a central tower emerges from the surrounding leads. The tower is surmounted by a second hall, originally called the 'High Hall', but later called the 'Prospect Room', a name still used today. At each corner of the house there is a tower which culminates in a turret chamber rising above the leads (plate 3). These might have been intended as banqueting or picnic rooms but, viewed from some distance, the corner turrets combine with the central tower, with its bartizans, to give the building a castle-like appearance and no doubt this was part of the overall intention.

The house faces north-west but for the sake of simplicity it will be described as if it faces north. The plan is symmetrical and consists of a square (including terraces on the north and south sides which were integral to the design), with an additional square tower at each corner. The main north and south walls are offset to accommodate the terraces, so that jutting corner chambers were created, adding interest to these facades. An elevation drawing by Smythson of one of these corners is thought to be the earliest English architectural elevation drawn in perspective (**ill. 4, overleaf**).

Smythson's proposed plan or platt survives (**ill. 5**), and shows that the design of the house also embraced its immediate grounds and outbuildings. The house itself was to form the central unit of a three by three square. The square immediately to the north, the front of the house, was to consist of a courtyard approach, entered by a gatehouse, with an arcaded covered walkway to either side rather like that depicted at Holland house, London, c.1606-7.[1] The topography of the site, surmounting a hill, dictates a rising approach to the building, so the house imposes itself impressively in front of the visitor. On the south side three squares were to be given over to formally laid-out gardens with direct access from the house, via the terrace, by an informal or postern doorway, 'the garden door'. In the centre of each side of the overall site square a long thin rectangular outbuilding was planned. To the north this was a gatehouse, to the west a brewhouse and bakehouse, to the east the stables, to the south a dairyhouse. The purpose of the remaining four squares of the plan is not specified, but we may presume the square in the centre of the west side formed a service courtyard, with traffic between the bakehouse and brewhouse. Both the service entry and a direct entry to the original Ale Cellar were located on this side of the house and decoration on the west facade, excluding the towers, is sparser and plainer than on other elevations (**ill. 10,** on page 15). This has been partly attributed to refacing by Wyatville,[2] but the stonework shows no substantial signs of this. There might

---

[1] Girouard (1983) 37.
[2] Linstrum, 1972, 66. This author notes, however, that there is no evidence that the decoration on the west facade ever matched that on others.

have been a similar courtyard arrangement to the east connected with the stables, as an informal or postern doorway once lay on this side of the house. The remaining two squares, flanking the courtyard on the north side, complete the plan and it was possibly intended that these should be landscaped to enhance the approach to the house.

There is no direct evidence that the outbuildings were constructed in accordance with this design, although there are hints that they might have been. There is a design drawing by Smythson in the R.I.B.A. library for a building thought to be the Wollaton gatehouse,[3] and there are other documentary references. A description of 1610 praises 'a most perfect and well-shaped house', with specific reference to 'the gatehouse, curtelages, gardens, orchards, stables, etc.'[4] A household inventory of 1609 refers to bedding delivered to 'the dairy house',[5] and Smythson's platt shows the outbuildings as having staircases, as if they were two storey structures with servants' accommodation above. There are, however, problems with these sources. Although the inventory clearly refers to the new hall for the main rooms, and probably means the new dairyhouse here, we know that the old hall continued in use and one cannot rule out the possibility that the old outbuildings were still servicing the new hall. In an attempt to corroborate this documentary evidence, a geophysical resistivity survey was carried out to the north of the house to try to determine whether the gatehouse had ever been built. Its supposed site revealed a degree of disturbance and scatter consistent with the demolition of a building (see Appendix II, p.112). Moreover some evidence of the collonaded walkway on the west side of the entrance courtyard shown in Smythson's platt was revealed in the second phase of the survey, when a seventeenth century subterranean Ale Cellar lying immediately to the north-west of the house was investigated (**ill. 37,** on page 40). One stretch of ashlar stone walling in an otherwise brick structure was revealed (**ill. 62**). This aligned precisely with the supposed location of the west wall of the collonade and may well be a vestige of that structure.

More evidence remains for the landscaping of the grounds. A painting by Jan Siberechts of about 1697 in the collection of Lord Middleton (**plate 2**) shows the house and gardens from the south-east side after landscaping by Thomas Willoughby and his sister Cassandra, who refers to reforming the gardens with the advice of a Mr Pratt, formerly of the Chelsea Physick Gardens.[6] The essential elements of the Smythson plan

[3] R.I.B.A. Smythson II/12.
[4] Wood (1958), p.70: the account is by Thomas Ridgeway, father-in-law of the son of Bridget and Percival Willoughby
[5] Mi I 16.
[6] Friedman, 1989, 160.

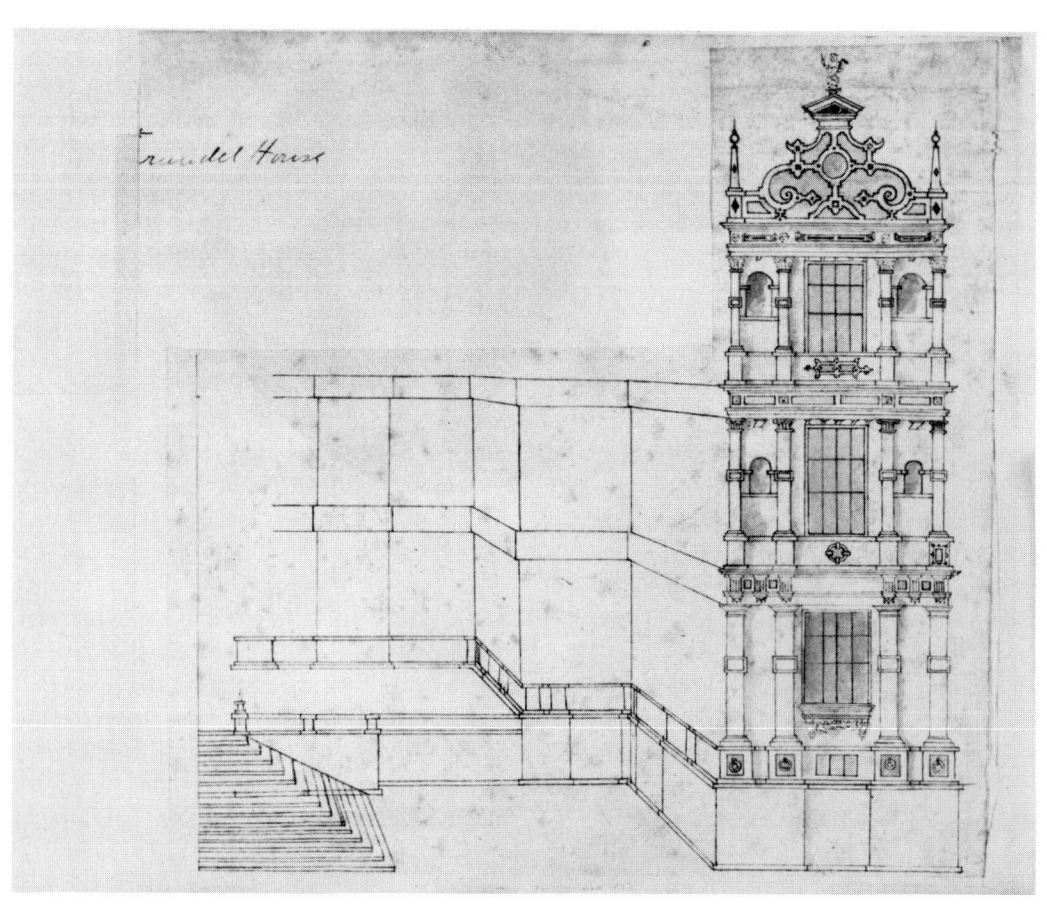

Ill.4: *Drawing by Smythson of a corner of the Hall, showing a tower, jutting corner chamber and part of a terrace. This is thought to be the earliest elevation drawing shown in perspective by an English architect. By courtesy of the British Architectural Library, R.I.B.A., London. [Smythson I/25(2)].*

Plate 1: *Wollaton Hall from the north-west. (Photo by Pamela Marshall.)*

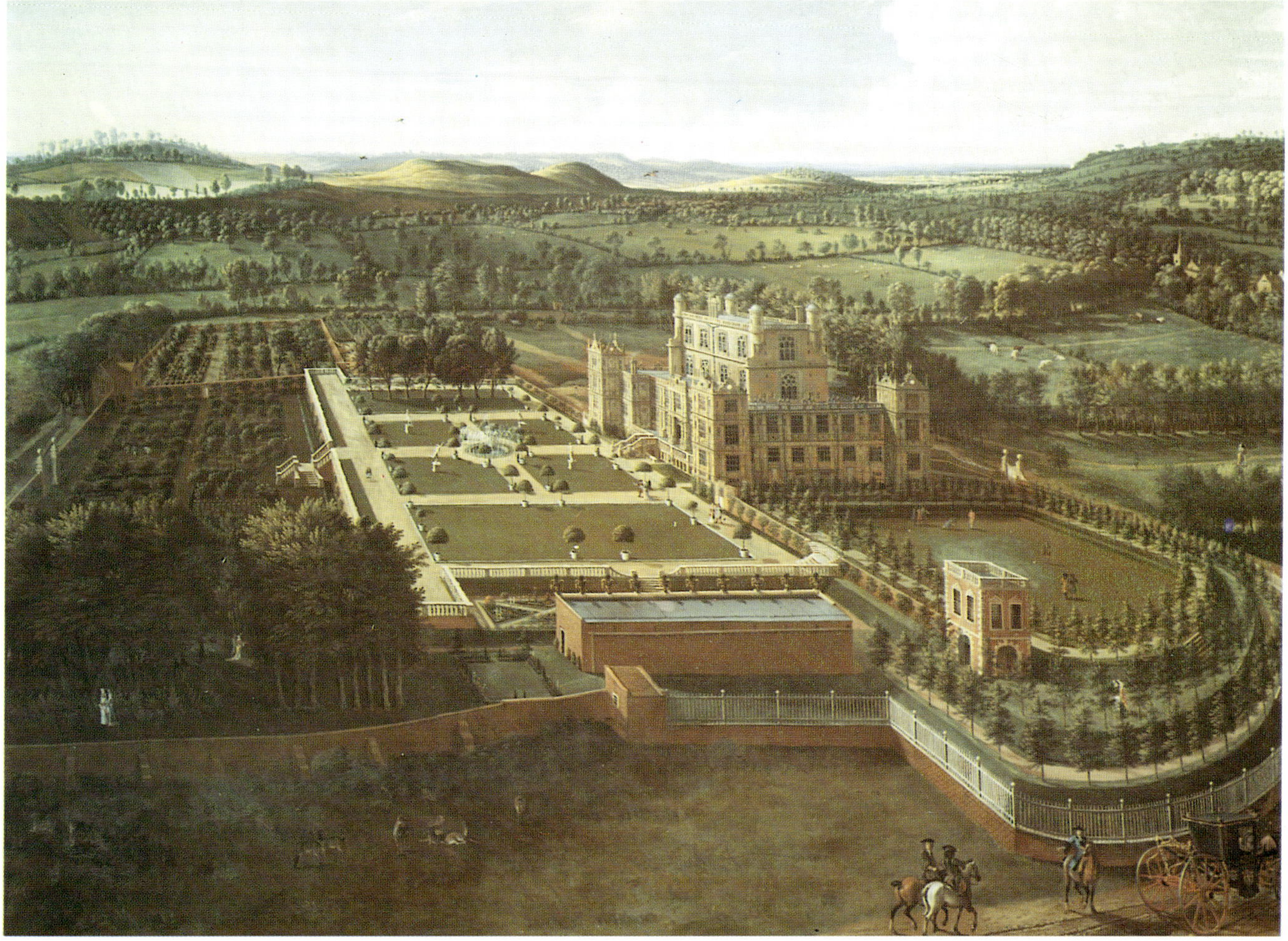

Plate 2: *A bird's eye view of Wollaton Hall from a painting by Jan Siberechts, 1697. By courtesy of Lord Middleton.*

Plate 3: *A turret pavilion seen from the roof of the central tower. (Photo by Pamela Marshall.)*

Plate 4: *The High Hall or Prospect Room, looking west. (Photo by Pamela Marshall.)*

Plate 5: *The Great Hall and Screen. (Photo by Philip Dixon.)*

Plate 6: *A cutaway drawing of Wollaton Hall c. 1590 by David Taylor. Furnishings shown are based on information from the household inventories.*

Plate 7: *The Screen. (Photo by Chris Salisbury.)*

Plate 8: *The Regency Saloon. (Photo by Philip Dixon.)*

Plate 9: *The hammer beam roof in the Great Hall, looking east. The slit windows in the far wall lit staircases to the High Hall and leads. Note they are present on both sides.*

Plate 10: *Hammer beam roof: detail.*  **Plate 11**: *Hammer beam roof: detail (Photos by Pamela Marshall.)*

Plate 12: *Wyatville's entrance hall. Wyatville opened up the space by removing the Porter's Lodge and Wardrobe and created a direct entry into the Great Hall (on the left). (Photo by Philip Dixon.)*

Plate 13: *The north state staircase. (Photo by Chris Salisbury.)*

[7] *Mi A70 (205).*

Ill.5: Design platt by Smythson for Wollaton Hall. The house is shown in the centre of a symmetrical plan which also embraces the immediate grounds and outbuildings. By courtesy of the British Architectural Library, R.I.B.A., London. [Smythson I/25(1)].

can still be traced, although the outbuildings are absent, perhaps swept away during this reorganization. The formal gardens with the circular feature indicated on Smythson's platt (**ill. 5**), are still in place, although by this date they have been extended yet further south beyond the terrace. More ground has been encompassed to both east and west, the eastern section landscaped into a huge D-shaped bowling green defined by a ha-ha. Other than the platt, there are no direct references to landscaping in the Tudor records. However, there is a 'Booke of extraordinary payements at Wollaton, Anno Domini 1591'[7] which refers to the new house and records many payments for 'stonne-getting' to one Richard Gamble and his fellows, for collecting and carting stone from Lenton Priory. Since the house had been completed in 1588, we must consider this reclaimed stone was used in landscaping the grounds, possibly to consolidate the artificial terrace on the south side. This reference might also throw some indirect light on the fabric used in the foundations and basement of the building, for some masonry fragments from an early 12th century church of some status were found in the walls of room 4/

14 (**ill. 6**). It is likely that a great deal of reclaimed stone was used in the early stages of building, probably also robbed from the decayed priory. Unfortunately the building accounts for the first two years (1580-82), which would have confirmed this, are missing.

Sir Francis Willoughby's motives for rebuilding Wollaton Hall have been discussed in chapter 1 and the design of the house supports the idea that it was conceived as a vehicle for superior entertainment. The first floor was reserved for two suites of state apartments, while the ground floor housed the main living area. The half roof or leads were designed for recreation (**ill. 7**), with four pavilions in the turret chambers (**plate 3**) and, most striking of all, the 'High Hall' crowning the central tower (**plate 6**). Given such innovative features, combined with Smythson's treatment of the external appearance of the house, one is struck by the conservative nature of the internal planning. The hub of the house remained the Great Hall, with its traditional screens passage (**plates 5 and 7**). Strict conventions of social orientation, with 'high' and 'low' ends to the reception rooms, were

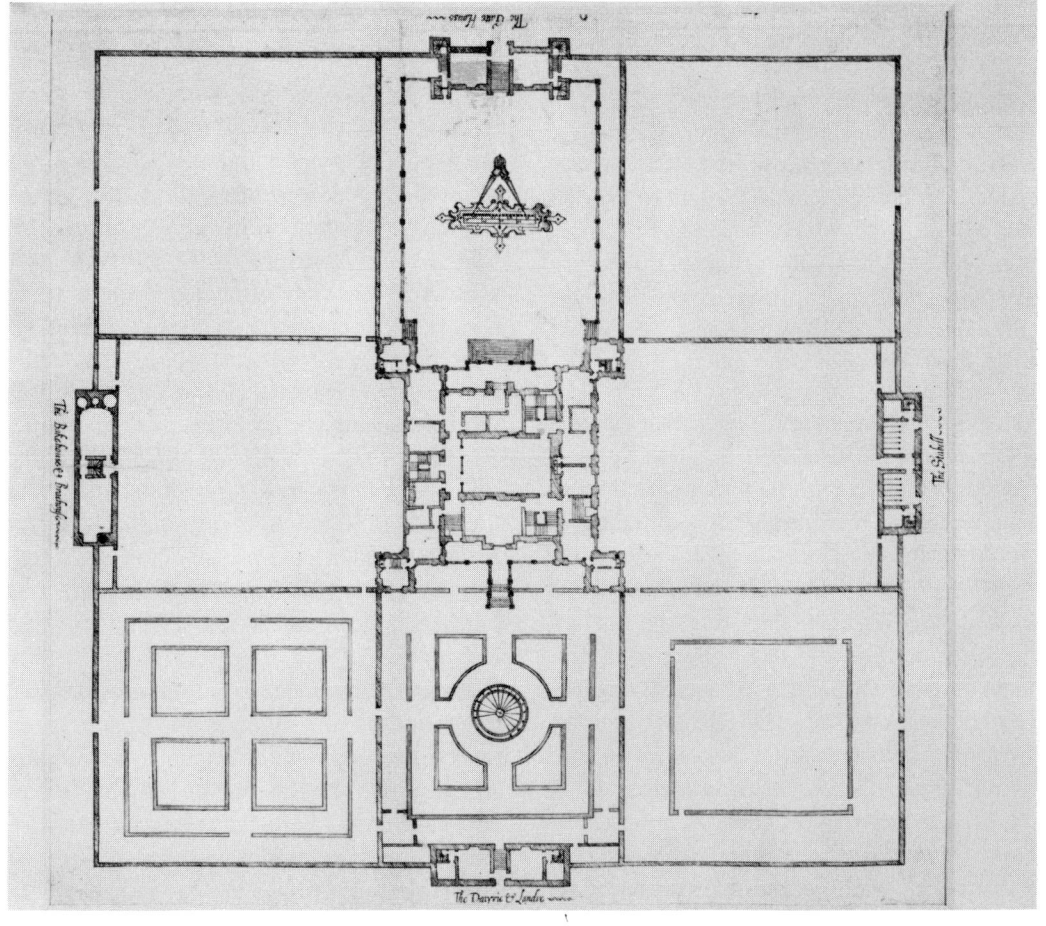

Ill.6: The south wall of room 4/14, which incorporates fragments of masonry robbed from an early Romanesque church. (Photo by Philip Dixon.).

observed: this is discussed in more detail in chapter 3. However the services necessary for entertaining on a lavish scale were not neglected. Well planned facilities and accommodation for servants were placed in the basement. Finally, a discreet and cleverly engineered waste disposal system was provided in the form of two sewers (**ill. 37,** on page 40). It is perhaps a further comment on Willoughby's character, however, that the old hall remained in use for the remainder of his life, so that he maintained an 'everyday' and a 'best' house.

There is some evidence to suggest that the High Hall, or Prospect Room (**ill. 7, plate 6**) was a late addition to Smythson's plan and that the central tower was originally envisaged as incorporating the clerestory of the Great Hall only. Smythson's building is characterised by a tendency to over-caution in structural matters, yet in connection with this feature, risks were taken which have resulted in a profound weakness. To span the 10m width of the Great Hall ceiling, the architect adopted the 'Chinese lattice' method of short joists interconnected in a kind of grid (**ill. 8**). The idea featured in Serlio's influential work *Architecture*,[8] and although the adoption of the method was undoubtedly partly due to the difficulty of acquiring sufficiently long timbers, one cannot help suspecting that Smythson was seduced by the opportunity to try out an innovative scheme. Genuine hammer beam trusses could have tackled the job with more success. While conventional tie-beams would have served to counteract the outward thrust on the central tower walls, the strain placed upon the joints in this grid-like arrangement was virtually guaranteed to result in their failure. Smythson's decision is puzzling in view of the structural caution he displayed elsewhere, but the method would have presented less risk without the additional burden of the High Hall. The failure of the High Hall floor joints was probably quite rapid and led to fear of outward movement of the Prospect Room walls. Buttresses were added below the bartizans at the corners of the central tower, their bases set on thick supporting walls belonging to the original structure. On a print of the Hall by Hollar, published in 1677,[9] no buttresses are depicted, but they are present in Siberechts' painting of 1695 (**plate 2**). Although the work has been

[8] S. Serlio, Lib. I, edition of 1566, 15.

[9] Thoroton (1677), 223.

2: DESCRIPTION OF THE HOUSE 13

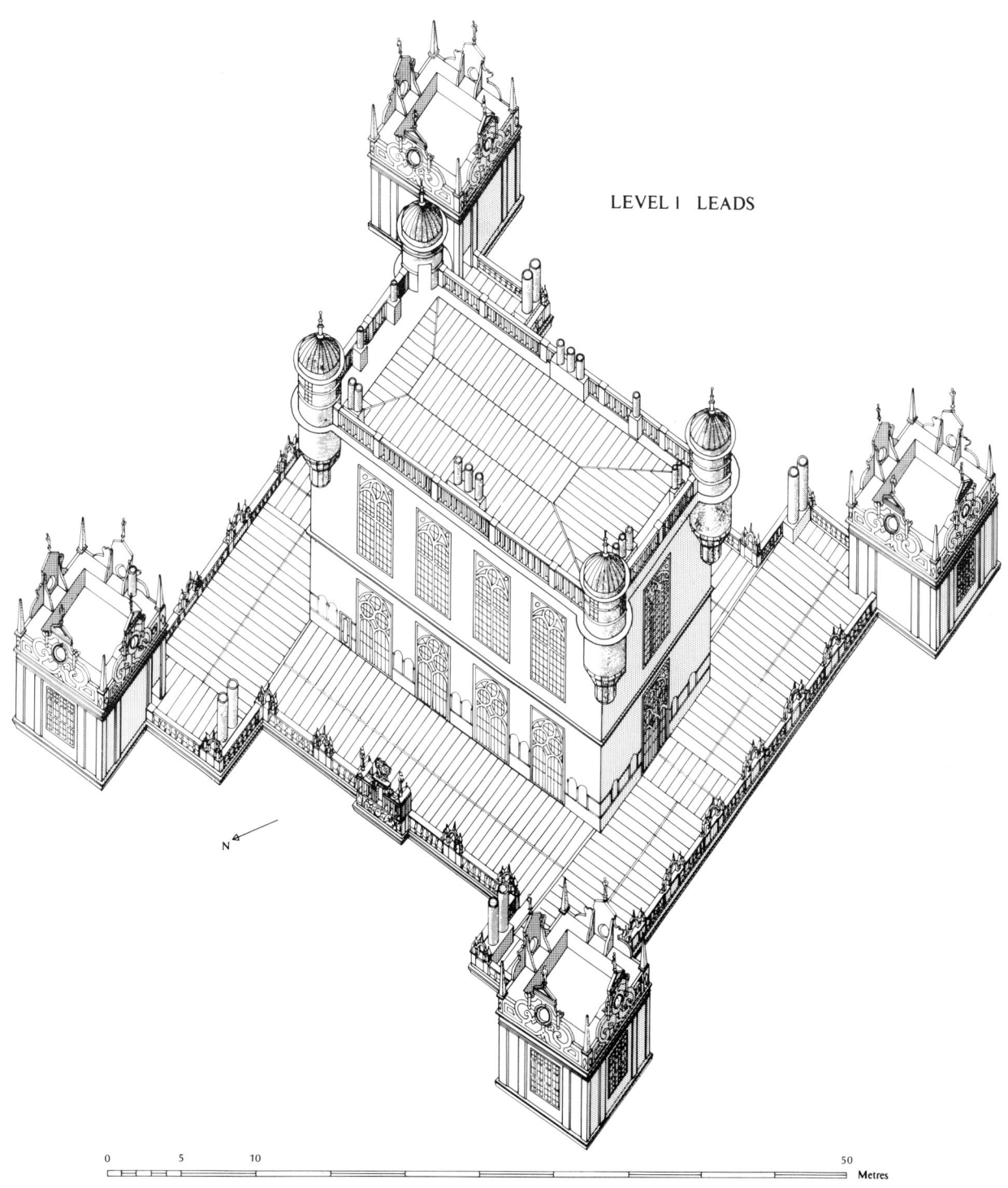

LEVEL 1 LEADS

Ill.7: Axonometric drawing of the leads (level 1).

well executed, there are some irregular joints on the outer faces. The best evidence, however, can be found on the inner corners, where the butt joints are quite clear and the coursing is out of line (**ill. 9**). During the 1960s the Prospect Room floor was stabilised by internal bracing by Nottingham City Engineers Department (**plate 4**), but it remains unusable.

The alterations which were later made to the building represent the efforts of subsequent ages to adapt the Tudor house to the changing needs of the time. A system of underground tunnels on the east side of the house (**ill. 37**) was probably built in connection with improving the water supply, possibly during Phase 2 under Thomas and Cassandra Willoughby. They were responsible for much work on the grounds, but

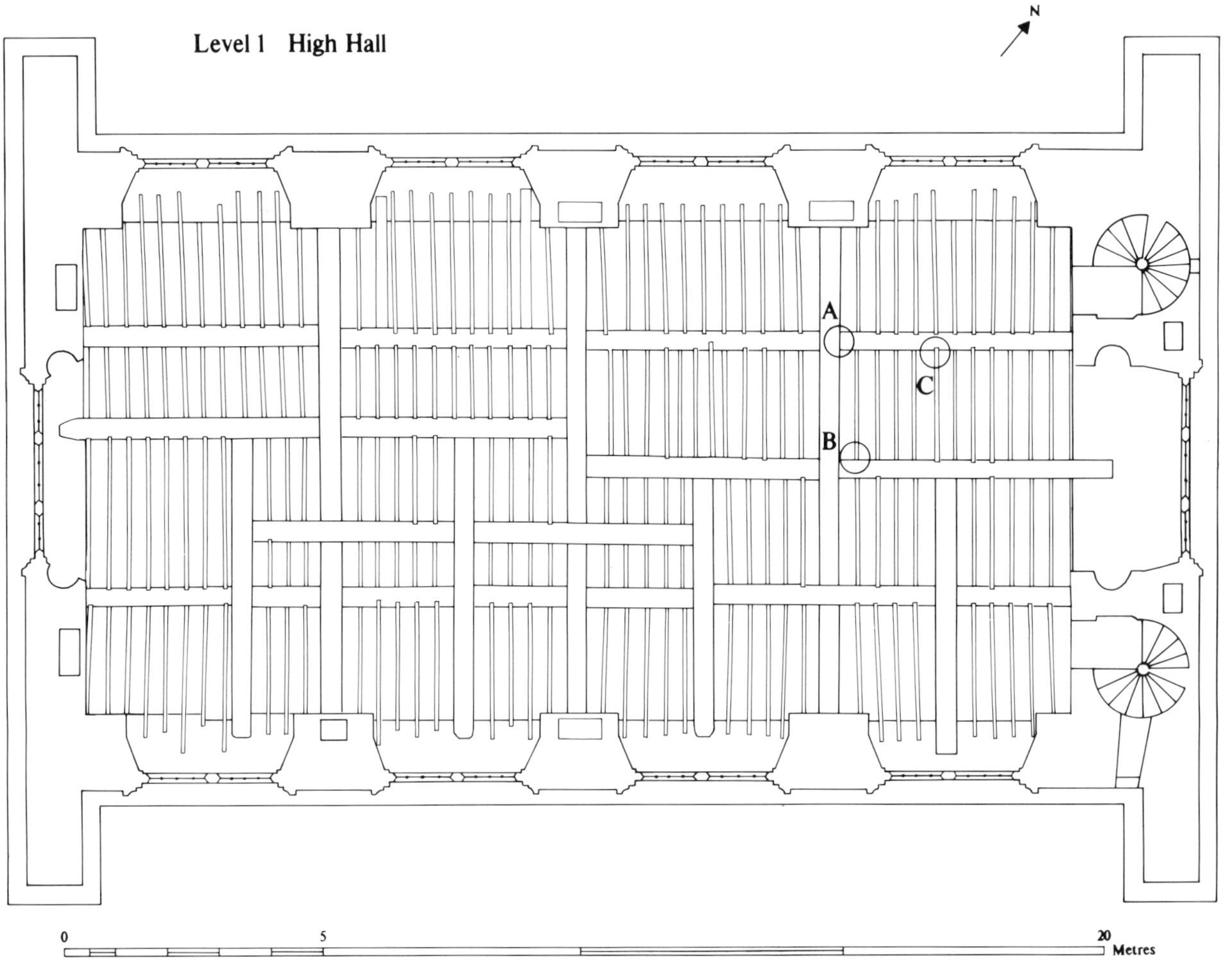

Level 1   High Hall

Ill. 8: *Plan of the High Hall. (Joint types A, B and C are shown in ill. 47).*

Ill. 9: *One of the buttresses of the central tower (photo by Philip Dixon).*

only four significant changes to the house itself can be attributed to them with any certainty. The first was to add buttresses to the central tower, the second was to install easier access to the leads, and the third was to provide a servants' hall. By now social distinction had made the custom of communal meals for the extended household obsolete. A large vaulted ale cellar in the basement (4/9) was converted for servants' use and was substituted by the fourth major change, the addition of its replacement, a subterranean Ale Cellar off the western service courtyard.

During Phase 3 Jeffrey Wyatville's alterations at the behest of Lord Middleton were far more wide-ranging. His brief was to update the house to serve an era in which social conventions and domestic expectations had changed completely. In 1809 Britton wrote of Wyatville's reputation as an architect 'who has manifested much skill in converting the interior of old, ill-arranged mansions, to the present, and more comfortable modes of domestic life.'[10] The exact dates when he was employed at Wollaton are not known, but he is thought to have started c.1801[11] and seems to have worked on the reception rooms first.

Some of his alterations appear in Britton's *Architectural Antiquities*, published in 1809 (**ill. 16**), although his work was not complete at this date. Between 1823-25 Wyatville was employed again at Wollaton, on a service extension which was added to the west side of the house (**illustrations 10 and 34**). A fundamental overhaul was made of the basement rooms as an adjunct to the addition of the new wing. At the same time he was building Lenton Lodge, a new gatehouse at one of the entries to the estate, following the form of an Elizabethan gatehouse probably designed by Smythson. Wyatville is likely to have been responsible for the design of the Camelia House situated south-west of the Hall.[12] In 1832 Lord Middleton was alarmed by riots stirred by the Reform Act. Nottingham Castle, seat of the Duke of Newcastle, was burned and Wollaton Hall attacked. The Baron asked Wyatville to design 'two circular lodges something of the martello kind' with a secure ground floor, blind and inaccessible from outside. He also stipulated that 'they should flank each other, with narrow slip (sic.) windows to fire thro', similar to old Castles. Some sort of Battlements in unison with the ornaments of the house might be contrived, to hide a cannon on the top.' They were each to house a family in two-roomed tenements.[13] The result was Beeston Lodge, another gatehouse on the perimeter of the estate,

[10] Britton, 1809, ii, p.116.
[11] The Builder, 13 April, 1889, also quoted in Linstrum, 1972, 255.
[12] Ibid. 66.
[13] A letter from Lord Middleton to Wyatville, dated 2 Feb, 1832, in the collection of Mrs. J.M.Don, quoted in Linstrum, 1972, 64-65.

Ill. 10: An elevation drawing by Wyatville c.1823 showing the proposed extension to house a servants' wing. When the work was carried out a central porch was added to the design. By courtesy of Department of Manuscripts and Special Collections, Hallward Library, University of Nottingham. [MiP3 p.3.]

and further work aimed at security was carried out within the Hall itself at this time.

Linked with Wyatville's modernisation came a veritable campaign to multiply accommodation within the walls of the house. This was partly achieved by the addition of rooms, or even suites, at mezzanine level between floors (**ill. 11**). The division of cells within the structure almost draws comparison with a cancerous organism. The Tudor house provided limited accommodation for servants in proper apartments. A.T.Friedman, in her study of the Wollaton household, has estimated that the house was run by 45 to 50 people in the 1570s, predominantly men with only a handful of women.[14] A number of the servants came from good yeoman or local gentry families, and some of these were linked by marriage with the Willoughbys themselves. The new Hall could not have accommodated all of these in private rooms. The servants were socially graded and the top level, whose status would have been quite high, appear to have been awarded a room within the house. These included the personal attendants of the family or guests, the cook, the porter, the butler, the gardener and the five occupants of 'the Yeomen's lodgings', stewards who are occasionally referred to by name. Many more servants must have lived elsewhere and taken meals in the Great Hall. The household inventories are helpful here. That of 1596 lists bedding 'forth of the house' and mentions the Lodge and the Brewhouse as well as naming four individuals in possession of bedding without

[14] Friedman (1989), 41-6

Ill. 11: *The corridor to a mezzanine level suite of rooms built over the south end of the Long Gallery during Wyatville's replanning of the house interior. The staircase is contrived in the Tudor window recess. (Photo by Philip Dixon.).*

stating their whereabouts. The inventory of 1599 speaks of 'the little chamber in the gardine' [sic], the 'maids' chamber', the 'warrener's lodge' and 'the house where the kitchen boys lieth' [sic]. The 1609 inventory speaks of delivery of bedding to the dairyhouse. Smythson's platt indicates staircases in the outbuildings, suggesting upper floor accommodation in these. It was, however, common practice for servants to sleep anywhere and the large quantities of bedding about the main house suggests that mattresses and bedding were brought out into the public rooms at night for servants of lower status and cleared away in the morning. The 1596 inventory lists ten featherbeds in the Parlour and twelve in the Wardrobe. Others might have used truckle beds or beds which folded up to look like chests. [15]

[15] I am grateful to David Durant for his advice on this matter.

Part of Wyatville's brief was clearly to provide a great deal of very unobtrusive sleeping accommodation for living-in servants. The Georgians wished more servants to be housed less visibly and were indifferent to the quality of their accommodation. Throughout the house the resulting mezzanine rooms are often cramped, poorly-lit and airless. The difference between the work of the two architects is quite striking. Smythson shows a consistent attention to air, space and to finished detail, even in the service quarters. Although Wyatville replaced most of the Tudor finished detail above stairs in line with current fashion, he fortunately left it in the service rooms. There are chamfered door surrounds with moulded stops and capitals and bases to the kitchen columns. The finish is comparable with that which survives in the upper apartments, for example the door moulding on the gallery door above the screens (2/12) and around the central tower doorways from the leads. Similarly, the design of the service staircase is close to that of the two state staircases as shown in Smythson's plan. Wyatville, by contrast, paid no attention to finish or detail in the service areas, where his alterations were often quite clumsy.

During Phase 4 (the museum phase, after 1926) little alteration has taken place. Many features are obscured by the conversion of rooms to museum galleries, but there has been minimal destruction, save the removal of the original floor joists in the south Great Chamber and timber gates to a yard in Wyatville's service extension.

3. FLOOR BY FLOOR ANALYSIS

The Ground Floor (ill.12, 13)

The ground floor contained private and public apartments and a few service rooms. Dominated by the traditional Great Hall, the remaining accommodation comprised a private Dining Parlour, six bed-chambers, five with inner chambers, three main staircases and two 'postern' staircases. Despite its complex layout and Renaissance shell, the plan was conservative, with strong echoes of the Middle Ages. The focus was still the Great Hall (3/5: **plate 5**), used for communal meals and complete with screens passage (**plate 7**). Here the three customary service doors gave access to the Pantry (3/16), Buttery (3/17) and kitchens. The Hall was set longitudinally to the front of the

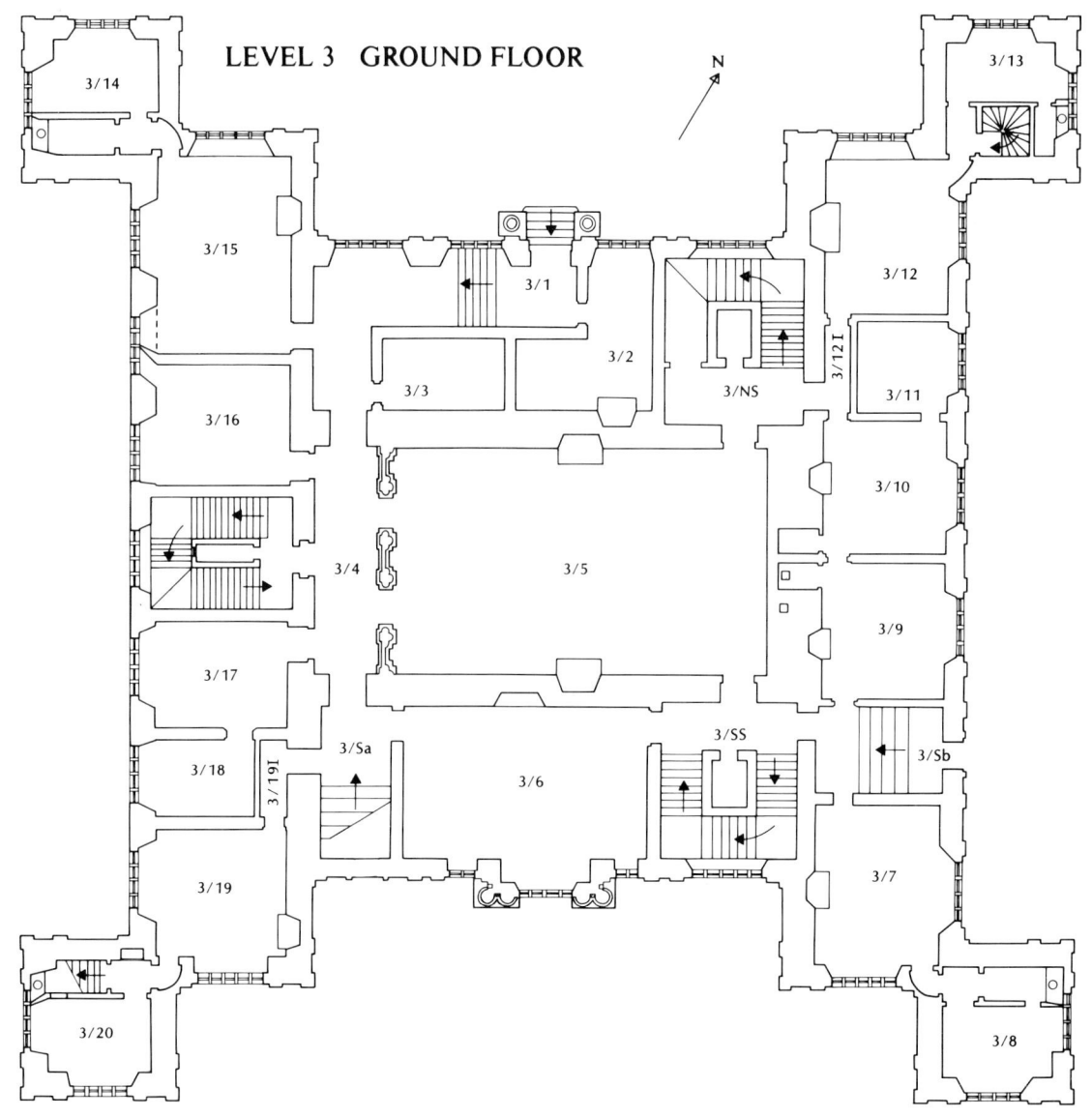

Ill. 12: Reconstructed plan of the Tudor ground floor (level 3).

[16] National Trust Guidebook (1975), 6 and plan on p.14.

Ill. 13: Axonometric drawing of the Tudor ground floor.

house, in the traditional manner, and was entered by the screened cross-passage (3/4). Because the main entrance to the house (3/1) was set in the centre of a symmetrical Renaissance facade and at a lower level than the Hall, the conflict which thus arose between an old-fashioned plan set in a modern shell had to be resolved. Entry involved a right-angled turn to the right, a short flight of steps, and then another turn to the left into the cross-passage (3/4). The entrance arrangements were further constricted by the positioning of a Porter's Lodge (3/2) and Wardrobe (3/3) beside the main doorway, so the entry into the house must have been something of an anticlimax in architectural terms after the external approach. Only three years after the completion of Wollaton Smythson abandoned this traditional form at Hardwick, where the hall was transformed into a grand entrance, placed axially so that the visitor gained access to it immediately, passing under a columned gallery which became a mere vestige of the traditional screens.[16]

At Wollaton there were no central doorways into the Hall, preserving the medieval concept of a 'lower' screens end, with more exclusive

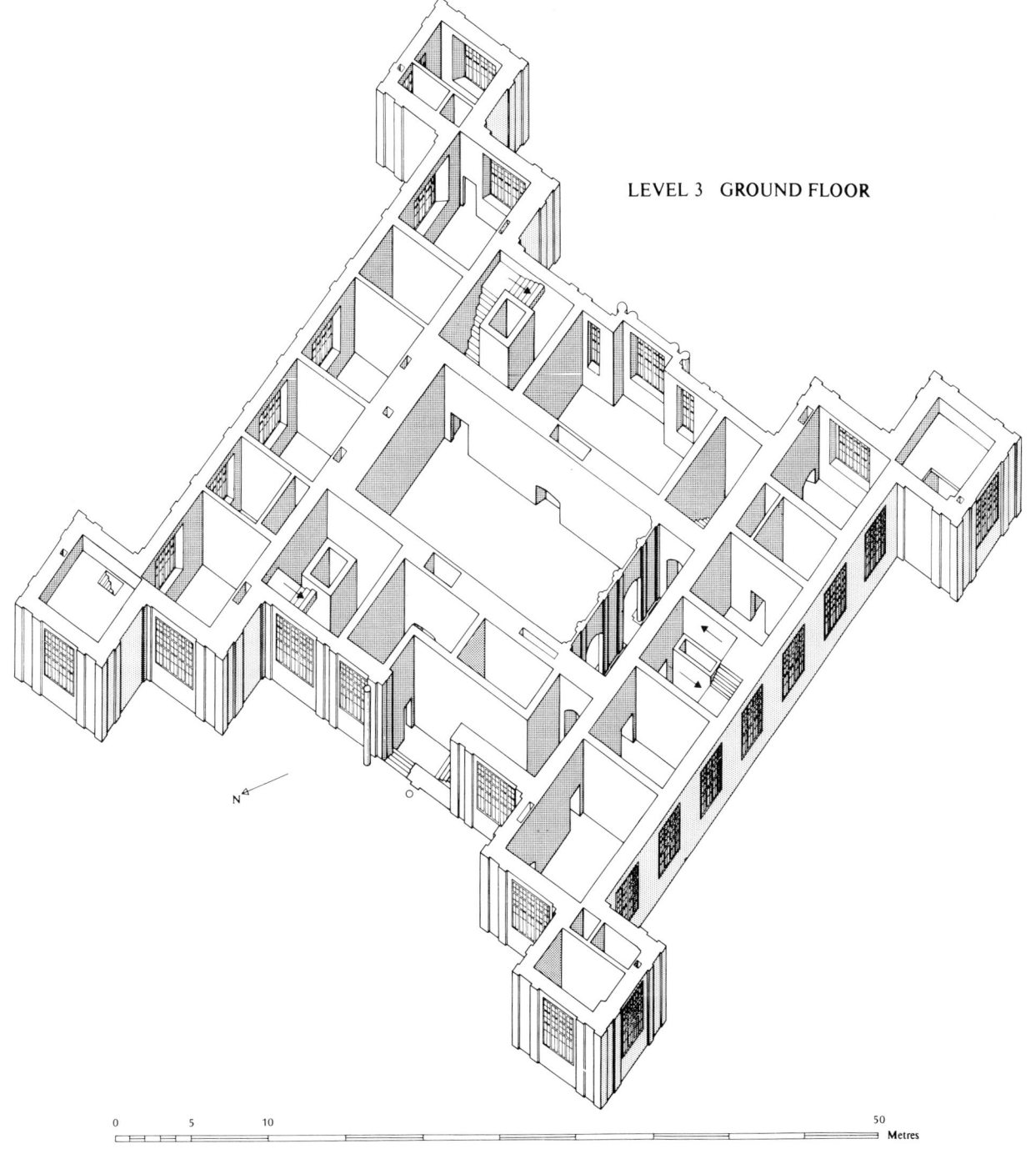

LEVEL 3   GROUND FLOOR

entrances at the opposite, 'high', end for the use of the family and special guests. Smythson's design drawing for the Screen survives (**ill.14**). The gallery above, wrongly termed 'the minstrels' gallery' was used as a service route to the Great Chambers on the first floor. At the south end of the cross-passage was the customary exit, here to the garden via a short staircase (3/Sa) and a terrace. Overhanging the hall is an elaborately decorated hammer-beam roof (**plates 9, 10, 11**: the shields and pierced panels were probably added by Wyatville.[17]) It is not structural and, in view of his patron's tastes, it is perhaps significant that, however innovative the 'Chinese Lattice' method of spanning the Hall ceiling might have been, the finished product was made to look more traditional.

The private Dining Parlour (3/6) on the south side of the house was reached from the head of the Hall, with a 'low' entry near the screens for service. The wine cellar was located at the east end of the basement, its route through rooms 3/13 and 3/12 being designed to link with the 'high' end of the Hall and Dining Parlour. The beer cellar shared the kitchen route via the service staircase (3/WS) at the west end, and most conveniently served the lower end of the Hall. Behind the screens were three traditional doorways associated with late medieval Hall design. The Buttery (3/17) and Pantry (3/16) were situated on the same level, while the central doorway led to the kitchens on the floor below. In the original house these entries led only to services and care was taken to provide alternative access, technically outside the screens, to the corner chambers, which were for the use of family and guests. Beyond the Buttery was the Butler's Chamber (3/18) which had an attached small mezzanine chamber accessible by ladder (3/18i). The household inventories of 1599 and 1601 indicate that one person slept here despite the fact it is little more than a cupboard, without light or ventilation. It is one of only two original mezzanine level chambers to survive in the house: the other is in the basement (4/3i). Three more are suggested by household inventories, all of them above inner chambers to bedchambers (see below).

By the 'high' end of the Hall were two state staircases, one for each of the suites on the first floor. A further short staircase (3/Sb) led down to a postern door on the east side of the house where it would have provided quick access to the stables placed across the eastern courtyard. Each

[17] Linstrum, 1972, 65.

Ill.14: Smythson's design drawing for the screen. By courtesy of the British Architectural Library, R.I.B.A., London. [Smythson I/25(7)].

[18] *The 1609 inventory accordingly names it 'The Duke's Chamber': Mi I 16.*

[19] *Nottingham University Ms, Mi A 60/5, f.iir.*

[20] *Archaeological evidence for similar cramped and often cupboard-like sleeping accommodation can be found elsewhere from the later Middle Ages onwards. The remains of an Elizabethan loft of the 1580s exists at Newark castle. In the first floor chamber of the south-west tower a floor was inserted at the point where a barrel vault began to spring. A short window was put high in the gable wall to light and ventilate the space, which was only tall enough to be used for storage or sleeping. Other evidence from the site indicates a preoccupation with increasing accommodation within the castle during the 1580s, so the latter use seems more likely, especially in view of the window.*

[21] *Inventories of 1599 (Mi I 8ii) and 1601 (Mi 15).*

of the corner chambers was a bedchamber (3/15, 3/19, 3/12, 3/7) and two more, the 'Painted Chambers' of the inventories, were situated along the east side (3/9, 3/10). The elaborate decoration implied here by the name is unlikely to have remained intact after the fire of 1642, which was concentrated at this end of the house. The rooms were of uniform quality, each being spacious, airy and well-lit, with a fireplace and access to a garderobe. All but one had inner chambers to accommodate personal servants (3/14, 3/20, 3/8 3/13, 3/11). These were smaller and unheated, but similarly light and airy and the garderobes were situated in cubicles within them.

The south-west corner chamber (3/19), with its convenient access to the garden, seems to have been one of the better rooms. It was first called 'the garden chamber' and later 'the Duke's chamber' after being assigned to the Duke of York, later to become Charles I, on his visit in 1604.[18] In 1601 it had a 'bedstead with tester and valance of crimson velvet and cloth of silver', some rich curtains and carpets, and some county maps hung on the walls. The household inventories of 1599 and 1601 suggest that this bedchamber had two inner chambers (see Appendix I), which raises the question of mezzanine level rooms in the original house which have been removed. Nothing remains of a second inner chamber here, although a short straight stair shown on Smythson's platt (**ill. 5**) might have given access to it. No doubt it was to accommodate the extra servants attending an important visitor, and in this respect the Garden Chamber was comparable to the north-east corner bedroom (3/12) and the Best Chamber (2/11) on the first floor, where two inner chambers are also listed. In both these cases mezzanine level rooms still exist, although the date of their construction is questionable, for they may be Georgian re-builds. Chamber 3/12 was possibly Sir Francis's personal suite, for in 1586 a payment was made for wainscotting in 'my M{aste}r's chamber by the north tower'.[19] The mezzanine rooms were probably little more than lofts.[20] The 1601 inventory refers to that in the north-east tower as a 'little chamber', which may indicate lack of height, and its furnishings are simple (see Appendix I). A parallel might be drawn with the surviving mezzanine Cook's Chamber (4/3i) in the basement or with the closet-like room attached to the Butler's Chamber (3/18i). In the 1599 inventory this is called an 'inner chamber', and it contained similar items to the 'little chamber' of the 1601 inventory. It is very low (1.52m) and unlit.

Perhaps the other chambers in question were little more than sleeping galleries.

There appears to have been no chapel at Wollaton although one might have expected that Willoughby's conservatism would have required one. There are intriguing references to 'the Chapel Chamber' in the inventories and it can be identified without doubt as the south-east corner chamber (3/7). The name suggests proximity to a chapel, but no room can be identified as such. The Chapel Chamber itself was always furnished as a bed-chamber, and was provided with a fireplace. The adjacent inner chamber (3/8) was unheated, faces east and had a niche in the north wall but on Smythson's proposed plan a garderobe is shown in the north-east corner. At all events this room, like its counterparts, contained bedding by 1596. The inner chamber to the second Painted Chamber (3/11) has neither a garderobe nor a fireplace, and faces eastwards, but it suffers the same disadvantages as room 3/8, in that its only access is via a bedchamber and it appears in the inventories as sleeping accommodation. Also it is not adjacent to the Chapel Chamber, so goes nowhere towards explaining the derivation of that name. It is possible that the delicate political climate of 1588, following the recent execution of Mary Queen of Scots and the imminent Spanish invasion, recommended the adoption of very public worship and that earlier plans to include a private chapel were abandoned, only the name lingering on.

From the evidence of the inventories, two different rooms fulfilled the role of Wardrobe for the storage of household necessities. At first it seems to have been the chamber off the buttery (3/18). This later became the Butler's Chamber, and the Wardrobe was moved to the small room by the entrance lobby (3/3) beside the Porter's Lodge (3/2).[21] The wardrobe contained a great variety of objects (see Appendix I), including much bedding, which was possibly stored here during the day and brought out at night.

Wyatville remodelled the ground floor to meet Georgian expectations, and what we see today is his plan (**ill. 15, overleaf**). He swept away all vestiges of 16th-century plasterwork and other architectural details in the polite rooms, including the wainscotting. His alterations involved much reorganisation of doorways, in the course of which the obsolete conventions of status within the medieval household were lost. High status rooms were now entered by ex-service doorways. Access to his new dining

Ill.15 *Phased Plan of Level 3.*

Ill.16 Plan of Wollaton Hall from Britton's Architectural Antiquities of Great Britain, *1809. The plan helps chart the changes made by Wyatville by this date.*

room, a polite room, was by the old Pantry door, which would have been unthinkable by the conventions which governed Willoughby's planning. Similarly, Lord Middleton's study was entered by the old Buttery door after further alterations c.1832. The insertion of centrally placed doorways into the Great Hall abolished its social orientation, as there was no longer a 'high' and 'low' entrance. The greater integration of classes in the Tudor household, where people ate and slept in close proximity, demanded that social hierarchy was maintained by strict distinctions manifest in the architecture and understood by all. Who sat where and which entrance they used had real significance. Now that the serving classes were kept separate, eating

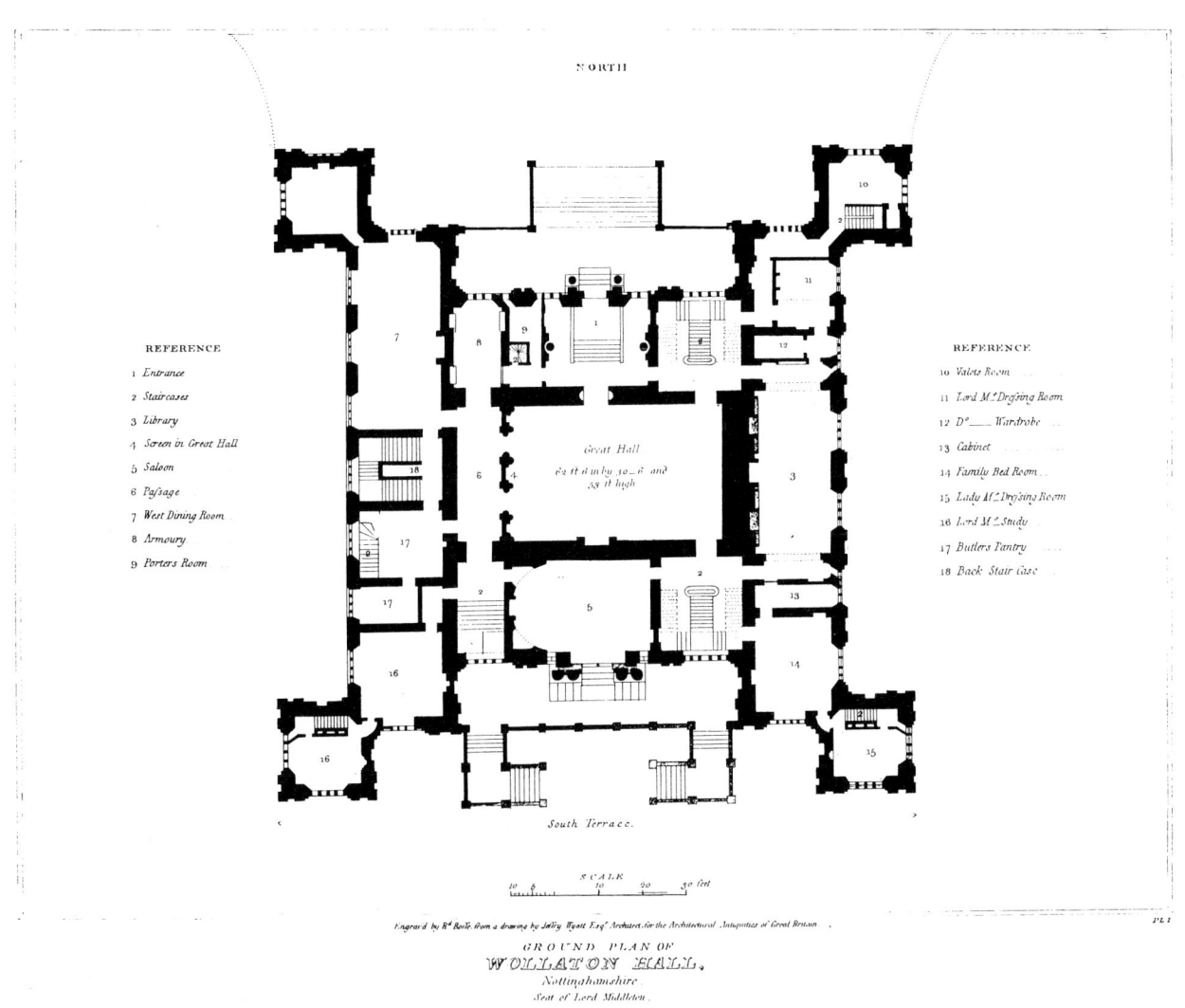

in their own quarters and housed invisibly at night, the need for these rules of architectural etiquette was removed.

Between c.1801-1809 the convoluted and asymmetrical entrance of the old house was completely reworked to provide a balanced entrance lobby of classical proportions (**plate 12**). The traditional porter's lodge and intrusive wardrobe were completely swept away. The long-changed function of the Great Hall, no longer the hub of an extended household, but a grand circulation area which could also serve as a ballroom, was now marked architecturally by a new and more direct approach from the entrance hall. The function of the screens passage had gone and there was no longer a need to retain architectural markers which had distinguished the 'high' from the 'low' end of the Hall and associated rooms. In 1832 Lord Middleton suggested that the central section of the screen might be removed to extend the Hall into the screens passage, but fortunately this was not done.[22] A new dining room was created in the north-west corner by combining the old pantry (3/16) and north-west corner chamber (3/15) into one. The south-west corner chamber (3/19) became a study and the inner chamber beyond (3/20) became a strongroom. Ironically Wyatville, who inserted mezzanine chambers all over the house, seems to have removed an original mezzanine room above this one. At the time of the Reform riots of 1832 (when Nottingham Castle was burnt by rioters) he inserted another, below the floor. This is vaulted to make it fireproof and was used to store muniments securely. He took out the state staircases, which must have seemed very confined, judging by the extant but slightly smaller western stair, and replaced them with cantilevered stairs (**ill.17**: compare **plate 13**). Radical changes were also made to the east wing of the ground floor. The staircase to the eastern postern door (3/Sb), the two painted chambers (3/9 and 3/10) and an inner chamber (3/11) were all removed and the external doorway to the staircase blocked. These spaces were combined to create a spacious library. The south-east corner chamber (3/7) remained a bedroom, with a wardrobe taking up some of the space made available by removing the postern staircase. The inner chamber (3/8) became Lady Middleton's dressing room. The north-east corner chamber (3/12) was considerably reduced in size, being partitioned to allow an access passage from the wine cellar stairs. This left the room, which became Lord Middleton's dressing room, undisturbed by traffic. Mezzanine chambers were inserted above the Buttery (3/17i) and the Butler's Chamber (3/18ii) and the south-east tower chamber (3/8i). Although a Tudor mezzanine room existed over north-east tower chamber (3/13i), it is likely that the mezzanine room which now occupies this position was re-built by Wyatville as part of a suite inserted over the north-east corner chamber (3/12i).

In 1832 Lord Middleton's anxiety over security led to further changes within the house. Bars were placed at the windows and the Tudor wainscotting in the Great Hall, despite being described as 'magnificent carved woodwork', was removed. It was seen as a liability in view of the recent 'deplorable example (at Nottingham Castle) how very soon a place may be consumed where there is dry wainscote.'[23] Rather perversely, it was replaced (**ill.18**). At the same time Middleton asked that wainscotting in his room (the study in the south-west corner chamber, 3/19) should be removed and a new

[22] Linstrum, 1972, 64,

[23] Ibid, 64: a letter from Lord Middleton to Wyatville, 2nd Feb 1832, in the collection of Mrs. J.M. Don.

Ill.17: The service staircase. Smythson's platt indicates that the original state staircases differed only in being slightly wider. (Photo by Philip Dixon.).

[24] Linstrum, 1972, 64.

entry made to it to accommodate improvements to the Saloon. Instructions were given 'to take down all the wainscote in the Salloon, and to fit up that Room in character with the rest of this building'. He wished to incorporate 'the space of the steps going into the garden' into it and 'if possible we may effect an exit to the Garden under the floor of the Salloon.'[24] It was at this time that the Regency sitting room (**plate 8**) took the shape it retains today, extending further west than its forerunner by the removal of the 'steps going into the garden' (3/Sa). A central doorway in the north wall allowed direct access from the Great Hall and French windows were opened on to the terrace. The garden steps (3/Sa), having been removed in accordance with Lord Middleton's wishes, were diverted from the terrace into the basement so that he also got his 'exit to the Garden under the floor of the Salloon'. The removal of the garden stairs necessitated a new entry to the study in the south-west corner chamber (3/19), which was achieved by a short corridor (3/19i) created by partitioning off a section of the Buttery.

Ill.18: A design drawing by Wyatville for replacement wainscotting in the Great Hall, 1832. The drawing suggested two choices, the left hand side being drawn on a flap which could be pulled down to reveal the right hand side as it would look over the whole elevation. Lord Middleton indicates in his own hand 'We wish to decide upon this (ie. the right), having four divisions, Because we think it will light better, & be nearer the old panels in the former wainscot.' By courtesy of Hallward Library [MiP3 p.15].

The First Floor (ills 19, 20)

In the Tudor house the first floor was reserved for entertaining. The central space was taken up by the upper part of the Great Hall and the entire east side was occupied by the Long Gallery (2/1) which measured thirty-seven metres. Access to the Gallery was by either of the state staircases and it is likely that of the first floor rooms, only the Gallery was used regularly. The tower chambers at either end of the Long Gallery (2/2, 2/3) seem to have been used as bedrooms. The northern chamber (2/2) is mentioned twice in the household inventories (in 1601 and 1609) and was better furnished than other tower chambers. It appears to have been unique amongst them in being heated, for a fire iron grate is listed in its contents and the north-east tower is alone in having an original flue.

The rest of the first floor was divided into two suites of twin apartments, one on the north and a slightly superior suite on the south side of the house. This duplication of sets of rooms so that the owner and his guest's household could be accommodated equally spaciously, has good

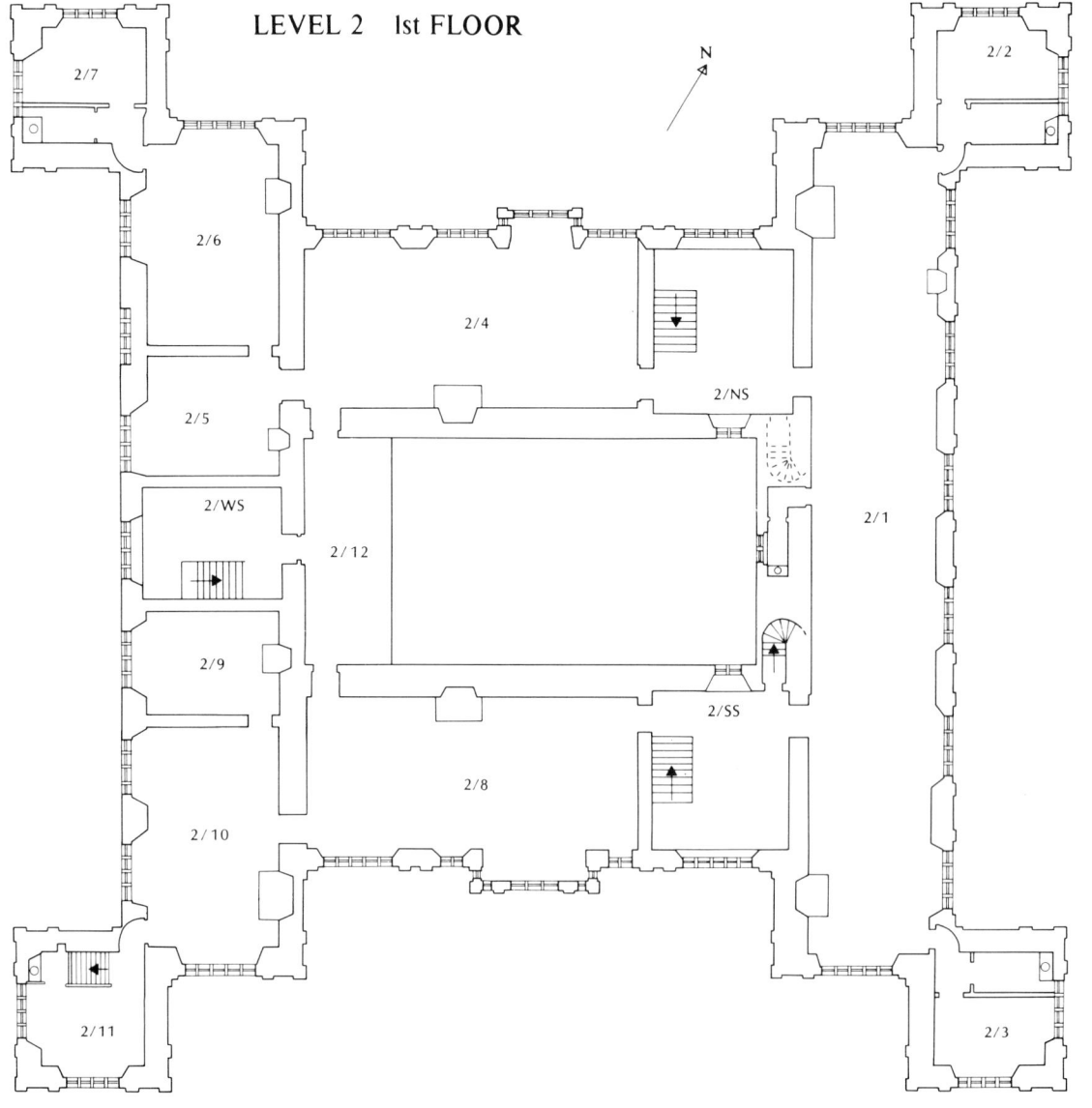

Ill.19. Reconstructed plan of the Tudor first floor (level 2).

[25] Faulkner 1963, 221-35.

Ill.20: Axonometric drawing of the Tudor first floor.

medieval precedents.[25] Each suite contained a Great Chamber (2/4, 2/8) with a principal entrance from a state staircase. At the other end of the room a doorway from the gallery over the screens (2/12) would have been used for service, for this gallery served as a sort of upper screens passage, being linked by the service staircase with the basement. The Great Chamber, like a miniature Great Hall, had its upper and lower end. Beyond the Great Chamber was a small withdrawing chamber (2/5, 2/9) and a corner bed-chamber (2/6, 2/10) with an inner chamber and garderobe in the adjacent towers (2/7, 2/11). The household inventories show the state rooms were lavishly furnished (see Appendix I).

However rooms 2/5 and 2/9 are referred to in three of the inventories as 'chambers at the kitchen stair head', which suggests that they were regarded as rather ancillary to the state suites. Their furnishings were less lavish, but they were reasonably well appointed and were probably intended for high ranking attendants. The north bed-chamber (2/6) is called the 'Queen's Chamber' in the inventory of 1609, no doubt recalling the visit of Queen Anne in 1603. The southern bed-chamber (2/10) is identified by the first four inventories as the 'Best Chamber', and by the inventory of 1609 as the 'Prince's Chamber', suggesting that it had been used by Prince Henry in 1603. The 1601

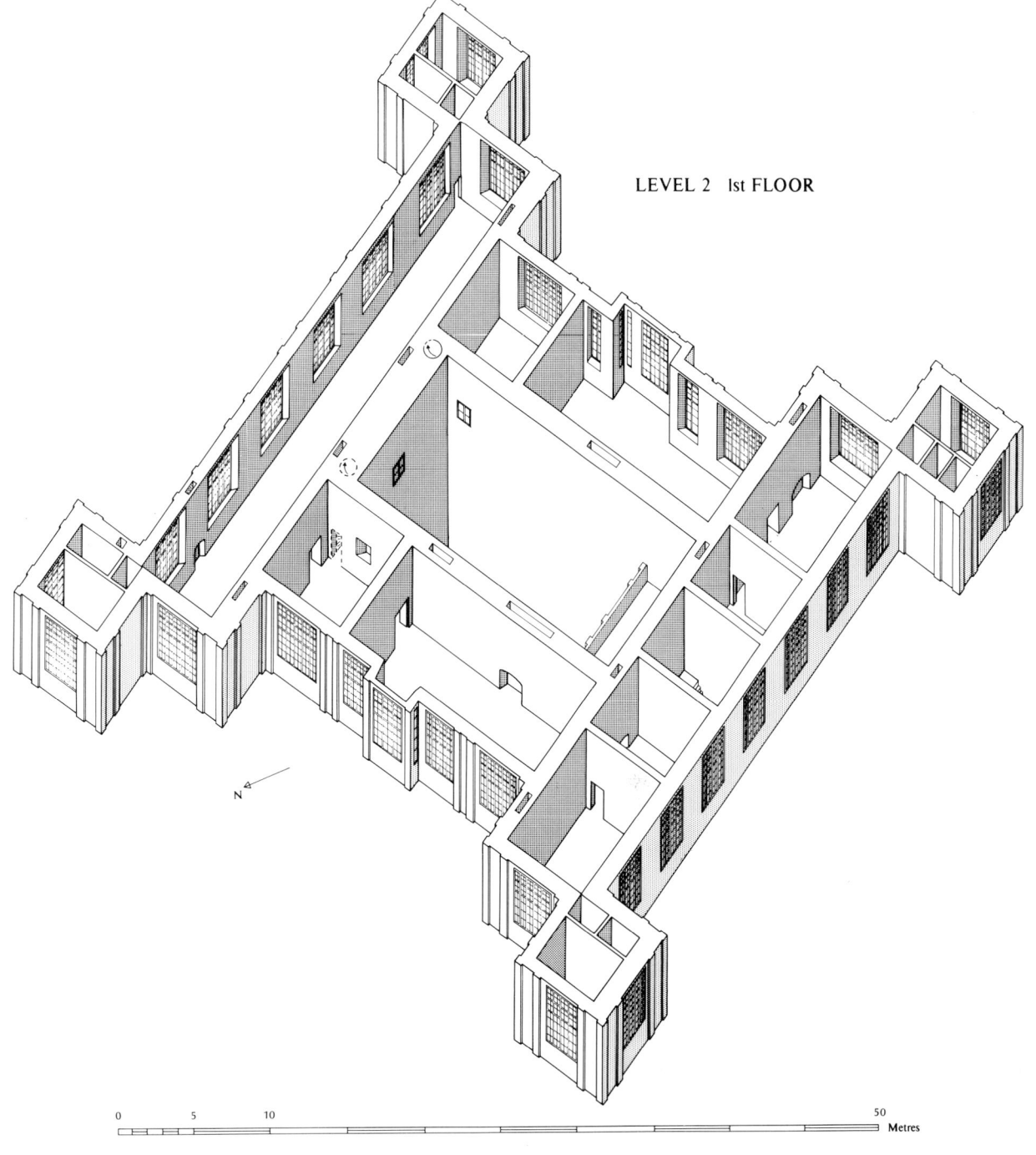

LEVEL 2   1st FLOOR

Ill.21: *Phased plan of the first floor (level 2).*

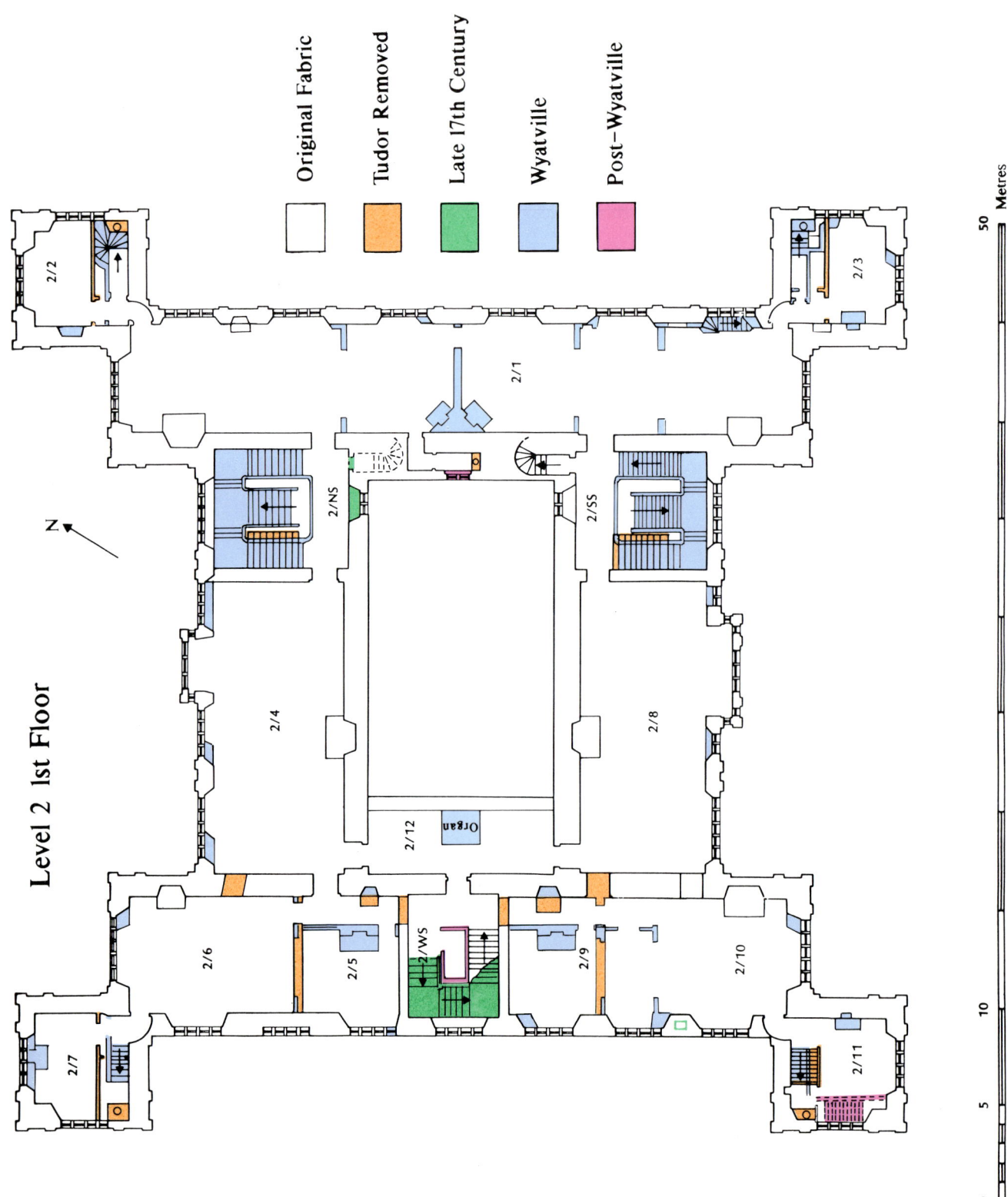

inventory speaks of a second chamber over the inner chamber (2/11), dealing with it as part of the southern state suite. There is still a mezzanine level chamber in this position, although it might be a Georgian replacement. The timber staircase to it is relatively modern and continues to the turret chamber on the leads, which was certainly not the case in the Tudor house. Examination of the floor joints in the mezzanine room, which was not possible during the survey, or their dendrochronological dating, might clear up this point.

During the tenure of Thomas and Cassandra the state staircases were decorated by Laguerre and Thornhill,[26] both fashionable artists. The execution of murals on the landing of the north state staircase might have prompted the blocking here of an access to a vice to the leads (see below). On the ground floor an elaborately carved door frame was inserted into the Great Hall opposite the northern staircase.

Wyatville multiplied the number of rooms on the first floor. He divided the Long Gallery into four and radically reorganised room divisions and entrances in the state withdrawing chambers (**ill. 21**). Here too, the medieval conventions of status attached to entrances were swept away. The withdrawing chambers (2/5, 2/9) could now be entered by arches driven through the landing of the service staircase. The 1609 inventory suggests that there might have been a mezzanine level chamber over the south gallery chamber (2/3), but Wyatville is likely to have been responsible for one now in this position, which is part of a mezzanine level suite inserted by him above the south end of the Long Gallery (**ill. 11**). A twin suite was placed above the north end of the Gallery. These rooms, less than 2 metres high and situated just beneath the leads, would have been unbearably hot in summer and very cold in winter.

[26] *Laguerre was working in 1699 and Thornhill in 1711. I am indebted to Elaine Guilding for this information.*

Ill.22: *The central Tower and half roof viewed from the leads. (Photo by Philip Dixon).*

The Leads (ill.7, page 13)

The whole of the roof area formed part of a recreational complex. The half roof of the main house, called 'the leads' (**ill. 22**) was used to enjoy the views and take some exercise in the open air, a sort of long gallery out-of-doors. A garderobe (1/6) was even provided. At each corner of the house turret chambers (**plate 3**) were gained only from the leads, their internal accesses dating only from the nineteenth century. They were perhaps intended for intimate banquets and picnics, like four of the turrets on the roof at Longleat.[27] The north-east turret chamber has an original flue (which probably served room 2/2), so it could have had a fireplace, otherwise none of the tower rooms were heated until the nineteenth century. Catering must have been simple in view of the distance from the kitchens and the awkwardness of the access. The earlier inventories do not include the turret chambers at all, and the later ones, of 1601 and 1609, show them to contain bedding. However, multiple use of rooms is indicated elsewhere in the house, as with the presence of bedding in the Dining Parlour (inventory of October 1596). It seems certain that the turrets were used occasionally as sleeping accommodation, but perhaps infrequently. Their inconvenient access across the open leads, and their sole convenience (a garderobe in the thickness of the central tower east wall, also accessed from the leads), suggest that they would be assigned to servants, perhaps the retinue of visitors.

The leads were reached by a narrow spiral staircase off the landing of the south state staircase, which also goes on to the High Hall and central tower roof. This stair is initially lit by borrowed light from the Great Hall through small loop windows. The presence of parallel lights at the north end of the Hall east wall suggests that a twin access was originally possible from the landing of the north state staircase. If so it must have been blocked during

[27] Girouard, 1983, 46. Here orders were given that four 'types' (ie. small domed turrets) were "to have little stairs won from the roof so as they may serve as banqueting houses."

Ill. 23: Timber staircase built during Phase 2 to link the first floor (level 2) with the leads (level 1), avoiding the more constricted Tudor access. The stair extends the west service staircase, which stopped at first floor level, where it is vaulted over. The base of the later stair well is therefore a solid floor, so the space was used to build a bathroom, probably early in the 20th century (Photo by Philip Dixon).

the late 17th century when the murals decorating this landing were executed. A staircase on the north side of the central tower now begins at leads level and rises to the High Hall and roof, mirroring the southern stair. No obvious evidence of a blocking can be discerned at its base, although the spiral is irregular at this point. However, well executed conversion work would not necessarily leave positive clues. (This is discussed in more detail in chapter 4.) The well-finished balustrades at the top of these stairs show that they were not merely meant to be used and seen by servants and artisans. They culminate in 'types', small studia or circular domed chambers which also form bartizans at each of the four corners of the tower, adding to the romantic appearance of the building.

The High Hall (**ill. 8**), later called the Prospect Room, is one of the most striking features of Wollaton. It is a large secondary hall which appears to float on top of the house, and is to a considerable degree responsible for the imposing appearance of the building (**plates 1 and 6: ill. 7**). In practical terms the apartment is almost useless: it was never heated, and its access very narrow and barely negociable in a farthingale. Servants could not easily have brought refreshments there, and its furnishings were sparse. Its sole appearance in the household inventories records 'certain mats and a joint stool' in 1601. It seems to have been designed, as its later name implies, as a room to walk in and admire the view, and is correspondingly well furnished with large windows. The High Hall is decorated with painted *trompe-l'oeil* drapery at the windows, dating from the eighteenth century[28] (**plate 4**).

[28]*Linstrum, 1972, 63.*

Thomas and Cassandra Willoughby by-passed the original means of gaining the leads by extending the western service staircase upwards in timber (**ill. 23**). A dome-shaped structure, covered in lead, was built against the western outer wall of the central tower at clerestory level to accommodate its exit. The young owners perhaps replaced the recreational function of the leads area to some extent when they built a new garden house in the grounds, depicted in Siberechts's painting (**plate 2**). Wyatville installed internal access to all the turret rooms and blocked the external doorways of the north-east and south-east turret chambers. He altered the external appearance of the leads further by installing extra chimney stacks, most notably the curved clusters of four stacks which meet over each turret to give a suggestion of a cupola (**plate 3**).

The Basement (ill. 24, 25)

The basement is built around a central core of solid Bunter sandstone which forms the foundation of the Great Hall and central tower. The floor level varies considerably as the natural topography of the site has been exploited, the soft sandstone having been levelled off and cut back to provide foundations.

In the Tudor house the basement was divided into two quite separate suites which were not directly accessible from each other. The first of these occupied the south-east corner and consisted of accommodation linked by an L-shaped corridor (**ill. 26**). It seems to have housed the upper servants of the household, and can be identified with the 'Yeomen's lodgings' of the 1601 inventory (see below, Appendix I). Under this heading five units of accommodation are listed, each furnished to a similar standard, which relate well to rooms 4/12, 4/13, 4/14, 4/17 and 4/18. The south state staircase descended to the basement to give access to the Yeoman's Lodgings, which is perhaps an indication of the occupants' status within the household. It is also significant that the rooms were kept distinct from the services, although they shared the same floor. The accommodation was comfortable, well lit and ventilated and had good access to sanitation, for there was a garderobe situated in the corridor (4SSii). It is possible that chamber 4/18 had its own garderobe. 4/13i, 4/11 and 4/16 were small chambers in spaces beneath staircases. A further entry in the 1601 inventory, 'The Gardener's Chamber', might conveniently represent room 4/15 in the south-east tower, which had direct access to and from the garden but could not be reached from inside the house.

The second, larger block of basement apartments occupied the entire north and west wings. Concerned with the preparation and storage of food and drink, it formed the service suite. Its main doorway from the western courtyard (**ill. 27**) led into a lobby (4/1) which was also the servery, with a hatch from one of the kitchens (4/2). Food was passed from here to the waiting staff and conveyed, via the western staircase (4/WS) to the Hall, Dining Parlour, and in the event of important visitors, to the Great Chambers on the first floor. As the liveried servitors were no doubt co-ordinated by butlers and stewards, two large niches were provided at the foot of the western staircase as a setting down place in the event of them having to wait. A blocked window on the first landing of the service stair overlooked the servery. Borrowed light was not necessary at this point for either stairs or servery and the window is more likely to have been used as a look-out point for one of the stewards orchestrating the business of conveying the food. From here he could see both down to the servery and up towards the Hall.

Preparation of food took place in five rooms (4/2 to 4/6 inclusive). There were two connecting kitchens with fireplaces (4/4 and 4/2). The first (4/2) contained the serving hatch and is called the 'outermost kitchen' in the inventory of 1601. Beyond it, in the north-west tower, was a small Pastry Kitchen (4/3). Above this room an original mezzanine chamber (4/3i) has survived. The inventories of 1599, 1601 and 1609 show that it was assigned to accommodate the cook. This must refer to the head cook and his family, as many more kitchen staff must have slept elsewhere. There is structural evidence to suggest that the second kitchen (4/4: **ill. 28**), the 'inner kitchen' of the 1601 inventory, had been conceived as a larger room. Both 4/4 and 4/5 are ceiled with quadripartite vaults supported by pillars, but the dividing wall between the two

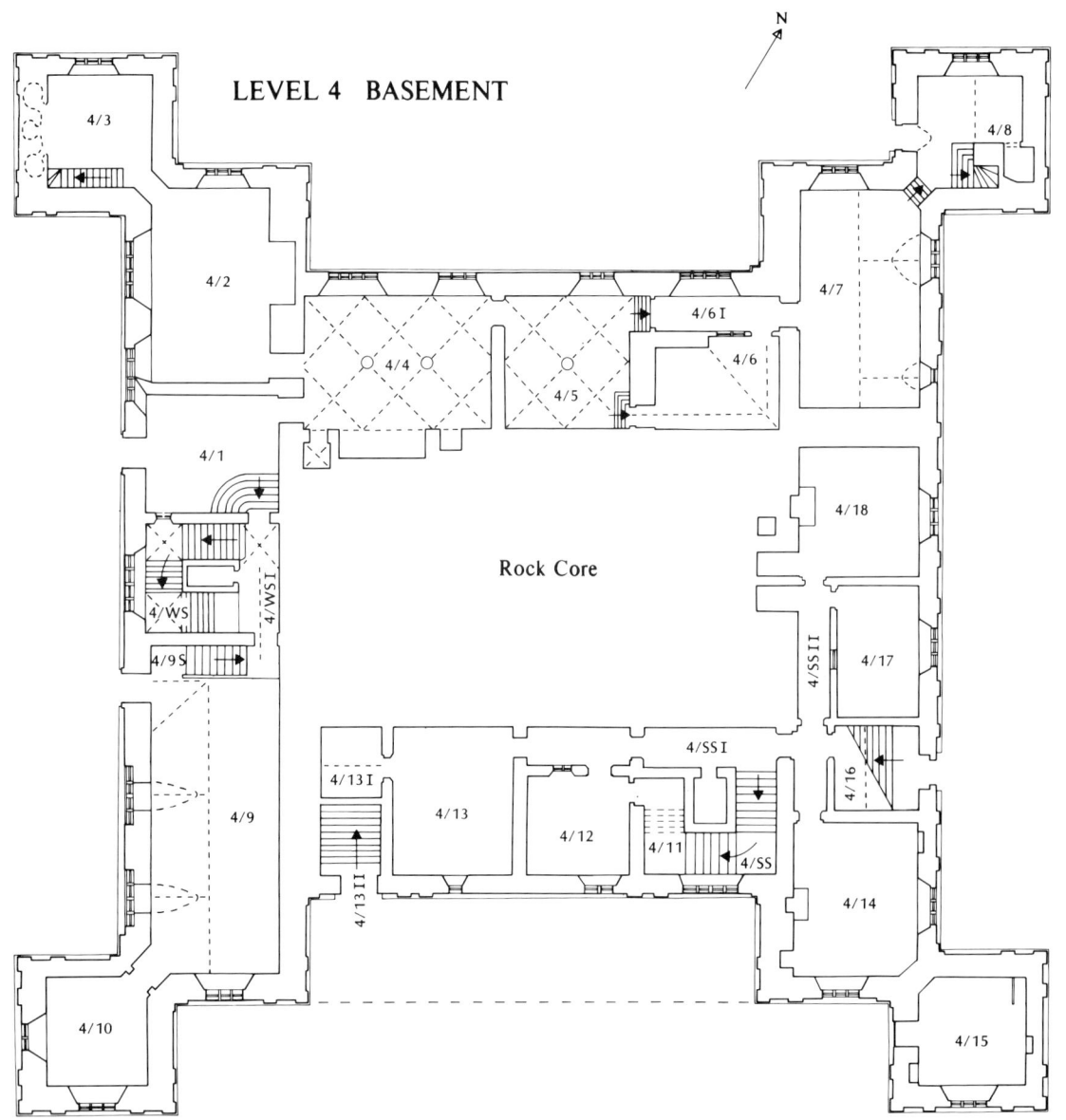

Ill.24: *Reconstructed plan of the Tudor basement (level 4).*

fouls the vault arrangement (see **ill. 24**). Had the two rooms been designed from the beginning as separate apartments, this would hardly have been necessary. It seems likely that a fourth pillar was envisaged where the wall is situated but the plan was changed at a relatively early stage in the building process, for the chamfered stone doorway which connects these rooms is entirely in keeping with the first build of the house. The wall stands directly beneath the position of a former dividing wall between the Porter's Lodge (3/2) and Wardrobe (3/3) beside the entrance hall on the ground floor (**ill. 12**). It seems that Smythson was unwilling to trust its weight to the vault. Room 4/5 is called the 'Larder' in the 1601 inventory. It was perhaps later converted to a scullery when a stone sink in this room was connected with the drains on the west side of the house (see chapter 4.). A 'Saucery' (4/6) completed the food preparation suite.

The north-east and south-west corners of the service block were devoted to the management of drink. The north-east corner was occupied by a vaulted wine cellar (4/7), which is indirectly

Ill.25: Axonometric drawing of the Tudor basement.

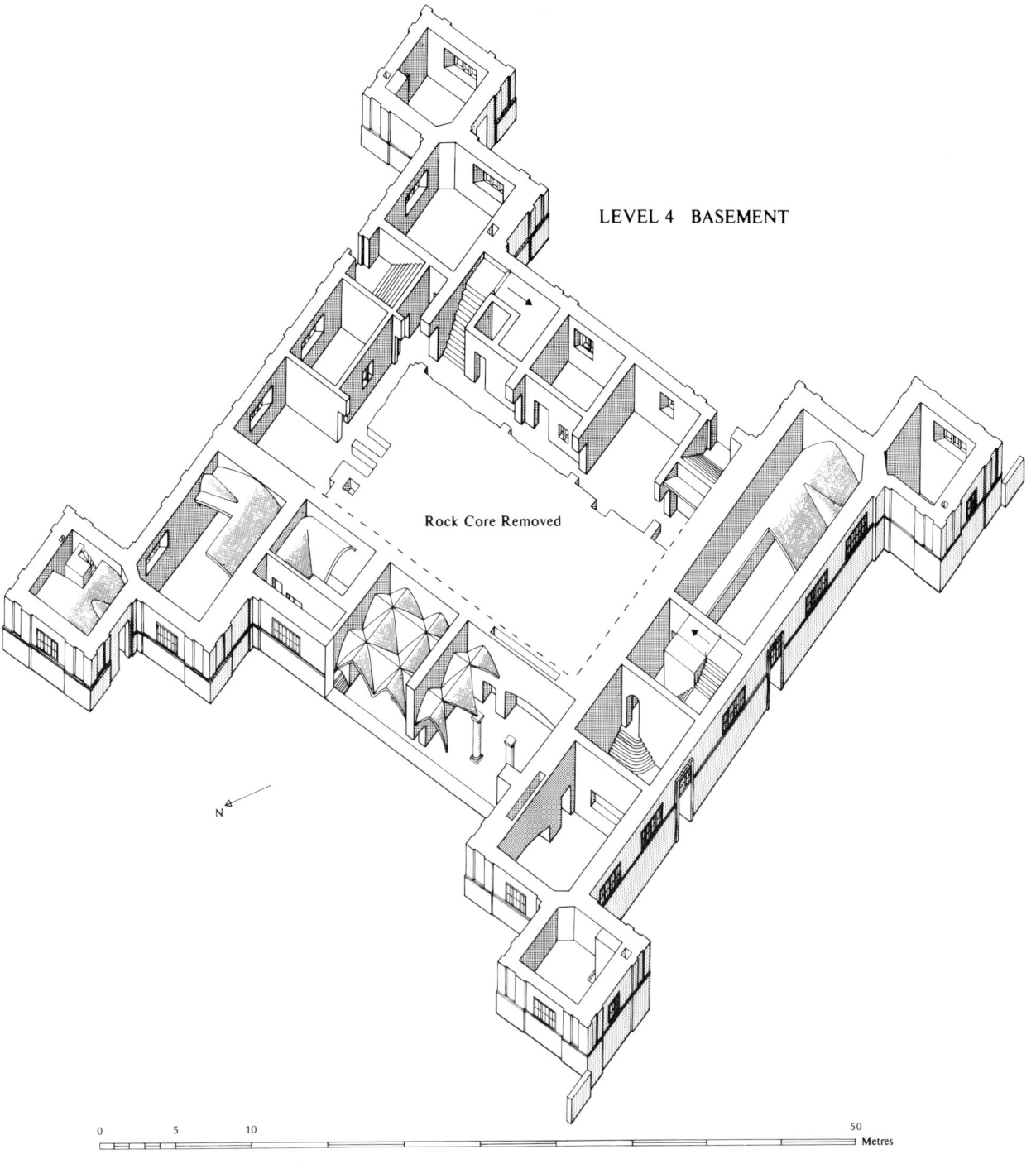

LEVEL 4 BASEMENT

Rock Core Removed

referred to in the inventory of 1596. The wine would be brought in by the wide exterior door in the adjacent north-east tower room (4/8: **ill.29**) and stored in the cellar. There was access from the cellar to the Saucery and Larder by a short passage (4/6i), and from thence to the kitchens beyond. However a separate staircase in the turret room (4/8), was provided to convey wine from the cellar to the upper end of the Hall without having to follow the more lengthy route to the western service stairs.

In the diametrically opposed south-west corner of the basement a similar vaulted cellar (4/9) dealt with ale. Again a wide doorway, now blocked, was provided to bring it in. This doorway architecturally matched that to the Lobby (**ill. 30**: cf. **ill. 27**), as the two would balance each other on the west facade. According to Smythson's platt (**ill. 5**), the brewhouse was situated just across the western courtyard. The cellar was situated next to the western service stairs by which the ale was conveyed to the lower end of the Hall. However, because the ground dropped naturally in this corner of the house, the floor of the ale cellar is about 2 metres lower than the foot of the western staircase (4/WSi), so a straight flight of stairs (4/9S) was necessary to reach it. These were set parallel to the western staircase and linked with the corridor at its foot (4/WSi). In Smythson's platt a staircase is drawn directly from the Buttery (3/17: **ill. 5**). While a stair directly linking the Buttery with the cellar would have been expected, in this position it would have cut the intersection of two barrel vaults (for details of this see survey of the basement, chapter 4) and therefore for structural reasons it cannot have been built as planned. It would also have blocked the external doorway to the courtyard. It seems likely that in drawing up his plan, Smythson had not taken account of a greater than expected drop in land surface at this point and had to modify the design on the ground.

During Phase 2 (late 17th century) a new subterranean ale cellar was built on the north side of the western courtyard (**ill. 37, 39, 40**). The old cellar (4/9) was converted to a servants' hall, with a fireplace inserted in the north wall, its flue emerging on the leads cleverly disguised in a baluster (**ill. 32**).

Some time after 1823 Wyatville added a single storey service block to the west side of the house (**ill. 10, 31**). A rough plan for this extension survives in Wyatville's hand (**ill. 34**). It included a new servants' hall, porch and rear entrance hall as well as extra rooms and it enclosed two yards. (Further additions of a workroom and public lavatories were made after 1926 when the building became a museum.) As well as the extension, Wyatville made some radical alterations to the Tudor basement. The floor area was increased yet further by the insertion of mezzanine level rooms over 4/9. A

Ill. 26: The southern arm of the corridor which linked rooms in the accommodation wing of the basement, the 'Yeomens' Lodgings'. The window shed borrowed light from one of the rooms (4/12) into the corridor (4/SSi) (Photo by Philip Dixon).

secure muniment room was also placed into the upper space of the tall south-west tower chamber (4/10). A lower ceiling vaulted in brick was inserted to make the floor of the strong-room and the north and south walls were thickened to carry the thrust of another vault above it, which formed its ceiling. Access to the muniment room was by a trapdoor in the floor of the ground floor room (3/20) above it.

More significantly, the distinction between service and accommodation blocks was abolished by driving a circulatory corridor around the whole floor. This was no easy task, for it meant breaking through two thick dividing walls and, more dauntingly, negotiating substantial changes in floor level. It was necessary to introduce a mezzanine floor in one corner and resort to tunnelling in another. Stretches of Tudor corridor were used where they already existed (4/SSi and 4/SSii) and new stretches were created where necessary by truncating rooms, eg. 4/13 and 4/13i were cut back to make a new stretch of corridor (4/SSia). The determination to form a complete circuit is perhaps best illustrated in the north-east corner, where joining corridor 4/SSii with the wine cellar (4/7) involved cutting back room 4/17,

Ill. 27 (above, left): *Doorway from the western courtyard into the Lobby/Servery (4/1). The service extension added c.1823-25 has made the doorway an internal one (Photo by Philip Dixon).*

Ill. 28 (left): *The 'inner kitchen' (4/4), converted to a boiler room when the building became a museum. The quadripartite vaults are supported on two pillars (Photo by Philip Dixon).*

then tunnelling below the floor of room 4/18. Some of the basement rooms were still used as staff accommodation, some of whom would have been fairly high-ranking: it was probably at this time that room 4/14 became known as the 'Steward's Room'. However there was no longer any division between the service and residential functions of the basement, which Smythson had clearly marked architecturally.

With the provision of a new servants' hall c.1823 the function of the seventeenth century hall (4/9), originally the Tudor ale cellar, was changed again. It was split horizontally and its access stair rebuilt. Wyatville's drawing (**ill. 34**) labels this area 'old servants' Hall to become bedrooms' and indeed the split cellar provided two large dormitories. A mezzanine floor, inserted into the upper space of the cellar under the barrel vault, was partly used to create the circulatory corridor, the rest being divided into two rooms (**ill. 33**). The smaller of these (4/9i) incorporated the upper space of the old cellar

Ill. 29 (left): *External door to the Tudor wine cellar in the basement of the north-east tower (4/8) (Photo by Philip Dixon).*

Ill. 30 (below): *Blocked external doorway to the Tudor ale cellar (4/9). Originally giving on to the western courtyard, but now enclosed by the service extension of c.1823-25.*

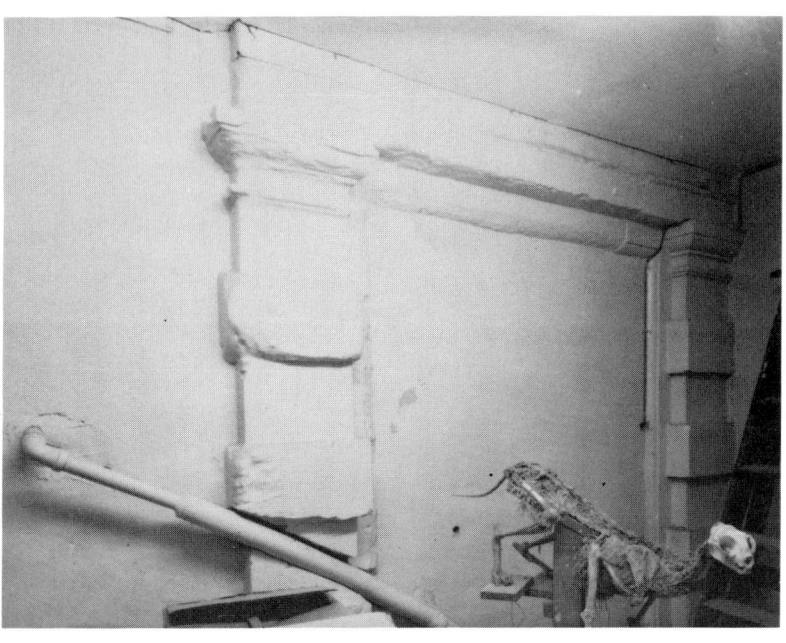

3: A FLOOR BY FLOOR ANALYSIS   37

Ill. 31: Phased plan of the basement

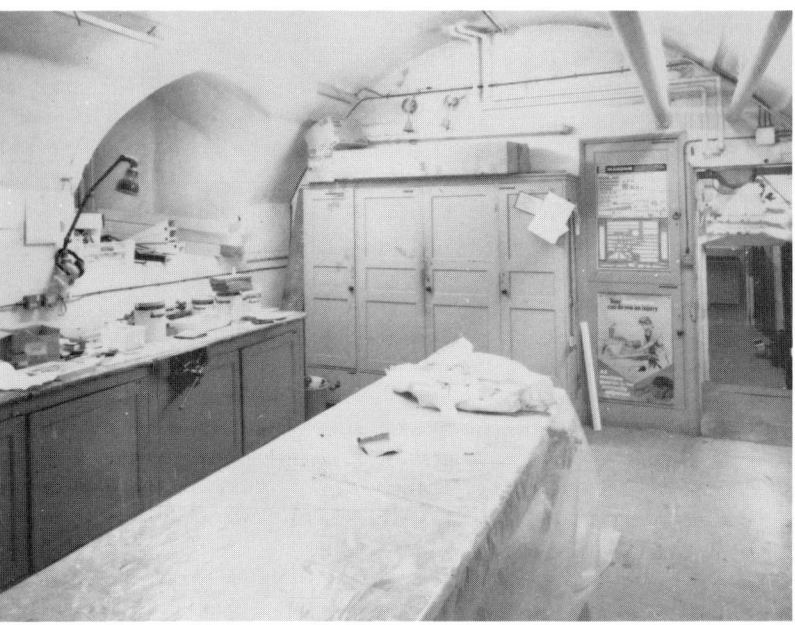

staircase (4/9S), the lower part of which was bricked up.

In 1832, in response to a request from Lord Middleton to alter the Saloon, Wyatville diverted a stairway from the south terrace (3/Sa) directly into the basement (4/13ii). The stair was conveyed into a small barrel-vaulted room (4/

Ill. 32 (above left): *Chimney disguised in a baluster on the leads. The smoke emerged through the niche (Photo by Philip Dixon).*

Ill. 33 (above right): *Mezzanine level dormitory placed under the vault of the Tudor ale cellar (4/9i) c.1823-25. Now one of the museum workrooms (Photo by Philip Dixon).*

Ill. 34 (below): *Wyatville's roughly drawn plan for the service extension c.1823. By courtesy of the Hallward Library [MiP3].*

13i) which had been designed by Smythson to bear the weight of its Tudor predecessor.

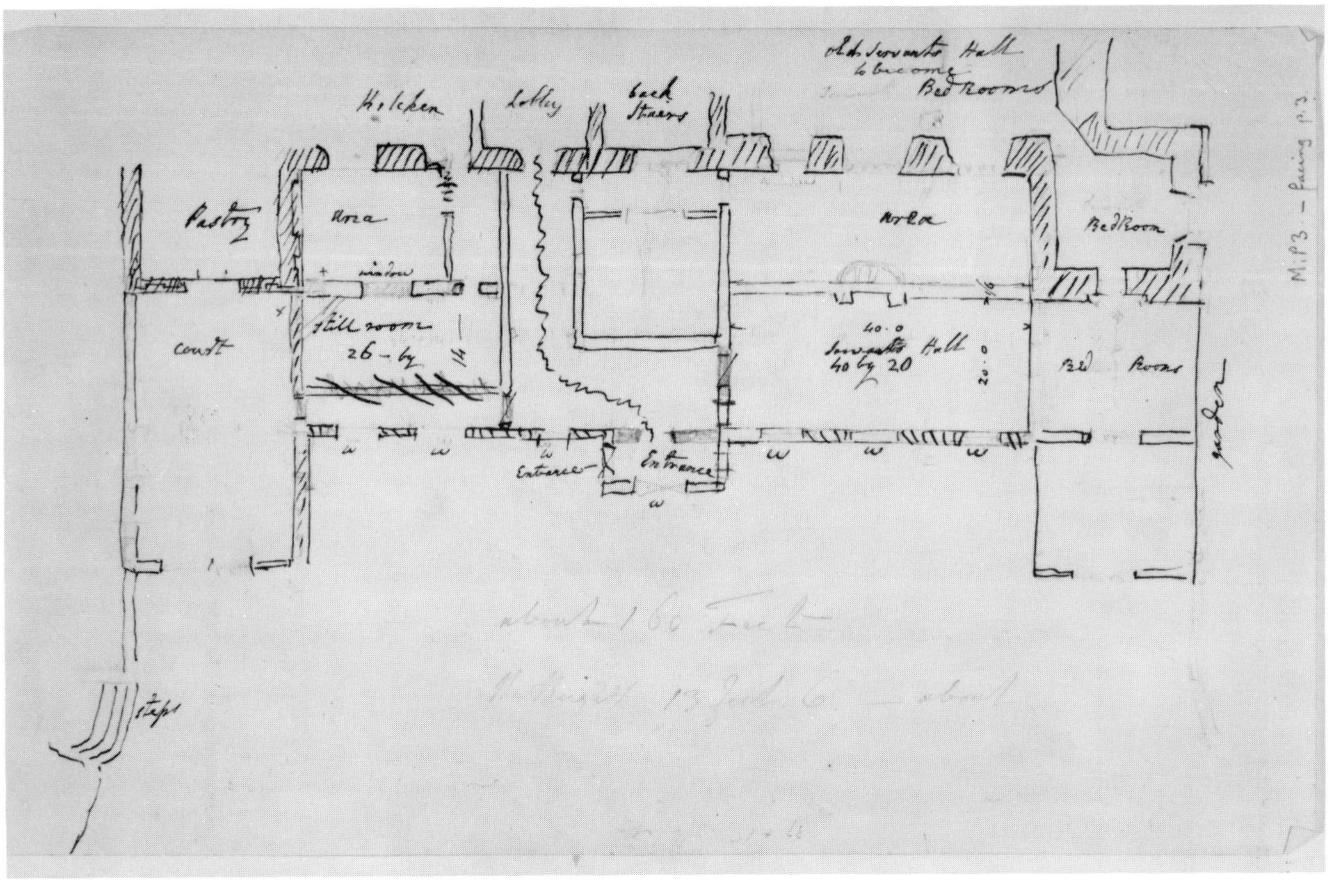

The Underground Works

The Tudor Drains (ill. 37)

In the original house sanitation was provided by two separate underground drainage systems, one on the east and the other on the west side (**ills 38, 39**). Each consisted of a long main sewer with shorter culverts leading from the bottom of vertical chutes, within the thickness of the house walls, which carried away waste from the garderobes. Only one chute is still visible inside the house (in room 3/20), but most are clearly seen from within the sewers themselves.

The chutes are sited precisely where garderobes are expected from Smythson's design plan (**ill. 5**). Each of the tower chambers had corner garderobes on both the ground and first floors. In the south-east tower the basement room was used as accommodation (4/15: the Gardener's Chamber), and it is quite likely that there was a garderobe provided in it. The Cook's Chamber was situated in the diametrically opposite north-west tower. This was merely a mezzanine room above the pastry kitchen, but the stone stairs which lead to it stop short of the south-west corner, where the garderobe chute is found in the wall thickness. This might have been deliberately contrived to give access to a sink or slop-out in the corner of the pastry kitchen, in an age when hygiene was imperfectly appreciated. It is technically possible that the cook's small apartment had a garderobe. The north-east and south-west tower basements were next door to cellars, where swilling and slopping out would be fairly regular occurrences, and so direct access to the drains would be useful. There is evidence that the north-east tower room (4/8) had access to the garderobe chute behind the

Ill. 35 (right): The main passage in the eastern sewer system (Photo by Chris Salisbury).

Ill. 36: Culvert from the south-east tower, with garderobe chute at the far end (Photo by Chris Salisbury).

Ill.37: Location plan of the underground works

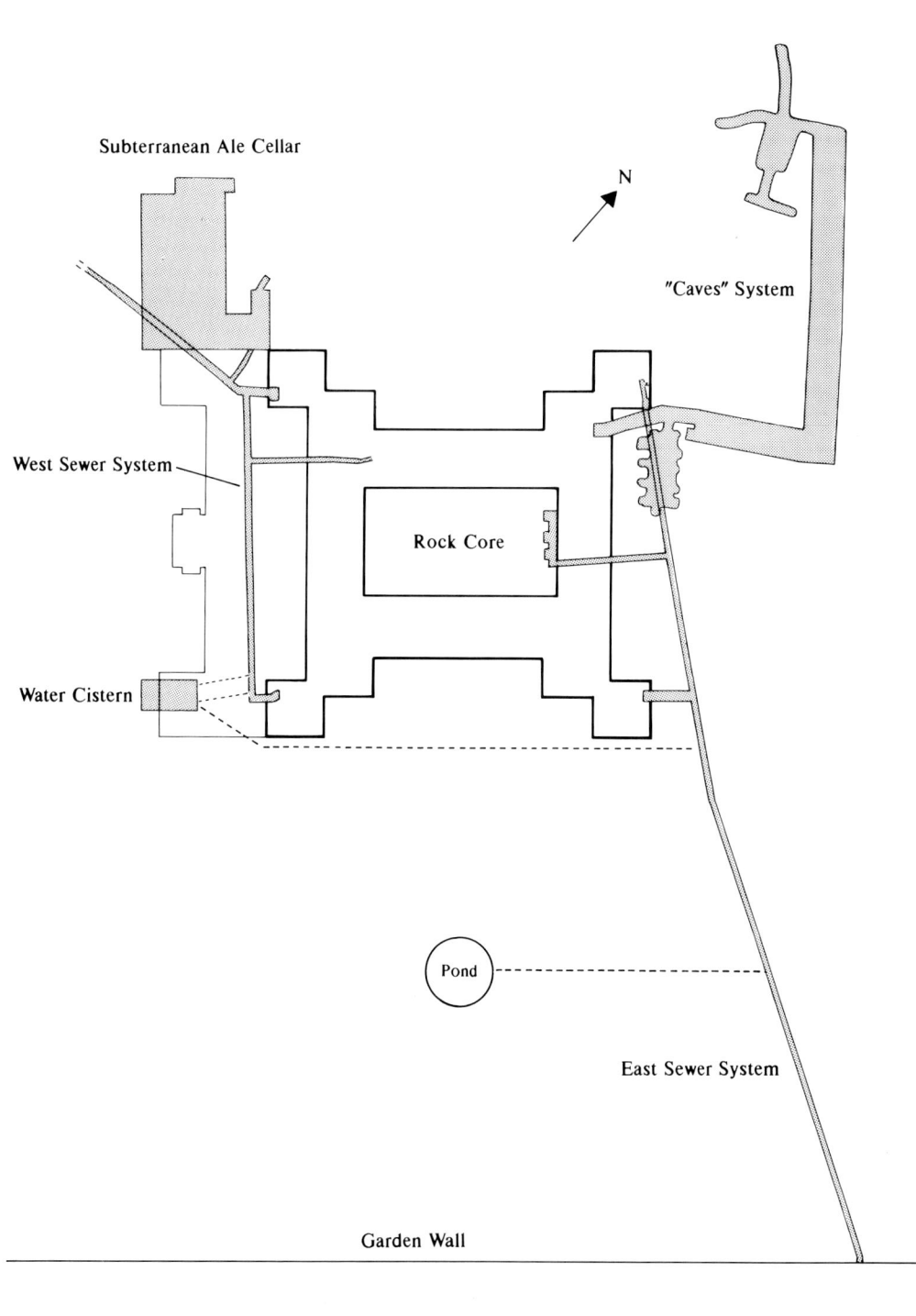

wine cellar stairs. In this position it was perhaps more likely to be used as a slop-out than a toilet. In the south-west tower basement (4/10) next to the Tudor Ale Cellar, the west wall was thickened in brick by Wyatville in connection with the insertion of a vault to create the muniment room (4/10i) above. However, near the floor in the appropriate corner is an arched opening, now blocked, whose best explanation is perhaps a floor level drain which was preserved when the wall was thickened.

On the east side of the house (**ill. 38**) there was an additional set of three garderobe chutes in the thickness of the central tower wall. These served a convenience on the leads, one off the Long Gallery on the first floor (2/1), and one in each of the Painted Chambers on the ground floor (3/9 and 3/10). In the basement they provided a communal toilet in the corridor (4/SSii) for four of the five Yeomen's Lodgings (4/13, 4/12, 4/14, 4/17) and very likely a private garderobe in the remaining one (4/18).

The sewers are constructed in brick, with barrel-vaulted roofs (**ill. 35**) and have been designed to maintain a steady fall, with slightly V-shaped brick floors so that liquid would easily have drained away. It might well have been common practice to flush out the culverts, where there is generally a steeper fall, by pouring water down the chutes, but in the main passages the slope is universally too gentle to ensure that this would remove solids. The main tunnels must have been regularly and manually cleaned and are tall enough for a man to stand upright in. Although often lower, headroom in the culverts would still allow this practice (**ill. 36**). Both systems survive for considerable lengths but have been cut short by later work, so it is impossible to say how they originally terminated. We may speculate that they ended in soakaways at a reasonable distance from the house. The circular pond in the centre of the south garden is connected with the eastern system by a narrow drain, so that it could be emptied as necessary. A pond in this position might have been an original feature, as formal gardens featuring a circular centrepiece appear on Smythson's design plan (**ill. 5**).

On the west side (**ill. 39**) the sewer system originally connected only with the tower garderobe chutes, but two further culverts were added later. During Phase 2 a drain was connected to the newly built Ale Cellar and, probably during Phase 3, another was inserted under the house to serve the kitchens area (possibly a sink in the Larder, 4/5). A brick-lined cistern just west of the south-west tower might date from the same period. It was designed to store water conveyed into it by drain-pipes from the roof. An overflow connects the top of the cistern[29] with the south-west corner of the sewer so that in the event of overfilling the surplus would run into the drainage system, helping to flush it out. In parts the sewer had to be strengthened where later work was built over it. The south-west corner of the Ale Cellar overlies it, causing a considerable stretch to be reinforced, and this was dated by a sherd of pottery to the late 17th or early 18th century (Phase 2). A similar step was taken by Wyatville when his service extension was built above another part, although here only one point was strengthened.

[29] *I am indebted to Nottingham City Engineers Department for this information.*

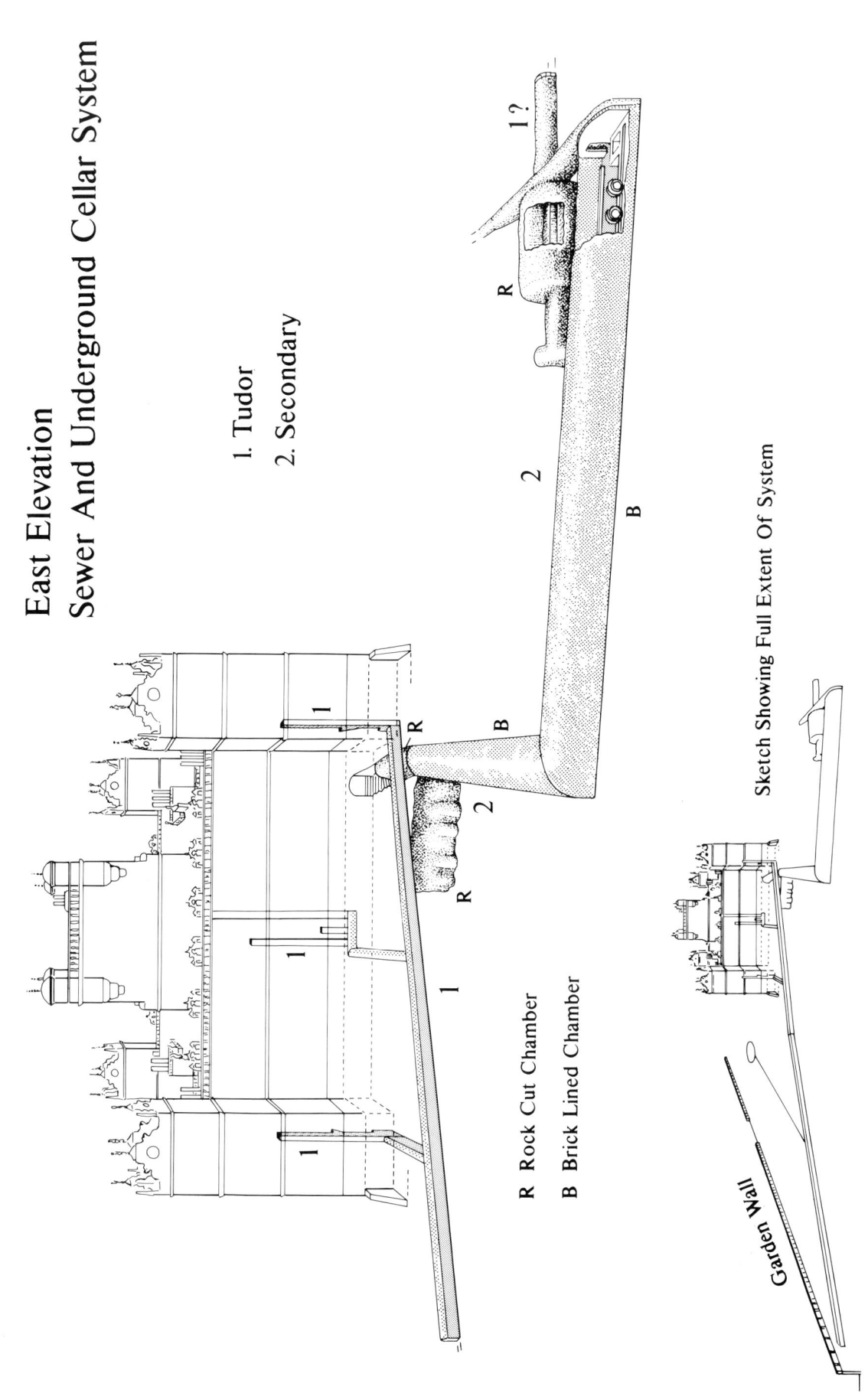

Ill. 38: Perspective elevation of the east side of the house, showing underground works.

3: A Floor by Floor Analysis   43

Ill. 39: Perspective elevation of the west side of the house, showing underground works.

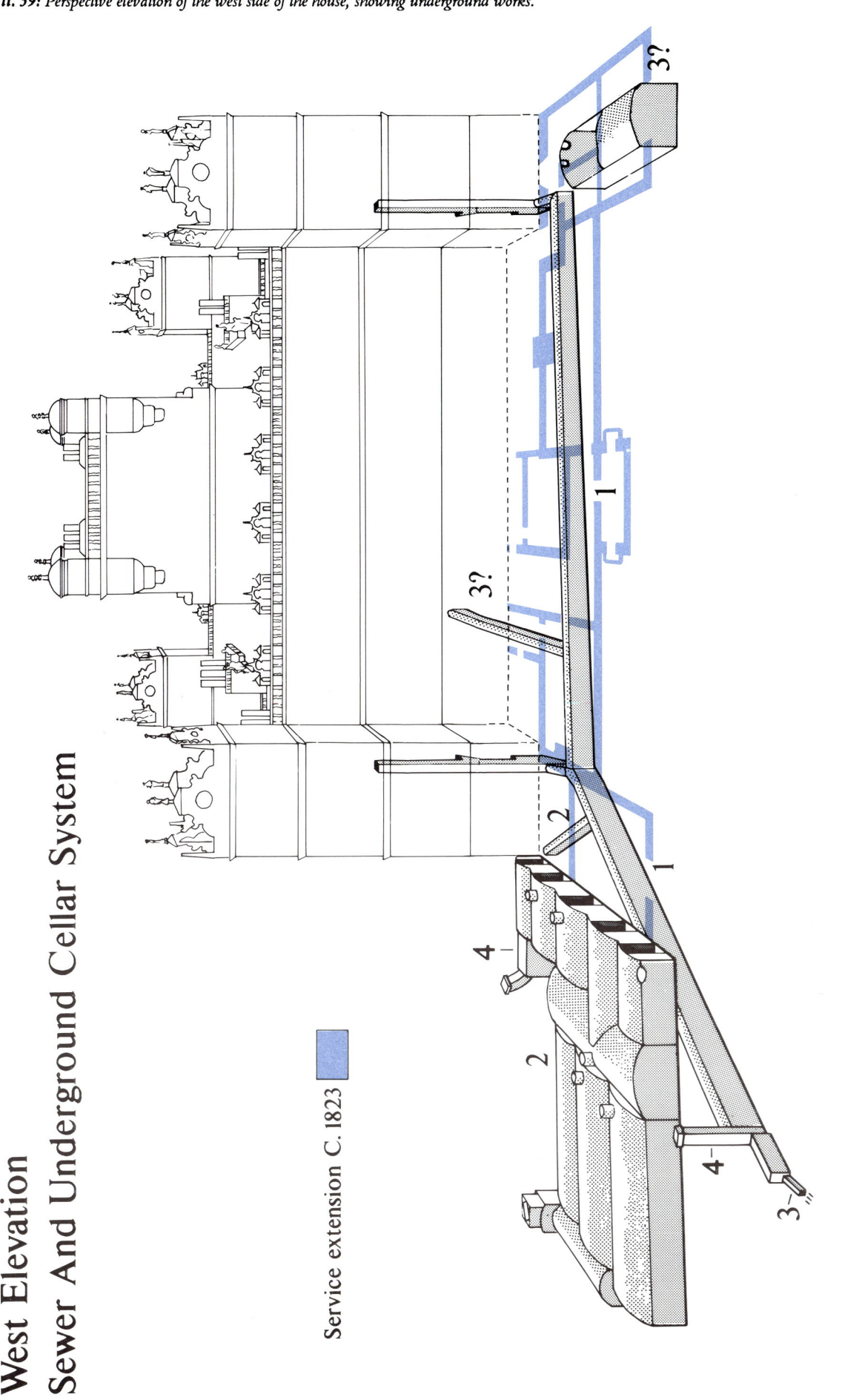

West Elevation
Sewer And Underground Cellar System

Service extension C. 1823

The Subterranean Ale Cellar (ills 37, 59)

Thomas and Cassandra Willoughby made few important changes within the house which can still be discerned, but one of these was to convert the Tudor Ale Cellar (4/9) into a servants' hall. The loss was remedied by the construction of a much larger Ale Cellar by the north-west corner of the house (**ill. 37**). The building consists of a series of brick vaulted chambers (**ill. 40**) and it runs northwards to a length of over 19 metres. The south front of the cellars formed a new facade on the north side of the service courtyard and this elevation, at least, was built at ground level, with a row of five doorways into the courtyard (**ill. 39**). Only this and a very short section of wall at the south end of the west facade could be seen above ground, for the rest was completely covered in earth. Without excavation it is impossible to tell whether the building was erected at ground level then buried or whether the site was excavated from existing higher ground and reburied. In any case, the intention was always that the cellars should be subterranean, for ventilation shafts were placed in the roof. The builders were no doubt anxious that the architectural impact of the house should not suffer from the close proximity of such a utilitarian structure.

Three of the five wide doorways in the courtyard elevation were blocked by Wyatville's service extension, which included a yard (marked 'court' on **ill. 34**: see also **ill. 31**). His design sketch shows the radiating steps which still exist by the south-west corner of the cellar, with the westernmost of the five doorways also blocked. On the same plan a gap is left inside the yard and it seems likely that the remaining doorway (second from the west end) was retained within the yard as the only access to the cellar. It remains so today, although Wyatville's yard now houses public lavatories. At a later date, probably the 20th century, one bay of the Ale Cellar was extended and two others altered to create a coal cellar.

Ill. 40: Subterranean Ale Cellar *(Photo by Chris Salisbury).*

The Eastern 'Caves' System (ills 37, 38)

Beneath the ground on the east side of the house is a complex of wide passages and small chambers which has become popularly known as the 'cave' system or the 'Admiral's Bath' complex. The spaces have been tunnelled from the soft sandstone which forms the natural geology of the site, although most are lined in brick. In the absence of either documentary evidence or stylistic detail, it is impossible to date the complex, except to say that its entry post-dates the original build of the house, but the plan suggests a possible interpretation.

The complex (**ill. 44**) is entered by a doorway cut into the east wall of the Wine Cellar (4/7), where a flight of stone steps descends sharply. The original wall of the house was roughly hacked through and not made good. The steep descent was necessary to avoid the eastern sewer, which crosses just above the staircase. As there is no sign of damage to the sewer having been repaired, we must assume that the entry represents a very competent piece of engineering. At this point

Ill. 41 (top, left): Staircase leading to the 'caves' system from the Tudor ale cellar (Photo by Chris Salisbury).

Ill. 42 (left): The rock-cut cistern known as the 'Admiral's Bath'. (Photo by Chris Salisbury).

Ill. 43 (below): View of the main passage in the 'caves' system, leading to the 'Admirals' Bath'. (Photo by Chris Salisbury).

46 WOLLATON HALL

Ill. 44: Plan and sections of the 'caves' system at the NE corner of the house.

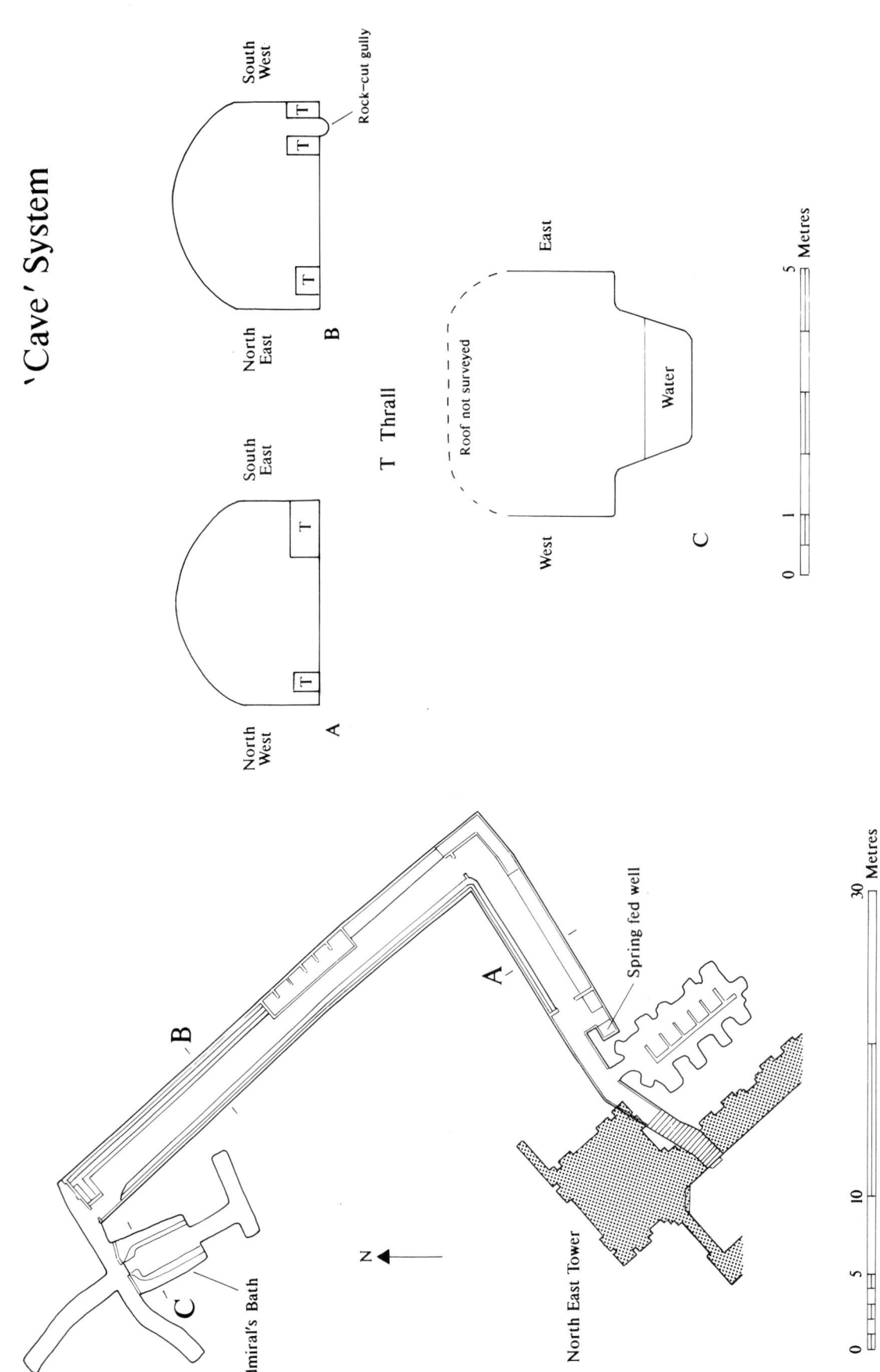

the stair passage is quite roughly cut from the sandstone (**ill. 41**), but when it reaches the bottom it is lined with a brick barrel-vault. There is an irregular-shaped chamber cut from the natural rock off to the south-east, which is furnished with brick wine-bins and a barred gate. As the doorway has been cut through the bricks of the passage wall, the room appears to be a late addition. Recent and regular rock falls within this chamber perhaps demonstrate why the greater part of the complex was brick faced.

Not far beyond this the passage widens and later turns northwards (**ill. 43**), eventually linking up with a system of narrower, more roughly cut passages approximately 30 metres away. The centrepiece of these is a large rock-cut cistern (**ill. 44**), popularly called the 'Admiral's Bath' because of a tradition that Rear Admiral Sir Nesbitt Willoughby (d.1849) bathed in it daily while resident at the Hall. The cistern fills naturally and is never dry, and it may explain the motive for building the 'caves' complex. The two legs of the main L-shaped passage have been furnished with brick thralls to store barrels, but the use of this complex as an additional cellar for the storage of liquor might be secondary to its main purpose, which is more likely to be concerned with water supply. The 'Admiral's Bath' and the adjoining blocked passages are different in character from the rest of the complex. The passages are irregular, as the miners appear to have followed natural veins and fissures in the rock while tunnelling them out. It might be significant that the rock around the cistern itself seems quite stable, as if a particularly hard section has been chosen in which to fashion it. Associated passages, one running north and the other west, have both been blocked by rock falls but might represent earlier accesses to the cistern. Whilst it is impossible to date a rock-cut, featureless cavern, it may be that the cistern is part of a water storage system belonging to the original house, accessible only from outside by passages which became dangerous. Water supply to a house built on top of a hill must have been something of a problem, and it should be remembered that the Willoughby family fortune was partly based on successful coal-mining. The creation of artificial caves has also been part of Nottingham's building tradition since the Middle Ages. The 'caves' complex also encompasses a natural spring-fed well, which is always full of clear water (**ill. 45**). The continual fetching of water from a source outside must have been a burden. This well might have been one of several in the immediate vicinity of the house, but was conveniently placed to be incorporated into an underground passage not too far from the kitchens.

Ill. 45: Spring fed well in the 'caves' system (Photo by Chris Salisbury).

The following interpretation of the 'caves' system can therefore be made. The 'Admiral's Bath' area survives from an original water supply system, which might have been more extensive, but was inconvenient as it was only accessible from outside the house. A plan was therefore devised which would enable the cistern (and possibly others whose access is now lost) to be reached more directly, and which would also incorporate access to a spring. The resulting space, in cool, dark conditions, was exploited as extra cellarage, and this was later extended by the addition of a further chamber on the south side.

4: SURVEY OF THE HOUSE

After the discussion of the development of the house in the previous chapter, we must turn to an examination of the details of structure and to a description of the individual rooms in the house. The present chapter begins with the discussion of a series of themes, and then surveys the house room by room from the roof downwards.

Part 1. STRUCTURE AND FABRIC

The foundations of the house have been cut from the Bunter sandstone core of the hill on which the building stands. In the basement the load-bearing walls are of stone, some of it probably robbed from Lenton Priory,[1] and the rest quarried at Mansfield. Mansfield stone would have been chosen for courses up to and including the plinth as this fine-grained sandstone does not readily absorb moisture and acts as a sort of damp-course. Its source was quite local (14 miles away), and its colour blends well with Ancaster stone, which was chosen for the facades. This honey coloured limestone was the best building stone in the region and was brought from a distance of 35 miles. The building accounts show that Smythson spent some time at the Ancaster quarry personally supervising the stone-getting. His efforts were worthwhile, for the stonework remains in very good condition and, except where openings have been altered and the work made good, the building has not been refaced.[2] Above the plinth, the hall is basically a brick building with a stone facade. Where the inner walls have been exposed,[3] the rear-arches of all the original openings are in brick, although the dressed door and window surrounds are of stone. Smythson shows himself to have been a cautious builder in making supporting walls excessively thick.

In places, oyster shells can be seen to have been used as packing in the fine joints of the masonry, a practice unlikely to have occurred on a subsequent refacing. The balustrade on the half roof or leads mostly appears to be original, with oyster-shell packing occasionally visible in the joints. The coping and balusters have been leaded in. On the east side, however, new coping has replaced the original, which appears on Siberechts' painting as matching that on the west. The shield on the south facade bearing the Middleton Arms was added in Ketton stone, the same material used for statues in the garden. Masons' marks are not often seen and when they do occur they appear to be piece-work banker marks. The more elaborate work is unmarked on the face, suggesting that a particular craftsman undertook a particular stretch of decoration, and the building accounts tend to confirm this.[4]

The roofs are covered in lead. The roof of the central tower was originally flatter than the present one and at least some of the original timber structure is visible through a trap door. However it was not investigated as part of this survey.

The surviving stretches of the original sewer system are of vaulted brick with brick floors (ill. 35). Some secondary culverts have been added in the same material. An underground cellar for storage, probably of ale, built beside the NW corner of the house during the 17th century, is also of vaulted brick with brick floors (ill. 40). This complex was extended during the 19th century.

Surface water drainage

A collection gutter runs along the cornice outside the central tower where the Great Hall joins the High Hall and the slightly pitched roofs of the Prospect Room, half roof and turrets all have drainage channels. The water was conveyed by lead down-pipes which cut through the string-courses on the facades. The drainpipes fed underground channels along the south front of the building which were located by excavation by the City of Nottingham Drains Dept.[5] The water collected in an underground brick-built tank in the south-east corner of the west service courtyard, which appears to be secondary. From here it could be drawn and any overflow was conveyed into the west sewer system.

[1] *The first two years of the building accounts (which would confirm or deny this conjecture) are unfortunately missing.*

[2] *John Key, Nottingham City mason, confirms this.*

[3] *Information from Prof. Barley.*

[4] *Rossell, 1957, 44.*

[5] *Information from Mr P. Coveney, Nottingham City Drains Department.*

Chimneys

a) Half Roof Level

Overlooking the recesses of the N and S facades were sets of double chimneys which served the corner bed chambers and long gallery. The SE set may also have served room 4/14 in the basement. On the S front an extra chimney has been added to the SW group, the straight joint in its base clearly visible. The chimney stacks are in Mansfield stone and probably replaced Tudor originals, perhaps c.1774, when the stable block was faced in Mansfield stone. Of the SE group one stack is in Mansfield and looks older; the others were replaced in Ancaster by Lord Middleton's mason in the 1920s.[6]

The curving chimneys over the turrets are built in brick and rendered over (**plate 3**). They do not appear in early pictures of the house and were added by Wyatville when he inserted fireplaces into the tower chambers. He also submitted plans to rebuild the turret chambers completely, but this was not carried out.[7]

On the W side there is a chimney worked into the balustrade (**ill. 32**). This dates from the late 17th century when the Tudor Ale Cellar was converted to a servants' hall.

b) Central Tower Roof

Here a central stack of 3 chimneys on the N side served fireplaces in the kitchens, Great Hall, Porter's Lodge and North Great Chamber. A similar set on the south side served the South Great Chamber, Dining parlour and probably room 4/13 in the basement. On the W side a pair of chimneys towards each end served the state withdrawing chambers on the first floor. On the E side there was only one pair of chimneys for the Painted Chambers and possibly room 4/18 in the basement. Siberechts' painting of 1697 shows only one set of chimneys on the W side. Of the five Yeomans' Lodgings in the basement, two were certainly unheated (4/17 and 4/12). The remaining three could have had fireplaces if flues were extended to basement level, but this cannot be known for certain. They may have remained unheated until Wyatville's alterations.

Buttressing to the Central Tower

The buttresses under the bartizan turrets on the central tower appear to have been added late in the 17th century. Although the work has been extremely well done, there is some discrepancy in the coursing and something approaching a straight joint can be occasionally be detected on the outer faces. Butt joints at the inner angle of the buttresses, where they join the north and south walls of the central tower, are more plainly noticeable (**ill. 9**). At this point on the north east corner the buttress has fouled a niche, which has been continued into the side of the buttress in an attempt to mask the fault.

The Terraces

The terraces to N and S, both integral to the original design, have been replaced, probably by Wyatville. The N terrace seems to have been rebuilt on a similar plan to the original, although the ghost marks of the original balustrade are discernible on the E and W walls of the jutting corner chambers. The S terrace is depicted in the earlier paintings as similar in plan to the northern, that is with centrally placed stairs. It has been rebuilt on a different plan with flights of steps at either end facing E and W, which turn through 90 degrees to reach the terrace. Tucked away behind the flanking flights on either side are short flights of eight steps which descend to a gallery under the terrace. These steps are in Linby stone and are very worn. They may have been reused from the original Tudor terrace, its replacement being in Mansfield stone. Beneath the S terrace is a long barrel-vaulted chamber measuring 18.70m by 2.62m, popularly known as the 'skittle alley'. It is entered through small lobbies whose barrel vaults run at right angles to the main gallery. It is constructed in brick with a low stone plinth to the N, W and E walls and a quarry-tiled floor. The bricks are Georgian in appearance with lime mortar and lined joints. The S wall is pierced by five arched openings, each having 3 stone doric pillars on the outside. In the N wall are 2 blind brick arches, each 4.05m from the end walls.

Alterations to Doorways

A doorway on to the W end of the S terrace was altered when the internal staircase at this point (3/Sa) was remodelled by Wyatville to make way for an extended Saloon. The doorway now leads into the basement. The stone coursing can be seen to be disturbed and comparison can be made with a pre-alteration drawing of the S facade which shows a round head to the opening.[8] A new doorway was inserted at the E end of the terrace when the S state staircase was rebuilt and French windows replaced the original 4-light bay window in the centre of the facade. On the E facade towards the S end an exterior doorway

---

[6] Information from Mr John Key

[7] MiP3, p.17, nos. 2, 3, 4, 4v. One of these designs was for octagonal turrets.

[8] Britton 1809, between p.108 and 109

was blocked in white Hollington stone when Wyatville removed staircase 3/Sb. This stone is not a good match but was used for the plinths of statues in the garden, which date from the same period. The balancing doorway further N in the same facade was filled in Ancaster stone and shows the same degree of weathering as the rest of the building. This was never actually an opening, but was included only to maintain the symmetry of the east facade. The external doorways from the NE and SE turret chambers on to the leads were blocked, almost certainly by Wyatville.

Part 2. ROOM BY ROOM SURVEY

During Wyatville's renovation the whole house was refurbished in the Georgian style and little Tudor decorative finish survives above stairs. Where earlier features exist, they are specifically referred to; otherwise it may be taken that all plasterwork, architraves, fireplaces etc. were replaced during the nineteenth century. The original height of many reception rooms has been reduced by approximately 30cms in the course of replacing the ceilings and some voids exist. It is possible that earlier features might survive in these, but it was not possible to investigate them. Where mezzanine chambers have been inserted, the reduction in original ceiling height is considerably more. Below stairs and in service rooms on the ground floor much more of the Tudor architectural finish has survived intact.

The main staircases are described first, followed by each floor treated separately as follows:-

1) Leads level.

2) First floor.

3) Ground floor.

4) Basement.

MAIN STAIRCASES

The State Staircases (NS and SS: Inventory Table)

Both Tudor state staircases were removed prior to 1809 when their successors are shown on a plan published by John Britton (**ill. 16**). Smythson's platt (**ill. 5**) shows them to be slightly wider than but very similar to the W staircase, which probably gives us a model for the others. The design is closely paralleled by staircases in the Little Castle at Bolsover, attributed to Robert or John Smythson.[9] As at Bolsover, the Wollaton stairs are shown with cupboards built into the closed well and one of these seems to be referred to in the inventory of 1601.[10] The same inventory lists a 'shorte table' placed 'at the stair head of the N Great chamber' and the 1609 inventory lists both stair head areas as usable spaces. At the top of the surviving W stair the stair-well is half vaulted over, making a half-floor, and we may surmise that the state staircases were similarly terminated. The N staircase connected only the ground and first floors: 4/8S in the NE turret connected the basement with the ground floor on this side. The S staircase, however, did descend into the basement as no other means of reaching the basement accommodation block would have been available in the original house. A vestige of the stairwell also survives in room 4/11.

Later alterations

As part of Thomas and Cassandra Willoughby's programme of restoration the walls and ceiling of the N staircase and the ceiling of the S staircase were decorated by Laguerre c.1699 and Thornhill c.1710 with paintings on classical themes. It is possible that there had been a doorway on the landing of the N staircase to a spiral stair in the central tower wall leading to the High Hall, mirroring the arrangement which still exists on the S side. This is based on loop windows high in the E wall of the Great Hall still existing on both N and S sides to light the lower part of the stairs. If so, the N access was blocked when the murals were executed. The cantilevered staircases which replaced the Tudor originals were the work of Wyatville (**plate 13**). An additional short flight from the S staircase at ground floor level leads to the S terrace by an inserted external doorway.

The Western Service Stairs (WS)

The W staircase was the main link between the service rooms in the basement and the two reception floors above. To span a floor, this staircase uses two main flights of straight steps with an intermediate shorter flight, each turning 90 degrees. These are roofed with a flat raked ceiling defined at each end by a round stone arch, those over the short middle flight springing from the window sill on the W side. Each landing is roofed by a groined vault. The central space is not left as an open well. At basement

[9] Faulkner, 1972, 52-3.

[10] 'In a little roome at the staire foote of the south great chamber'. It contained only 3 items.

level it houses two large niches, one of which is now blocked, perhaps used for setting down food ready to be carried upstairs. At ground floor level this space was open, but ceiled by a barrel vault, 1.14m high. It shed borrowed light towards the screens passage from an arched window in the W wall and it was consequently well finished in ashlar, as it would have been visible from the screens passage. At half landing level above here the central space is occupied by a rectangular cupboard 1.67m high x 63.5cms wide enclosed by a door. There is a square chamfered doorway in stone, rebated to take a door opening inwards. There are original pivots on the N jamb. As the space was enclosed, no care has been taken to finish the interior in ashlar, as below, and the ends of the stair-treads can be seen in the S wall. The staircase is lit by a total of three 4-light windows in the W wall. Of these, only the topmost was completely open on the interior. Of the lower two, only certain panes were utilised, the rest blocked by the vaults and the staircase itself. On the exterior, however, the full height of the windows was maintained for the appearance of the facade. At half landing level in the basement there was a window in the N wall of the staircase which overlooked the lobby/servery. Borrowed light was not necessary in this position and it was more likely for a steward to observe and orchestrate movement up and down the stairs from the servery to the Great Hall.

Later alterations

At ground floor level the barrel-vaulted central space of the staircase, designed to shed borrowed light onto the screens, became redundant when the original function of the Great Hall and screens became obsolete. The servants now ate in the servants' hall in the basement and there was less need for regular and heavy traffic between the basement and the ground floor. The central doorway leading to the kitchens, originally an open arch so that traffic was unimpeded, now had a door fitted. The barrel vaulted space was converted to a cupboard, the window in its W wall largely blocked, and a timber door-frame inserted at the E end. The door has a seventeenth or early eighteenth century latch. The staircase originally ended at first floor level, but an extension in timber was built to provide a more convenient exit on to the leads (**ill. 23**). The style of the balustrade suggests this belongs to the Phase 2 renovation of the house late in the seventeenth century. Samples from two of the stair-treads were dated by dendrochronology by Dr R. Laxton of the Department of Mathematics, University of Nottingham.[11] The samples were short on rings and without sapwood, but a date of c.1700 was suggested. The samples matched well with the chronology of the West Midlands, where the family had other estates from whence timber might have been sent. At the top of the timber staircase a dome-like structure was built to cover the exit of the new staircase on to the leads. The central tower wall has been cut back here partially to accommodate the final flight of stairs. At the very foot of the W staircase and also at the top of the first half flight, jambs were inserted to create doorways, probably the work of Wyatville. These were to limit sound carrying from the basement. The window in the N wall of the landing, overlooking the lobby/servery, was also blocked, perhaps for the same reason. At first floor level a chamber constructed of timber and frosted glass has been inserted into the open well of the 17th century staircase. This is popularly believed to have been Lord Middleton's bathroom, and probably dates from the early 20th century.

Level 1 - The Leads

The Central Tower (ills 7 and 8)

The central tower is formed by the upper part of the Great Hall with the High Hall or Prospect Room (1/1) above. The lower set of windows on the tower are the clerestory of the Great Hall (set at leads level) and the upper set light the Prospect Room, whose floor is about 5m higher than the leads.

The Central Tower Stairs

In both the SE and NE corners of the tower are newel stairs which rise to the roof, where the upper landings have ornamental balustrades and emerge in small circular bartizan turrets. There are exits to the leads on both sides which emerge just to the W of the buttresses. The doorways measure 1.75m x 0.77m and retain the original mouldings, which match another external doorway on the leads (originally to a garderobe, 1/6) in the E wall of the central tower, and also an internal doorway on the gallery over the screens passage.

The N doorway retains an original Tudor panelled door. An identical door, though cut down, has been re-used on one of the mezzanine chambers

---

[11] I am indebted to Dr. Laxton for this information.

(3/18i) inserted during the 19th century. On the N side the newel stair diverts from its course to reach the leads exit and ends at this point. The position of the two exits to the leads are not identical on each side. On the S side it is hard up against the buttress, with a niche to the W of it in the space between the doorway and the first of the clerestory windows. On the N side the doorway is positioned further W, immediately beside the clerestory window, with the neighbouring niche to the E. The SE vice carries on down to the first floor landing of the S state staircase and it is possible that in the NE corner it did so too, although evidence for this is ambivalent. There is no direct evidence of its blocking on either the first floor landing or at the leads, although well executed work could mask this. The external wall of the SE staircase is 1.10m thick. There are regular slit windows which overlook the Great Hall and the S state stairhead as well as the exterior. One, which overlooked the long gallery, has been blocked. In the NE corner loop windows overlook the Great Hall in a position where there is no longer a staircase (**plate 9**), and it is on this evidence that it is surmised that the NE stairs also descended as far as the first floor.

The High Hall or Prospect Room 1/1
(ill.8, plate 4: Inventory Table)

The Prospect Room, like the Great Hall, has four traceried windows in the N and S walls and one in each of the E and W walls. There is a doorway at each end of the E wall leading to the staircases. The window embrasure at the E end is much deeper than that at the W end as the wall thickness is much greater to accommodate the staircases. The N and S walls of both of these window recesses each have a classical niche with a shell motif in the top (**ill 46**). Mark Girouard records that a shell-decorated niche was uncovered in the angle of one of the Longleat bay windows, which are all drawn with similar alcoves on a plan of the house which survives at Hatfield. He cites shell-headed niches at South Wraxall Manor, the Hall at Bradford upon Avon and Charlton Park as all being derived from the Longleat example,[12] and it is likely that those at Wollaton have the same derivation. The motif might well have embellished other rooms which have not retained their original decoration. The walls are now decorated with *trompe d'oeil* drapery in the Regency style. The floor-boards have been taken up to reveal the joists, which are arranged in a 'Chinese Lattice' pattern (**ill. 8**). **Illustration 47** shows the joint types used in the construction of the floor. Type A has been used on the timbers of the main framework and type B on the smaller joists. Where these have been reinforced by the addition of secondary joists, in an attempt to stabilise the floor, type C has been used. Again, this might be Wyatville's work as a letter from the architect to Lord Middleton, dated 26th August 1830, discusses the state of the floor and possible remedial measures. A post-script advises that the number of people admitted to the room at one time should be severely restricted.[13] The failure of the joints can be seen in several places and the floor is still unsafe. The room has been braced

[12] Girouard, 1983, 62.

[13] MiP3 p.20.

Ill. 46: Niche with shell motif in the High Hall (Photo by Philip Dixon).

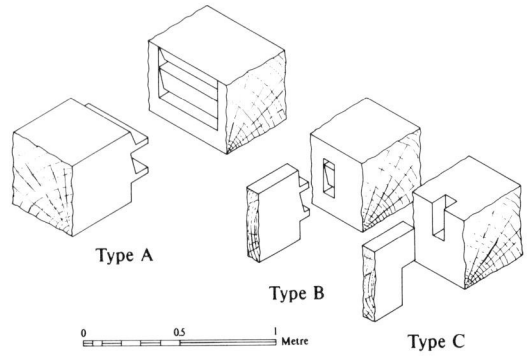

Ill. 47: Joint types used in the High Hall floor.

by the City of Nottingham Engineers Department but is largely inaccessible.

The Turret Rooms. (1/2, 1/3, 1/4, 1/5)

Originally access to these was only possible from the leads and they were furnished as bedrooms. The inventories of 1601 and 1609 mention all except the NW chamber.

NE Turret Room 1/2 (Inventory Table)

The room was lit by 4-light windows in the N and E walls and the doorway, now blocked, was in the W wall. There is an original flue (from room 2/2) in the S wall, emerging on the parapet, so the chamber could have been unique amongst the turrets in being heated.

Wyatville's alterations

The SE corner of the room was partitioned for a spiral staircase in timber which descends to the ground floor. The external doorway and the E window were blocked completely and the N window fitted with shutters.

SE Turret Room 1/3 (Inventory Table)

The room was unheated and had a ceiling height of 4.33m. It had 4-light windows in the E and S walls. The doorway to the leads was on the W wall and is now blocked, although a Tudor pivot on the N jamb and a catch on the S jamb remain.

Wyatville's alterations

The room was made accessible by stairway from the (inserted) mezzanine floor below. The mark of the original floor level is clearly visible on the N wall of this staircase. Within the room the E window was blocked but the S window retained. The N side of the room was partitioned off, with a cupboard in the W half which contains the blocked external doorway. The E half of this partition contains the landing of the stairway, the doorway between the room and landing being well-made with a good Georgian fanlight.

SW Turret Room 1/4 (Inventory Table)

The doorway on to the leads survives in the E wall and retains the original pivots in the N jamb. The room had a 4-light window in each of the S and W walls.

Modern alterations

A timber staircase has been inserted from first floor room 2/11. At this level it adjoins the W wall, emerging in the SW corner of the chamber. It has been screened off from the W part of the room by a partition wall. Although the stairs are quite modern, they might replace a Wyatville forerunner: the latch on the door at the top of the stairs is 17th or 18th century. The S window has been partitioned so that one light is directed on to the stairs, the other three into the chamber. The ceiling has been lowered to a height of 2.85m.

NW Turret Room 1/5

This room has been used as a masons' store and has lost much of its plasterwork, exposing the stone walls. At the S end of the E wall the original doorway to the leads retains Tudor pivots on the N jamb and probably the original lock, although the door has been replaced. The chamber is 4.24m high and was lit by 4-light windows in the N and W walls.

Wyatville's alterations

The SW corner of the room has been partitioned off where an internal staircase has been inserted. This begins in first floor room 2/7. The N window has been blocked and the W window has been divided, three lights into the chamber and one on to the stairs. In the E wall is a Georgian cast-iron fireplace. There is a squinch over the NE corner of the chamber.

Garderobe closet 1/6

On the E elevation of the central tower, towards the N end, is a doorway to a small closet which was originally a garderobe. It has a square niche in the S wall to hold a candle or lantern, for it has no window. Although blocked, its chute can be seen from within the E sewer system and the City mason, John Key, once dropped a plumb-line down its entire length through a small hole in the floor.[14] It has a modern door but its possible original, a match to the door to the central tower N stairs, may have been cut down and fitted to mezzanine chamber 3/18i. The moulding around the doorway matches that on the doorways of the central tower stairs and the gallery over the screens passage. The closet was probably intended for the use of guests using the High Hall and leads as a recreation area or possibly for servants occupying the turret chambers.

Level 2 - THE FIRST FLOOR (Ills 19, 20 and 21)

The first floor contained twin suites of state apartments and the Long Gallery as well as small chambers in the towers.

---

[14] I am indebted to Mr. Key for this information.

The Long Gallery 2/1 (Inventory Table)

The whole E range of the first floor was occupied by the Long Gallery which rose to a height of over 5m. It was lit by a 5-light window at either end and six 4-light windows in the E wall. It was entered by doorways from each of the state staircases. In the SE and NE corners were doorways to tower chambers which were probably infrequently used as bedrooms. Fireplaces could have been placed at any of four points along the W wall where flues from the rooms below could have been utilised but it is likely that they would have been placed at each end. In the thickness of the W wall was a garderobe with a window overlooking the Great Hall. It shared a chute with one of the Painted Chambers (3/9) on the ground floor and another off corridor 4/SSii in the basement.

North Gallery Chamber 2/2 (Inventory Table)

This room was originally approached only by a doorway in the NE corner of the Long Gallery. Lit by 4-light windows in the N and E walls, it was originally about 5m high. It is referred to in the inventories of 1601 and 1609 when it was used as a bedchamber and was better furnished than other tower chambers. The room might have been heated, as the NE tower is unique in having an original chimney and a fire iron grate is listed amongst the contents of the room.

South Gallery Chamber 2/3 (Inventory Table)

This chamber was approached by a doorway in the SE corner of the gallery and is mentioned only in the 1609 inventory when it had very little in it. It was unheated yet contained a pair of bellows and a fire shovel, which suggests it was used as a store-room. It also contained some bedding. It had 4-light windows in the S and E walls.

Wyatville's alterations (ill. 21)

Wyatville divided the Long Gallery into two long rooms, themselves sub-divided by arches which may have had partition doors. At the W end of the central dividing wall he placed diagonally-set fireplaces which tapped into existing Tudor flues in the W wall. The two central E windows were reduced to three lights and the S window to four. The southernmost window in the E wall was reduced to three lights and a timber staircase inserted in its recess, leading to a mezzanine floor above. The N and S portions of the gallery beyond the arches were reduced in height to 2.85m in order to insert mezzanine level suites above. The ceiling height of the central portion was reduced to 4.04m to retain some proportion. It was not possible to investigate the void which must have been created.

Chamber 2/2

The S part of the room was partitioned off for a timber spiral staircase which occupies the SE corner, the garderobe being removed. This staircase rises from the ground floor and is well-made with a fine curving banister. The E window was partitioned, the S-most light directed on to the stairs, the remainder into the room. A fireplace and flue was inserted into the W wall. The ceiling height was lowered to 2.51m for the insertion of a mezzanine room above.

Chamber 2/3

Wyatville inserted a fireplace in the W wall and reduced the S window to three lights. He partitioned off the N part of the room to house a timber staircase linking this level with the tower rooms below. This staircase is far more

Ill. 48: Plan of mezzanine level suite over the north end of the Long Gallery and north gallery chamber c.1809.

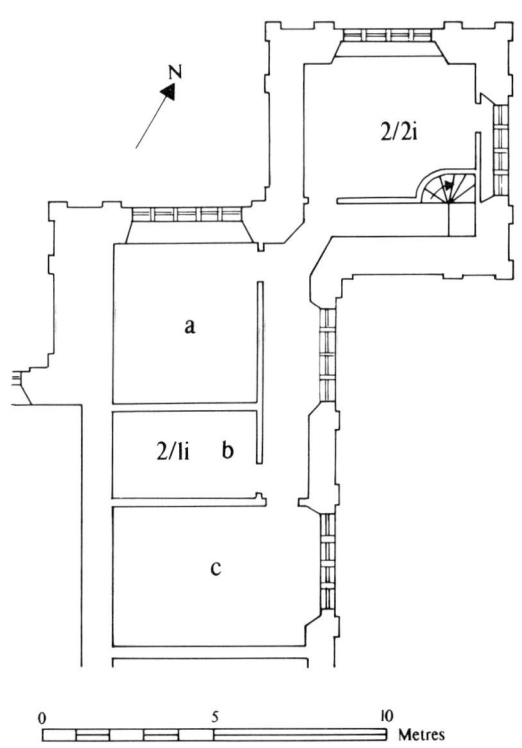

utilitarian than its counterpart in the NE tower. The E window was partitioned, with two lights remaining into the room, one directed on to the staircase, and one light blocked by the creation of a new N jamb for the chamber window. The height of the room was reduced to 2.30m by the insertion of a mezzanine chamber above.

Mezzanine Floors

Above the North End of the Long Gallery (Ill. 48)

This small suite of three chambers was gained by an inserted staircase in the NE tower and through a doorway cut in the angle between the main block of the house and the tower. There is only 1.34m headroom and the floor is lit at floor level by the top pane of the three available windows (two 4-lights to the E, one 5-light to the N). As the floor is partitioned into three rooms the central room has no external window, only a borrowed light in its E partition wall. These chambers just under the leads were unheated, cold in winter, and airless in summer and were clearly servants' accommodation.

Tower Mezzanine Room 2/2i (ill. 48)

This is approached by the spiral stairs inserted into the SE corner of the tower. The N side of the room has been partitioned off from the stairs. Only the top southernmost pane of the 4-light E window has been retained at this level to light the stairs while the remaining panes have been blocked and the window recess made into a cupboard within the chamber. The four top panes of the N window illuminate room 2/2i. The ceiling height is 2.41m. On the stair landing a doorway has been inserted into the SW corner leading to the mezzanine suite above the old Long Gallery.

Above the South End of the Long Gallery (ill. 49)

These mezzanine chambers are a mirror image of the suite at the N end of the Gallery (see above) but were reached by a staircase inserted in the southernmost window recess of the Long Gallery E wall (ill. 11). Several lights have been blocked off and a bite has been taken out of the soffit at the S end of the embrasure to give extra headroom at the top of the stairs. A doorway in the SE corner has been cut through the tower wall to reach a mezzanine room in the SE tower (2/3i).

Tower Mezzanine Room 2/3i (ill. 49)

This room is approached from the inserted mezzanine floor above the S end of the old Long Gallery by a doorway cut into the angle where the main block of the house meets the tower. The upper part of the windows belonging to the chamber below (2/3) are used to light the room at floor level. The E window has been reduced to two lights, as in the room below. The N section of the room is partitioned off to house a straight timber staircase which leads to the SE turret chamber (1/3) and a cupboard has been built under these stairs in the NE corner of the room. Room 2/3i is unheated.

The North State Suite (2/4, 2/5, 2/6, 2/7)

The North Great Chamber 2/4 (Inventory Table)

This was a spacious apartment, over 5m high, with windows all along the N wall and heated by a fireplace in the S wall. It was entered by a doorway at the E end from the state staircase. Another in the opposite wall led to the withdrawing chamber. There was a third at the W end of the S wall for service access from the

Ill. 49: Plan of mezzanine level suite over the south end of the Long Gallery and south gallery chamber c.1809.

gallery over the screens passage which led to the service stair beyond.

Chamber attached to the north state suite 2/5 (Inventory Table)

This room was most likely reached from the adjoining Great Chamber and was used as an ante-chamber to the state bed-chamber. It was fairly small and was lit by a 4-light window in the W wall. The N wall of the room, which divided it from the adjoining bed-chamber, has been removed but its position was dictated by the layout of walls on the ground floor and in the basement. The wall must have fouled the next window to the north and, although included on the exterior to maintain the symmetry of the facade, this is unlikely to have been open to the interior. There was probably a fireplace in the E wall.

The N State Bedchamber 2/6 (The Queen's Chamber: Inventory Table)

This was reached from the withdrawing chamber by a doorway in the S wall. It had a fireplace in the E wall and was lit by a 5-light window to the N and a 4-light window to the W. In the NW corner was a doorway to the inner chamber.

Inner Chamber 2/7 (Inventory Table)

Smythson's platt shows that the general arrangement in the Inner Chambers was a partitioning into three units; an entry lobby, a corner garderobe and the chamber itself which would have been occupied by personal attendants. There were 4-light windows in the W and N walls and one light of the W set was diverted by the partition into the garderobe.

Wyatville's alterations (Ill. 21)

The former North Great Chamber 2/4

A great deal of light was excluded from the room by Wyatville who blocked the easternmost 4-light window completely and reduced the two westernmost windows from five and four lights respectively to only three lights. Only the bay window remains intact. An extra doorway was inserted at the N end of the W wall to connect with 2/6, the Tudor bedchamber. This was cut at an angle to avoid a flue inserted into the W wall from the fireplace in his new dining room below. The fireplace in the S wall was retained.

The former Withdrawing Chamber 2/5 and Bedchamber 2/6

These two rooms were fundamentally altered. The dividing wall between them was removed and replaced by a flimsier partition wall pierced by a wide archway. Having removed the supporting wall on the floor below to create a dining room, Wyatville was unable to leave this one in place. Room 2/6 retained its fireplace but had a new doorway cut into the E wall from the Great Chamber 2/4 (see above). The N window was reduced to four lights to match the W one. Space formerly occupied by 2/5 was reduced by the insertion of a further partition wall on the E side. A short corridor was thus created between this and the original E wall, lit by a borrowed light in the partition wall. At its S end this corridor linked with the landing of the W staircase by an inserted archway. At the N end a doorway linked with the corridor with room 2/6. A third doorway at the S end of the partition wall led into the new room. The provision of this alternative access shows that it must have been possible to enclose this room by folding doors or the like across the large archway which divided it from room 2/6.

The original fireplace in the withdrawing chamber was blocked and a new one inserted against the partition wall, with an arch to carry its flue across the corridor and into the Tudor original in the E wall. The 4-light window was reduced to 3-lights.

The former Inner Chamber 2/7

This room was lowered in height to 2.68m by the insertion of a mezzanine chamber above. A timber staircase begins here and carries up through the mezzanine room and into the turret chamber on the leads. It occupies the S side of the room, where the entry lobby and garderobe were formerly situated. A new doorway into the chamber was made in the E end of the partition wall. There is a Georgian cornice, and a cupboard has been made under the stairs in the SW corner after the removal of the garderobe. A fireplace and flue have been inserted in the N window embrasure, blocking off all light from this direction.

Mezzanine Room 2/7i

This occupies the top space of the original room 2/7 and is gained by the inserted staircase, the landing of which takes up the SW corner. The staircase carries on to the turret chamber above. The W window has been partitioned so that one light illuminates the stairs. The N window has been blocked to accommodate the flue of the fireplace in the room below. The height of the room is 2.52m. There are signs of a blocked fireplace and inserted flue in the E wall, which curves inwards towards the S end, perhaps in connection with the flue.

The South State Suite (2/8, 2/9, 2/10, 2/11)

This is almost a mirror image of the N State Suite, although it has certain points of superiority, not least its south-facing aspect overlooking the formal gardens.

The South Great Chamber 2/8 (Inventory Table)

The main variation between this room and its counterpart on the N side is the larger bay window (compare these on **ill.19**). Almost the whole S wall was covered in glass, but this effect has been lost by the blocking of two windows by Wyatville. In February 1990 the floor of this chamber was taken up and the original joists replaced. Although no formal arrangements were made for the proper recording of this feature prior to its destruction, a record of the joist arrangement was made by Prof. M.W. Barley (**ill. 50**), who also recorded the type of joint used (**ill. 51**).[15] The joint is a type fairly typical of the 16th century.[16] There was no sign of the fire damage of 1642, which apparently did not extend to this area of the house.

Chamber attached to the south state suite 2/9 (Inventory Table)

This chamber was a mirror image of its counterpart in the northern suite, except that the position of its S wall, which was dictated by the wall dividing rooms 3/17 and 3/18 on the floor below, left insufficient room for a doorway off the South Great Chamber. The room must have been reached from the state bed-chamber or, less likely, from the landing of the service stairs. However it was in one respect better proportioned than its counterpart on the N side, for the dividing wall with the adjoining bedchamber was attached to a pier, allowing two full 4-light windows in the W wall of the adjoining bedchamber.

[15] I am indebted to Prof. Barley for this information and the drawings.

[16] C.A. Hewett, 1980, 282, fig. 305.

Ill. 50: Original joist arrangement in the south Great Chamber, recorded by Maurice Barley.

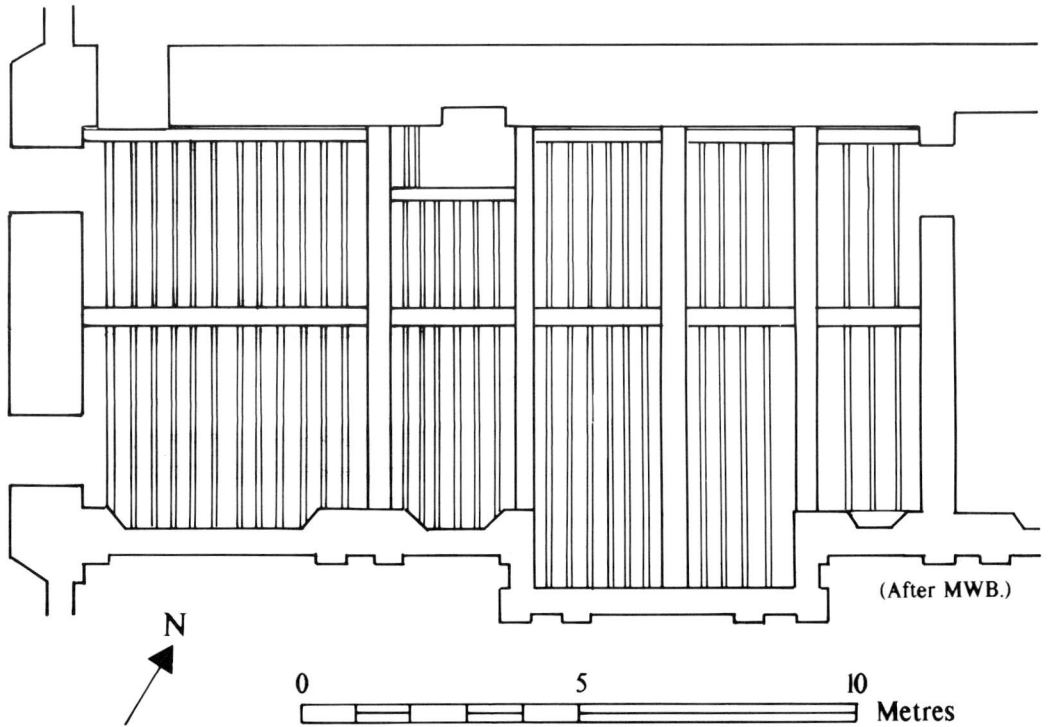

South Great Chamber   Arrangement of main beams and floor joists

The South State Bedchamber 2/10 (The Best or Prince's Chamber: Inventory Table)

This room was called 'the Best Chamber' in the earlier inventories, and 'the Prince's Chamber' after 1603. It was entered from the Great Chamber (2/8) and was heated by a fireplace in the E wall. It had a 5-light window to the S and two 4-light windows to the W. A doorway in the SW corner led to an inner chamber.

Inner Chamber 2/11 (Inventory Table)

As the inner chamber to the Best Chamber, this room would have housed the personal attendants of important visitors. There was a 4-light window in each of the S and W walls and in the NW corner was an unlit garderobe with a niche to hold a candle or lantern. The 1601 inventory suggests that there was a mezzanine room above, although one presently in this position seems more modern.

Later alterations

The former South Great Chamber 2/8

Two 2-light windows, one on either side of the bay, have been blocked. A doorway has been cut at the S end of the W wall to connect directly with chamber 2/10.

The former Withdrawing Chamber 2/9 and Bedchamber 2/10

In altering these two rooms Wyatville has followed a similar plan to that on the N side. The dividing wall was replaced by a flimsy partition wall, slightly further N than the original wall, and pierced by a wide archway. In this case there was no structural cause for moving the wall, but it might have been done to make room for an inserted doorway from the S Great Chamber, mirroring the arrangement on the N side. Room 2/10 retained its fireplace and the S window was reduced by one light. The space occupied by 2/9 was reduced by a partition wall to make a corridor on the E side. Like its N counterpart, this was linked with the W staircase landing by an inserted archway at its N end, and to the original bedchamber (2/10) by a doorway at the S end. A wide arch divided the new 2/9 from the old 2/10 and a further arch subdivided 2/9. There were additional doorways from the new corridor into each of these divided spaces, again suggesting that the wide archways could be closed off by partition doors. The original fireplace on the E wall was blocked and a new one inserted against the E partition wall, its flue carried over the corridor in an archway to link up with the original Tudor flue. The two W windows were reduced to three lights.

The former Inner Chamber 2/11

A fireplace has been inserted in the E wall and the ceiling height reduced to 2.74m by the insertion of a mezzanine room above. A timber staircase has been built against the N wall, turning through 90 degrees and continuing against the W wall. It leads to the mezzanine room and also to the turret chamber on the leads. Although it is a recent rebuild, it probably replaces one by Wyatville.

Mezzanine Room 2/11i

Inserted in the top space of room 2/11, this small room is lit by the top section of the 4-light window in the S wall. There are partition walls to the W and N, the staircase turning through 90 degrees beyond. A doorway in the W partition gives access to the room from the staircase.

Gallery Over the Screens Passage (Minstrel's Gallery) 2/12

Placed above the screens passage, this gallery acted as an upper service passage to the state chambers. The doorway in its W wall, which retains its original moulding on the E side, was originally the only link between the service stairs and the first floor. Doorways at either end of the passage led to the Great Chambers, but they have been remodelled in the Georgian style. The balustrade of the gallery is in stone and might be a Wyatville addition (**colour plate 7**). An organ which still occupies a central position on the gallery is shown in an engraving of the Hall made by Wyatville for Britton's *Architectural Antiquities of Great Britain*, published in 1809[17].

[17] Britton 1809, 108-9

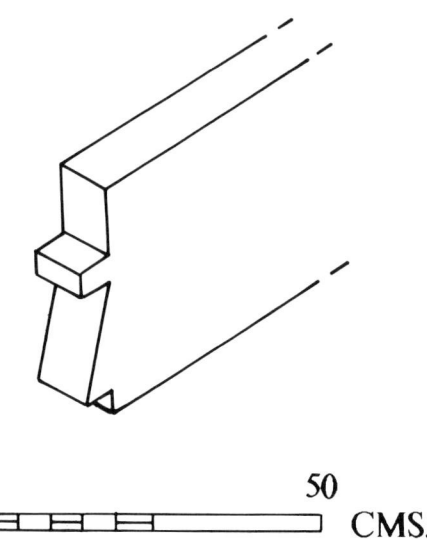

Ill. 51: Joint type used in the south Great Chamber.

Level 3 - THE GROUND FLOOR (ills 12, 13 and 15)

The main floor of the building is in fact above ground level as the basement is only partially subterranean, but is referred to as the ground floor for convenience. The front door is reached by the N terrace and a further set of five steps.

The North Range

Entry Arrangement (3/1, 3/2, 3/3 on ill. 12)

The threshold of the front door is set 90cms below main floor level, making an internal flight of six steps necessary to reach the latter. The position of these steps was altered during Phase 3 as part of a fundamental remodelling of the entrance arrangement. Originally the visitor would climb the few steps from the N terrace to the main door, as now, but he would then find himself in a relatively small lobby (3/1). To the E was a doorway leading to an L-shaped **Porter's Lodge (3/2: Inventory Table)**, which is referred to in all five household inventories. It was lit by a 4-light window in the N wall, from which the porter could also monitor callers, and had a fireplace in the S wall. The visitor would turn W and climb half a dozen stairs into a corridor (3/1a) which was well lit by two large windows on the N side. It was, however, rather narrow considering the expectations of grandeur raised by the exterior of the house. He or she would pass the household store-room on the left-hand side. Called the **Wardrobe (3/3: Inventory Table)**, this room was unheated and probably lit by a borrowed light in its N wall overlooking the corridor. In the earliest inventory (of October 1596) this room was called 'the chamber next to the gate', and was furnished as a bedroom, while the Wardrobe was located in room 3/18. However it had been moved to 3/3 by December of the same year when a second inventory was taken on Sir Francis' death. In 1599 room 3/18 is called 'The Old Wardrobe' and the Wardrobe was still in room 3/3 when the last inventory was taken in 1609. It contained all sorts of household stuff (see Appendix I), including bedding which might have been brought out at night for servants who slept in the public rooms.

No trace of features 3/1 to 3/3 survives, and the plan is known only from Smythson's platt (**ill. 5**). However the sub-structure in the basement lends credence to the accuracy of the plan. The N wall of the Wardrobe, which also formed part of the Porter's Lodge wall, was carried on a series of three columns in the basement below. A fourth was almost certainly planned but was replaced by a wall instead which divides the Inner Kitchen and Larder (rooms 4/4 and 4/5). Although contemporary with the first build, this wall sits so badly with the vault arrangement of both rooms that it must be an afterthought. Smythson may have deemed this wall necessary to support the weight of the N/S wall above, which divided the Porter's Lodge from the Wardrobe. Although the underlying vault would have been sufficient for this purpose, it is typical of the caution shown by the architect.

The visitor to the Hall might have been forgiven for some sense of disappointment at his or her first glimpse of the interior of a building which promised such splendour from the exterior, for the entrance arrangement was far from spacious and the apartments immediately encountered utilitarian. It was necessary to make another 90 degrees turn into the Screens Passage before the first view of the Great Hall might have justified the newcomer's expectations.

Wyatville's alterations (ill. 15)

3/1, 3/1a and 3/1b

It is perhaps easy to see why the internal arrangement described above was targeted for radical alteration by Wyatville before 1809 as part of his first assault on the house. At this date the ground plan published by John Britton (**ill. 16**) shows that Wyatville had removed the Porter's Lodge, blocking up its fireplace, and had also swept away the Wardrobe. The 4-light windows either side of the front door were narrowed to two lights to create more fashionable Georgian proportions. Retaining the E wall of the Porter's Lodge as the E extremity of his new entrance hall, he added a central classical niche flanked by columns and pierced the S end of this wall with a doorway leading directly to the N state staircase. He inserted a matching wall and doorway at the same distance to the W of the front door and raised the floor level of the newly created entrance hall to match that of the rest of the ground floor. The six entry steps, placed by Smythson to the W, were still necessary but were turned through an angle of 90 degrees so that visitors are now faced by them directly as they enter the house. The alterations were completed by piercing the N wall of the Great Hall with a grand doorway so that it can be entered directly from the entrance hall. The most impressive room on the ground floor is instantly attainable, without the convoluted preamble necessary in Smythson's arrangement. The new entrance hall was finished with cornices, plastered ceiling decoration and stair balustrades in keeping with the classical tradition and was redecorated in 1990 in the Georgian style (**plate 12**).

The space beyond the new W wall of the entrance lobby was divided into two small rooms, (3/1a and 3/1b on **ill. 15**; numbered 8 and 9 on Britton's plan, **ill. 16**). These comprised a new porter's room (3/1b) and an 'armoury' (3/1a), the latter no doubt inspired by picturesque notions inspired at the time by the Romantic Movement. The former is lit by a single light from the first window W of the front door, which was divided by the inserted wall. The armoury has the second window, narrowed from five to four lights so there is an equal amount of wall space on either side of the jambs. Britton's plan shows a slightly different method of dividing the available window lights of these two rooms. It also shows a spiral staircase in the porter's room, which can never have existed. It could not have descended to the kitchen below, breaking the vault there and neither does it make sense to have connected this room with the N Great Chamber above. There is no trace of a mezzanine floor above this space either. There are so many small inaccuracies in the 1809 plan that it seems likely to have been drawn from the architect's plans rather than from the finished alterations. These rooms could be approached either from the entrance lobby or from the screens passage. A Tudor doorway in the W wall of the armoury, which had previously led to the NW corner chamber, was blocked.

The screens passage (3/4)

Under the original arrangement an archway linked the entrance corridor (3/1) with the N end of the screens passage and another arch at the S end of the screens led to a short staircase (3/Sa: 'the garden stair' of the inventories) which gave out onto the S terrace. To the W were three service openings, that in the centre an arch which led to the W service staircase and the kitchens below. Originally open, a doorway with a fanlight above has been inserted. A doorway on the N side of this led to the Pantry, another on the S side to the Buttery. The stone screen was fortunately left unaltered, although Lord Middleton had envisaged removing the greater part of it in 1832. Smythson's design drawing survives and is lodged in the British Architectural Library of the R.I.B.A. (**ill. 14**).

The Great Hall (3/5: Inventory Table)

Rising through two-and-a-half storeys, the Great Hall formed the centre of the house. It was lit by traceried clerestory windows above first floor level, their sills sharply angled to convey light downwards. There are four windows to the N and S and one great window to the E and W (see **ill. 7**). The hall has five hammer beam trusses highly decorated with grotesque faces and bosses (**plates 9, 10, 11**).[18] The trusses serve no structural purpose, the ceiling of the Hall being spanned by a 'Chinese lattice' method discussed above (**ill. 8**).

The Great Hall was socially orientated, with a 'higher' and 'lower' end. Smythson's platt (**ill. 5**) shows a fireplace in the centre of each of the N and S walls. The visitor would enter the Hall at the 'lower', west, end from the screens passage. The family and honoured guests would enter by doorways at the 'high', east, end from their private apartments. These comprised bedrooms on the E wing of the ground floor as well as the state apartments on the first floor. The doorways led to each of the state staircases and above each of them, at first floor level, is a window which conveyed borrowed light between the Hall and staircase landings. The window on the N side was blocked by the addition of mural paintings to the staircase landing in the late 17th century. At the same level a similar window in the centre of the E wall conveyed borrowed light into a garderobe off the Long Gallery, which is no longer accessible because of museum display cases. The window is now covered by a clock. In the upper part of the E wall, at both the N and S ends are small loop windows. Those at the S end still light the newel staircase to the High Hall but those at the N end are redundant.

Wyatville's alterations (ill. 15)

It is not known how much Tudor plasterwork was removed from the Great Hall, but new wainscotting was designed and installed by Wyatville after 1832 when Lord Middleton insisted on the removal of the original 'dry wainscote' which he saw as a fire risk. A drawing survives in the Middleton Collection which offered a choice of two designs (**ill. 18**). It has written upon it, presumably in the hand of Lord Middleton, 'We wish to decide upon this, having four divisions, because we think it will light better and be nearer the old panels in the former wainscot'.

Before 1809 Wyatville pierced the N wall of the Great Hall with a doorway from the reworked entrance hall, presumably removing a Tudor

[18] *The building accounts show a bonus payment of £2 in 1586 to a plasterer named Ragge because Sir Francis was so pleased with his work in the Great Hall. Rossell (1957) 85.*

fireplace which is shown on Smythson's platt. Britton's plan (**ill. 16**) shows the S fireplace still *in situ* at that date. Around 1832 a remodelling of the Saloon (Tudor Dining Parlour) led to further changes in the Hall. A new doorway was placed in the centre of the S wall, giving direct access into the Saloon and the fireplace in the S wall had to be moved further E. The original flue would have been utilised, however.

The South Range

The south range overlooked the garden and housed the Dining Parlour and a staircase to the south terrace.

The Dining Parlour, later the Saloon (3/6: Inventory Table)

The central room on the S side, the private Dining Parlour in the original house, was approximately 3.5m shorter than it is now. It was lit by a 4-light window in a square bay and two 2-light windows, all in the S wall. The fireplace was almost certainly placed in the centre of the N wall as it appears on Smythson's plan (**ill. 15**), so that it could share a flue with the S fireplace in the Hall. There were two opposing entrances in the E and W walls, the eastern for the use of the family and the western a service door from near the screens passage.

Staircase 3/Sa

The Smythson platt shows a short flight of stairs S of the screens passage. Its landing had a doorway in the W wall leading to the SW corner chamber lobby (3/19) and another in the E wall leading into the Dining Parlour (3/6). The flight of about 6 stairs led to a doorway just below ground floor level which gave out onto the S terrace and is referred to in the inventory of December 1596 as 'the garden door'. On an elevation drawing made by Wyatville prior to his alterations,[19] the doorway is shown as being rounded-headed and intruding into the base of a 5-light window which lit the stairs.

This staircase was removed by Wyatville after 1809 but, in addition to the documentary evidence, two pieces of archaeological evidence for the existence of the staircase remain. A small barrel-vaulted chamber was constructed in the basement to carry the weight of the stairs and this survives (room 4/13i). Traces of some of the treads are still distinguishable in the basement, furthermore, on the W wall of the former stair well.

[19] Britton 1809, 108-9.

Wyatville's alterations

The Britton plan of 1809 (**ill. 16**, room number 5) shows a curved partition wall with niches at the W end of the room to give the Dining Parlour an apsidal end, no doubt representing interior *decor* influenced by fashionable Regency classicism. French windows had replaced the 4-light window in the bay, and the room was re-named the Saloon. The same plan shows that the Tudor fireplace in the N wall had been blocked and a new one appears, inserted into the centre of the now curved W wall. It is difficult to see how a flue could be inserted here, for the S Great Chamber on the floor above extends further W. However, a fireplace and flue were inserted at the E end of the room, and it seems likely that once again we see ideas rather than accomplished alterations in this plan.

The Saloon was extended westwards in c.1832, by the removal of the original W wall and the staircase beyond (3/Sa). This added a 5-light window, originally over the staircase, to the room. A doorway in the W wall, which had linked the garden stair with the SW corner 'Garden Chamber' (3/19), was blocked. The original 'garden door' on to the terrace was retained at basement level, but had to be made shorter so that it did not interfere with the Saloon. The stairs from the terrace were diverted into the basement (see below.) The fireplace in the N wall was moved further W to make way for a doorway giving direct access to the Great Hall.

As a result of Wyatville's changes there are now three entrances to the Saloon; from the S state staircase, from the Great Hall and from the S end of the screens passage (the last being temporarily blocked by a museum case). Any traces of earlier decorative finish were removed. The ceiling was replastered with a lozenge motif and plasterwork cornices were applied. It seems likely that the ceiling height was lowered from approximately 4.75m to 4.40m in the course of this work.

The East Range

The E side of the ground floor was originally given over to bed-chambers and a short staircase to the exterior.

SE Corner Chamber 3/7 (Chapel Chamber: see Inventory Table)

In four out of the five household inventories, this room is called the 'Chapel Chamber', although there is no evidence for a chapel in the house. It was entered from the landing of an adjoining short staircase (3/Sb) by a doorway at the W end of the N wall and was lit by a 4-light and a 5-light window in the E and S walls respectively. There was a fireplace in the W wall, and a doorway in the SE corner led to an inner chamber (3/8) in the SE tower.

Wyatville's alterations

The E window was narrowed to two lights and the S to four lights. When the Tudor S state staircase was remodelled, a new doorway was made into the room in its W wall; previously such an entrance would have been impossible. The original entrance to the room was retained as the doorway into a closet (see below).

Tower Room 3/8 (Inner Chamber to the Chapel Chamber: Inventory Table)

This was an unheated room lit by a 4-light window in each of the S and E walls. Its original height was approximately 4.75m and it measured approximately 4.75m square. The tower garderobes were situated in the NE corner. Here the N section of the E wall has been cut back, making it thinner than the other outer walls. This was perhaps done when a staircase was installed by Wyatville and it may have exposed the garderobe chute towards the corner, which was boarded over and plastered, for a hollow sound can be located by tapping here.

Wyatville's alterations

Wyatville cut room 3/8 both horizontally, to create a mezzanine chamber above, and vertically, as a section 1.30m wide was partitioned off to the N to insert a timber staircase. The partition wall is of modern plasterboard and abuts a brick pillar, which blocks one whole section of the E window lights. The height of room 3/8 is now 2.33m and it is lit by two lights of the lower part of the E window. The northernmost light is diverted into a closet in the NE corner under the stairs (now occupied by a modern lavatory). A fireplace has been inserted into the W wall. The staircase leads to the mezzanine floor above and also carries on to the first floor of the tower.

Mezzanine Room 3/8i

Created from the upper space of the original Inner Chamber 3/8, this room is 2.27m high. It is lit on the S side by the topmost panes of the original 4-light Tudor window, the next panes below having been blocked to form a sill. Only one pane of the E window remains unblocked in room 3/8i and the northernmost pane is directed onto the staircase. The original window arches and splays are clearly visible. The winding timber stair leading to the 1st floor has been replaced in modern times on the same plan, for traces of the Wyatville original survive in a cupboard under the treads. Room 3/8i seems to have been unheated.

Staircase 3/Sb

A doorway on the E side of the S state staircase led to the landing of a short subsidiary staircase (3/Sb) which in turn led to an external doorway in the E facade. A 4-light window above this doorway lit the stairs, which were supported on the barrel vault of room 4/16 in the basement. From the landing of 3/Sb one could gain access to the SE corner 'Chapel Chamber' (3/7) or to the 'Painted Chamber' (3/9).

Chamber 3/9 (Painted Chamber: Inventory Table)

The inventories of 1596, 1599 and 1601 all refer to this room as one of two 'Painted Chambers', the other being next door. It originally measured approximately 5.75m N/S by 5.30m E/W. It was entered by a doorway in the S wall from the landing of the adjoining staircase 3/Sb, and was lit by a tall 4-light window in the E wall. There was a fireplace in the centre of the W wall and a garderobe in the thickness of the same wall towards its N end.

Room 3/10 (Painted Chamber: Inventory Table)

The other 'Painted Chamber' of the inventories, room 3/10 was similar in size and facilities; it too had a fireplace and garderobe in the W wall and a 4-light window to the E. According to the Smythson platt, there was a connecting door between the two painted chambers, but 3/10 also had its own access in the NW corner. Unlike its counterpart, it had an inner chamber.

Room 3/11 (Painted Chamber Inner Chamber: Inventory Table)

This square room, approximately 3.75m by 4.00m served as the inner chamber to room 3/10 and was created out of equivalent space used for staircase 3/Sb on the S side of 3/9. It was unheated, and lit by a 4-light window in the E wall. Apart from a pier of masonry which once formed its NW corner (see **ill. 15**), it has been completely removed.

Room 3/12 (NE Corner Chamber: Inventory Table)

The NE corner chamber was originally approached from the foot of the N state staircase by a short passage (3/12i). It had a 4-light window

[20] Nottingham University Manuscript Mi A 60/5, f.iir.

in the E wall, a 5-light window in the N wall and a fireplace in the W wall. In the NE corner a doorway led to the tower. It is referred to in the building accounts as 'My Master's Chamber by the north tower'[20], but must have been something of a thoroughfare at meal-times, for the NE tower beyond it contained a staircase from the wine cellar, so the chamber was *en route* for servants fetching wine to the Great Hall and Dining Parlour.

Wyatville's alterations to E wing

The whole eastern range on the ground floor was radically altered. Chambers 3/9 and 3/10, the two painted chambers, were made into one large room by the removal of the dividing wall. The two Tudor fireplaces were blocked and a new fireplace installed in the centre of the W wall, blocking the entrances to the garderobes. The original end walls to N and S were pierced by wide arches as it would have been structurally imprudent to remove them altogether. Staircase 3/Sb was taken away and its exterior doorway blocked. Beyond the arches new N and S walls were constructed and the space between converted into domed alcoves with apsidal E ends. These are lower in height than the main part of the room. Their construction necessitated blocking out part of the 4-light windows which had previously served the short staircase 3/Sb and inner chamber 3/11. The new room became a long and elegant library with alcoved entrances and lit by the two remaining 4-light windows in the E wall. The height of the ceiling was reduced from approximately 4.75m to 4.50m in the main section of the room, much lower in the alcoves.

Access to the corner chambers having now been removed, new doorways were cut into the W walls of 3/7 and 3/12 from the bottom of the staircase areas. This was made possible by the installation of the new cantilevered staircases for their Tudor forerunners would have solidly occupied these blocks of space. The S half of the space which had been occupied by the short staircase 3/Sb was converted to a closet off room 3/7, accessed by the original doorway to that room. Later a doorway was made in the W wall of the closet and it is now converted to a lavatory. The N half of what had been room 3/11 was similarly converted to a closet beside room 3/12, which was used as Lord Middleton's dressing room. Each of these closets was lit by the remaining halves of the 4-light windows into 3/Sb and 3/11 respectively.

Room 3/12 was reduced in size by a new partition wall to the W and N. This arrangement created an L-shaped passage outside the room leading from the bottom of the N state staircase to the NE turret. The original Tudor fireplace was blocked and a new one installed on the W partition wall of room 3/12, its flue connecting with the Tudor flue in the original W wall by an arch which spans the new passage. The ceiling height over the area formerly occupied by 3/11 and 3/12 was lowered by approximately 1.65m by the insertion of a mezzanine floor above (called 'Jackson's Quarters'; see below).

Tower Room 3/13 (Inner Chamber: Inventory Table)

The NE tower room was always small in area (approximately 3m x 4.5m) for the staircase from the wine cellar emerged in its S half. On Smythson's plan (**ill. 5**) the staircase is shown as a newel stair, square in plan, with a garderobe closeted off in a space remaining in the SE corner and this accords with what remains today except that the garderobe has gone. The 4-light window in the E wall was divided so that half lit the garderobe and half served the chamber, and the masonry division can still be seen. The chamber has an additional 4-light window in the N wall and was originally unheated.

The 1601 inventory clearly refers to 'a little chamber over' it which might have been a loft-like sleeping gallery reached by ladder. The mezzanine level room which now occupies this position looks like Wyatville's work.

Wyatville's alterations

The Tudor staircase from the wine cellar still links 3/13 with the basement. The garderobe was removed and a timber newel staircase inserted in its place. This is unique in that it scales the full height of the NE tower from ground level. It is also superior to the other inserted tower staircases, with a curving handrail and plastered underside to the treads, suggesting that the rooms in the NE tower were rather better than their other counterparts in the Georgian house. On the N side of the staircase the room is partitioned off and is oak panelled. A fireplace and flue have been inserted into the W wall and the 2-light window in the E wall has been blocked. The mezzanine level chamber above has reduced the ceiling height to 2.5m.

Mezzanine Room 3/13i

This chamber is 2.12m high and uses the top section of the N 4-light window to light the room at floor level. The E 4-light window retains the original Tudor division. The southern two lights, which originally lit the garderobe, are now directed on to the staircase while the northern two lights, which originally lit chamber 3/13, have been blocked. The S section of the room has been partitioned off from the adjacent passage and staircase. In the SW corner of the passage a doorway has been cut through the wall where the tower joins the main block of the house. This leads to the mezzanine suite above 3/11 and 3/12, called 'Jackson's Quarters'.

Mezzanine suite above 3/11 and 3/12, called 'Jackson's Quarters' (ill. 52).

This small suite of cramped accommodation preserves the name of a previous occupant who acted as caretaker during the Second World War, when the museum was closed.[21]

Inserted by Wyatville, the suite is approached from the NE tower through an opening cut diagonally where the tower meets the main block of the house. It occupies what would have been the top 1.65m of rooms 3/11 and 3/12 and the ceiling height is only 1.35m. Only the top panes of the original windows light the suite at floor level. The dividing wall between 3/11 and 3/12 was removed and a very substantial timber beam was inserted, with a flimsy partition wall above. The section over room 3/12 is divided into three. A small entrance lobby ((a) on **ill. 52**) is lit by one pane of the divided E window. A small room facing N (b) utilises the top section of the N facing 5-light window. In its SW corner a block of masonry 76cms high is connected with the inserted flue in the room below. The remainder of the room (c) is lit by the remaining three lights of the E window and has a modern closet partitioned off in the SE corner, containing a bath, and with a borrowed light in its N wall. Two steps are necessary on either side of the doorway between rooms (c) and (d) to overcome the massive inserted beam. The space over 3/11 is occupied by (d) and (e). Only (d) is actually a room, very small, and lit by the 4-light window in the E wall. A trapdoor, probably put in for maintenance purposes, in the floor next to this window allows a good view of the entire window, originally to room 3/11, stretching out below. This has been blocked on the interior in the course of alterations to make the library. Area (e) is not usable space, but was partitioned off to accommodate the lath and plaster dome in the N alcove of the library below, the top of which can be seen through a cupboard door.

In the course of the alterations to the eastern wing the walls of room 3/11 were completely removed, except for a pier of masonry which had formed the lower part of the NW corner of the Tudor room. This was retained to carry the weight of the massive timber beam inserted at mezzanine floor level, now visible in 'Jackson's Quarters'. If the beam was inserted to support the new suite, it would have been simpler to leave the N wall of room 3/11 *in situ*. In fact this wall was to be largely replaced by a flimsier partition wall which forms the N wall of a closet. This odd sequence of removing a wall, replacing its support function with a beam, then rebuilding a flimsier wall in the same place might be explained in two ways. It could represent a change of plan, with Wyatville's original intention to make his room 3/12 bigger, but then deciding to create a closet mirroring that on the N side of room 3/7. However the beam in question at mezzanine floor level is odd in

[21] *I am grateful to Mr. D. Biggs for this verbal information.*

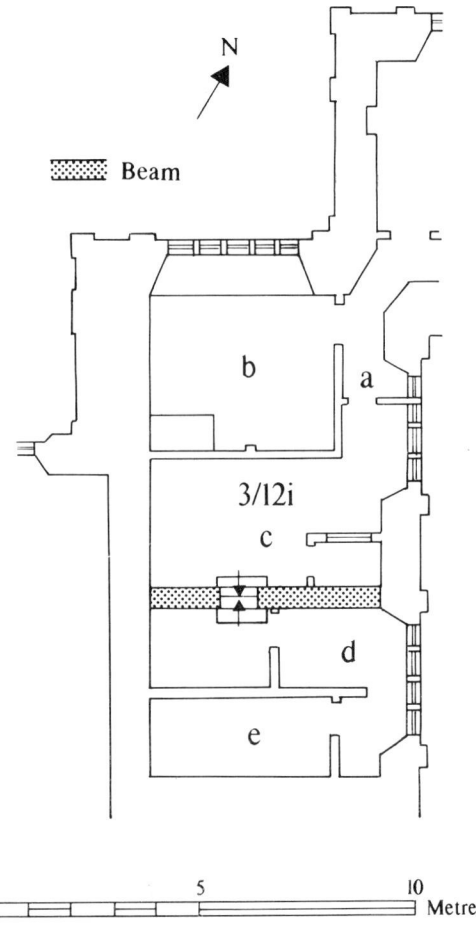

Ill. 52: Plan of mezzanine level suite, known as 'Jackson's Quarters', over the north-east corner chamber, constructed c.1809.

itself. It is so massive, steps have been provided within the mezzanine suite to climb over it. Whilst Wyatville's work in the less polite areas of the house tends to be less polished, nowhere else does he appear quite so clumsy. A second possibility is that it is connected with fire damage of 1642. If the wall was badly damaged, it might have been removed and the timber beam inserted as part of emergency repairs, when we know from Cassandra's *Account* that work was poorly executed.[22] Wyatville might have decided to utilise it to create a mezzanine suite at the N end of the ground floor. There is no comparable suite at the S end, in contrast with mezzanine suites above first floor level which form twin sets, one to the north and one to the south. Also there are no intrusions elsewhere as large as this beam. If the latter theory is true, we do not know what arrangement was put in place here between c.1687, when Francis Willoughby reopened the house, and the beginning of Wyatville's regime of alteration. A dendrochronological date from the beam might provide a satisfying answer to the puzzle.

[22] Wood 1958, 67.

The West Range

The corner rooms of this range were bed-chambers with inner chambers in the towers. The central block was taken up with service rooms and the service staircase.

Room 3/15 (NW Corner Chamber: Inventory Table)

This bed-chamber is mentioned in each of the inventories except that of 1601. It was entered by a doorway, now blocked, at the S end of the E wall, directly from the Tudor entrance hall (3/1). There was a fireplace in the E wall whose flue emerges on the leads. The room was lit by a 5-light window in the N wall and a 4-light window in the W wall. The position of the dividing wall between this and the neighbouring room (3/16) was dictated by the supporting wall in the basement (between 4/1 and 4/2) and did not coincide with a pier on the W side but abutted a window. This was possibly split to give two lights into each of the rooms, but was perhaps more likely to have been a sham, retained to maintain the symmetry of the W facade but blocked on the interior. The inner chamber was in the adjoining NW tower.

Tower Room 3/14 (Inner Chamber: Inventory Table)

Originally the inner chamber to the NW corner chamber, the room had a garderobe partitioned off in the SW corner. A 4-light window in the W wall was divided to light both garderobe and chamber and there was a further 4-light window in the N wall. The room survives to its original height of 4.76m.

Room 3/16 (Pantry: Inventory Table)

Originally the Pantry, this unheated room was entered from the northernmost of the three service doorways in the screens passage. It had a complete 4-light window in the W wall and possibly a further 2-lights of a divided window, also in the W wall (see above, room 3/15).

Wyatville's alterations (3/14, 3/15, 3/16)

Wyatville converted rooms 3/15 and 3/16 into a dining room by removing the dividing wall, thus opening up the central window in the W wall. He narrowed the 5-light window in the N wall to 4-lights to match the others, and inserted a decorative arch at the N end of the room, lowering the ceiling beyond to create an alcove. The Tudor fireplace in room 3/15 was blocked and a new one inserted into the centre of the E wall of the new, enlarged room. This entailed blocking the Tudor doorway from the entrance lobby. The Pantry doorway was retained for the dining room and a secondary service doorway, now blocked, was cut in the S wall from the landing of the W service staircase. In the tower chamber 3/14 the N 4-light window was completely blocked by Wyatville for the insertion of a fireplace and flue.

Room 3/17 (Buttery: Inventory Table)

This unheated room was originally the Buttery and was entered by the southernmost of the three doorways from the screens passage. It measured 4.5m x 5.75m but has been reduced in size. There is a 4-light window in the W wall and a doorway in the S wall led to an inner chamber (3/18). The N face of this doorway has retained the original Tudor chamfered surround and stops and the S face is rebated for a door.

Smythson's platt (**ill. 5**) shows a staircase against the W wall with a central section of eight straight treads and four wedge-shaped treads at either end. It would make sense to have the Buttery connected with the beer cellar in the basement, but it is impossible to see how this staircase could ever have been built as planned. It would have cut through the basement ceiling at a point where two barrel vaults intersect and would have blocked an external doorway in basement room 4/9, which is undoubtedly original. It seems this plan was abandoned and an alternative access to 4/9 was devised (see below). Although the staircase is repeated on Britton's plan of 1809 (**ill. 16**), this has many inaccuracies and seems to have been partially compiled from the earlier plan.

Room 3/18 (Butler's Chamber: Inventory Table)

In the inventory of October 1596 this room is referred to as 'the Wardrobe'. It is omitted from the December 1596 inventory, is called 'the Old Wardrobe' in 1599 and by 1601 it has become 'the Butler's Chamber'. It was lit by a tall 4-light window in the W wall and was linked to the Buttery by a doorway in its N wall which has remained unaltered although the door was replaced by a heavy iron door when the room was used by Lord Middleton to store silverware. The room was 1.25m shorter than the Buttery, for its E wall was a partition allowing space on the other side for an access passage (3/19i) between staircase 3/Sa and the corner chamber 3/19.

Mezzanine Chamber 3/18i (Inventory Table)

The space over passage 3/19i is occupied by a tiny mezzanine level chamber which was entered by ladder from the Butler's Chamber. This room, little more than a closet with no natural light, measures 1.32m x 3.24m with a height of 1.52m. It has a burnt lime floor and a ceiling of horsehair and plaster on wooden laths. The walls are lined with wooden planks and in the NW corner are two arched recesses in brick 1m above floor level. The doorway confirms, both in style and fabric, that the room is original to the first build. It measures 1.26m x 0.74m and is chamfered all round, including the threshold, with quirks in all corners except the top right, which has been repaired. The doorway has a brick rear-arch which is partially exposed. It is clearly not inserted and the bricks are identical to others found in the original fabric of the house. The room is referred to in the inventory of 1599, when one person apparently slept in it.

Passage 3/19i

This short passage linked the SW corner chamber (3/19) with the landing of the garden staircase, 3/Sa. Only 2.90m in height, it carries mezzanine level chamber 3/18i above it.

Wyatville's alterations (3/19i, 3/18)

Access to the SW corner chamber from the garden stair (3/Sa) was removed c.1832 when the Saloon was extended, so a new means of access to 3/19 was created. The Buttery was reduced in size by the insertion of a partition wall which cut 1.25m off the E end of the room and the space was used to extend passage 3/19i further N, linking it with the old Buttery doorway off the screens. A further doorway also had to be cut half-way along the passage through the original S wall of the Buttery. The partition wall was deliberately angled at the N end to allow for a new doorway to be provided into the Buttery from the service staircase landing. A plan of 1932[23] shows a further doorway between Buttery and passage in the partition wall opposite this point, but this has been blocked. A fireplace was inserted in the Buttery against the partition wall. Mezzanine rooms (3/17i and 3/18i) were inserted above the Buttery and Butler's Chamber respectively, reducing the ceiling height in these rooms to 2.50m. A straight timber staircase was installed against the Buttery S wall to gain access to these.

[23] *1932 Plans held in Wollaton Hall archives: Wallis Gordon drew this set of plans in 1932 when he was City Engineer for Nottingham.*

Ill. 53: Plan of mezzanine level suite over the Buttery and Pantry c. 1809.

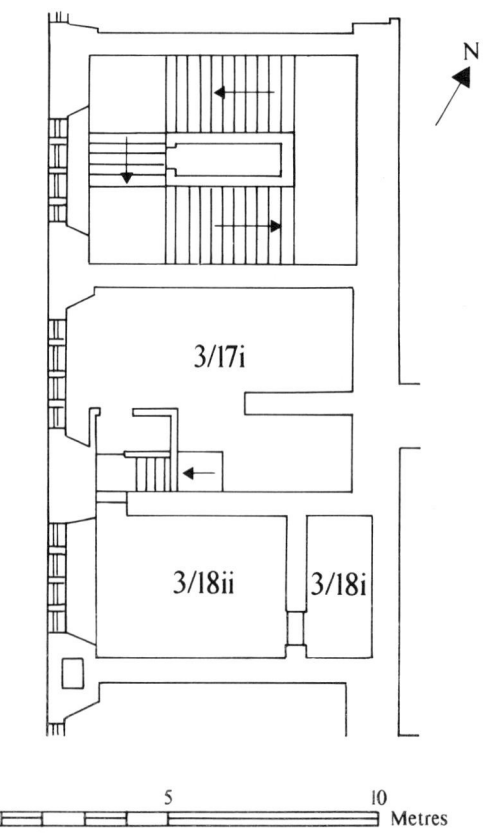

Mezzanine Room 3/17i (ill. 53)

At the top of the timber staircase a stair-well has been partitioned out of room 3/17i, which is otherwise the same size as the original Buttery. The top four panes of the Buttery window light the room at floor level. A block of masonry 0.54m x 2.48m against the E wall intrudes into the room to carry the flue of the inserted fireplace below, which taps into the flue of room 2/9 above (see **ill. 21**). A substantial timber ceiling beam 1.31m W of the E wall is probably original. The door to the room is 19th century but is fitted with a reused latch of late 17th or early 18th century type.

Mezzanine Room 3/18ii (ill. 53)

Access to the room is by the inserted staircase in the Buttery (3/17), at the top of which a doorway has been cut into the Tudor wall on the S side. At some stage this doorway has been deliberately narrowed to reuse a door, which is one of only two surviving doors which appear to be original to the house. It has decorative panelling and matches the door to the Prospect Room stairs on the N side of the leads. It has been shortened to fit the doorway, but otherwise its measurements indicate that it might once have belonged to the garderobe on the leads (1/6). The top four panes of the Butler's Chamber window light the room at floor level. The insertion of the floor has made the Tudor mezzanine chamber (3/18i) more easily accessible, but the ceiling height of 3/18ii is only 1.98m.

Room 3/19 (The Garden or Duke's Chamber: Inventory Table)

The SW corner chamber is included in all the early inventories and was clearly one of the better rooms in the house. By the time the inventory of 1609 was compiled it had acquired the name 'the Duke's Chamber', suggesting it had been occupied by the Duke of York in 1604. It was lit by a 4-light and a 5-light window in the W and S walls respectively and had a fireplace in the E wall. Smythson's plan (**ill. 5**) shows the fireplace further S than now. If this was so it has been moved to a more central position by Wyatville, but it should be remembered that Smythson's platt was drawn as a design, not as a record of what had been built. A doorway in the SW corner led to an inner chamber in the adjoining tower. The main door in the N wall has been re-hung, for the original pivots survive on the opposite side.

Tower Room 3/20 (Inner Chamber: Inventory Table)

This room would have housed the personal servants of important guests and there is documentary evidence that it had an additional mezzanine floor above it. The evidence rests on the inventories of 1599 and 1601, supported by the Smythson plan (**ill. 5**), which shows a straight stair against the N wall. This plan also shows a garderobe in the NW corner under the stairs and indicates that the northernmost light of 4-light W window was divided off and directed into the garderobe. The N jamb of this window is still squared off, whereas the other jambs are all splayed, and the brick-lined chute of the garderobe is still visible through a door in the jamb of the window recess. There was a further 4-light window in the S wall and no fireplace.

Wyatville's alterations

It seems ironic that in other towers Wyatville has inserted mezzanine floors and staircases where they did not previously exist, but here he has removed one. To create a study the room was restored to a square shape with full height windows and a fireplace was inserted in the E wall. As a strong iron door was fitted, valuable documents were apparently kept here. In the floor in front of the S window a trapdoor and ladder led to an even more secure muniment room.

Mezzanine Room 4/10i (Muniment Room)

Sandwiched between room 3/20 and basement room 4/10, and with a brick vault above and below it, this chamber would have been virtually fire-proof. It still retains brick and stone shelves on the N and E walls where documents were stored. It measures 4.23m N/S by 3.45m E/W, with a maximum height of 2.22m. A shallow 3-light window in the S wall originally lit room 4/10 in the basement. This has been fitted with shutters. The E and W walls of the basement room below (4/10) were thickened to carry the thrust of the inserted vaults. Room 4/10 was barrel-vaulted in an E/W direction to form the muniment room floor, while the ceiling of the strong-room itself was barrel-vaulted in a N/S direction.

Level 4 - THE BASEMENT (ills 24, 25, 31)

The foundations of the house were cut out of the Bunter sandstone which forms the core of the hill on which the building stands. In the basement the central space is occupied by a solid block of this rock, which supports the Great Hall and central tower, while the basement rooms are arranged in four wings around it. The stone is quite soft and the inner walls were carved from it, lined with brick or stone and plastered over. Occasionally flues and garderobe chutes intrude into the rock core.

Relative Floor Levels

As the natural topography of the site rose and fell around the summit of the hill the foundations of the basement were cut away at different levels, reaching a particularly low point in the SW corner. In order to convey the extent of these varying levels, for the purposes of the survey the entry lobby from the W courtyard (4/1) has been designated level 0 and each subsequent room is assigned a plus or minus level relating to this. For example, kitchen 4/2 is on the same level as 4/1, so is described as level 0 but the floor level of room 4/13 is higher (+1.65m) and room 4/9 is lower (-1.16m).

As the basement is partially subterranean, most of the windows are shallow and set near the ceiling. Exceptions to this occur on the W side where the natural ground level falls so much that the external walls are more normal in height. Here deeper windows were possible.

In the original house the basement rooms were divided into two separate suites or blocks, one containing service rooms, and the other providing some accommodation. There was no direct communication between these blocks at basement level.

The Service Block

Entrance Lobby / Servery - room 4/1, level 0

The lobby is entered by a doorway in the centre of the W wall 1.37m wide x 2.40m high. This was originally an external doorway to the W courtyard, but now links with Wyatville's single storey extension added after 1823. On the exterior the door surround is square-headed with rusticated quoins and voussoirs in the style of Serlio (**ill. 27**: compare the matching blocked doorway to room 4/9, **ill. 30,** which was also originally an external doorway). The rear-arch is curved on the interior. The S jamb is square with three deep horizontal rebates to accommodate the strengthening bars of the door; the N jamb is chamfered. The door is extremely heavy, of plank construction strengthened by three bars and many studs.

The lobby is 4.88m high and lit by a shallow 4-light window high in the W wall towards the S side. A further single light in the extreme NW corner is divided from a 4-light window serving both this lobby and room 4/2 to the N. The jamb of the embrasure has been cut at a sharp angle to convey more light into the lobby.

A further window, now blocked and not visible from the lobby, existed high in the S wall, which forms the N wall of the W staircase. It is unnecessary to convey borrowed light between the staircase landing and the lobby, so it was more likely a lookout point for a steward directing the conveyance of food from the servery up to the Hall. In the centre of the N wall a serving hatch probably represents the position of the Tudor servery; ghost marks on the wall show that this was once larger than it is now. The existing doorway at the W end of the N wall was inserted by Wyatville to give secondary access to his extension (see room 4/2).

At the northern end of the E wall a doorway leads into room 4/4 (the Inner Kitchen). It is typical of the Tudor doorways throughout the service apartments, with a square chamfered heading, chamfered jambs and a curved rear-arch. It measures 1.85m high x 0.92m wide with chamfers 65mm wide. In the SE corner a flight of six stone steps abuts the E wall and curves to abut the S wall. At the top of these steps is a round-headed arch, 1.39m wide x 2.51m high, chamfered all round with chamfer stops 0.30m from the bottom of the jambs. It leads to a short corridor (4/WSi) at the foot of the service stairs. The arch was converted to a doorway by the insertion of a timber frame with fanlight above during Wyatville's renovation. The addition of two further doors to the service stairs themselves indicates a preoccupation with limiting noise from the basement from reaching rooms above stairs. It is likely that the window on the stair landing was blocked at the same time and for the same reason.

The lobby is floored with diamond-shaped flagstones. A stone circular bowl has been cut into the centre of the E wall at floor level with a round-headed and domed niche over. This was perhaps to provide drinking water for a dog.

Room 4/2 *(The Outermost Kitchen: Inventory Table) level 0*

Identified from the household inventories, this room was one of two main kitchens. The E wall is thick enough to house a fireplace and a flue emerges on the leads, but the fireplace is now blocked. An original doorway at the southern end of the E wall connected this kitchen with another (the inner kitchen, room 4/4).

Room 4/2 is lit by a tall 4-light window in the W wall and a shallow 3-light window high in the N wall. High up at the southern end of the W wall three lights of a shallow 4-light window are directed into the room, the remaining light being directed into the lobby (4/1).

Later alterations (ill. 31)

A doorway at the W end of the S wall was inserted by Wyatville adjacent to another, at the S end of the W wall, which led into his service extension built c.1823. A plan of 1932 shows a curving wall forming a passage to divide these two doorways from the kitchen. It was lit by the three lights of the divided 4-light window mentioned above. This curving wall has been removed since 1932.

Along the W wall is a brick range over three arched openings for coals, one blocked. This would have been used to keep food hot. A similar range with a circular copper is shown on the 1932 plan along the N wall, but is now inaccessible.

In the NW corner, a short passage cut diagonally leads to the basement level of the NW tower (room 4/3). The square doorway is chamfered all round and is 1.85m high by 0.81m wide. It is rebated for a door to open into the tower chamber and one Tudor pivot remains.

Room 4/3 *(The Pastry Kitchen: Inventory Table) level 0*

This tower room is identified as the Pastry Kitchen by the 1601 inventory and is marked as such on Wyatville's extension plan of 1823 (**ill. 33**). It is 4.5m square, with a shallow 3-light window high in the N wall. The W wall is 0.25m thicker than the corresponding outer walls of the other towers and it seems likely that this was to accommodate pastry ovens in its thickness. (The central portion of the wall where the ovens would have been has been removed: see below). The room is only 2.44m. high as there is a mezzanine chamber above. This is reached by a flight of stone stairs against the S wall made up of seven straight treads and four winders. On the exterior face of the E wall there is a recess and an apparent lintel, signs that a doorway has been blocked, but no trace of this remains on the interior. Such a doorway would have balanced a corresponding doorway into the NE tower opposite, which was used for the delivery of wine.

Mezzanine Room 4/3i *(Cook's Chamber: Inventory Table)*

This is interpreted as the 'Cook's Chamber', mentioned in the household inventories of 1599, 1601 and 1609. Formed from the upper space of the Pastry Kitchen, it is only 2.12m. high. In 1599 it contained two sets of bedding, but only one set in 1601. It might have been merely an open loft over the kitchen as the partition from the staircase which now exists is 19th century.

Wyatville's alterations

Room 4/3.

Wyatville planned a yard to the W of the pastry kitchen (**ill. 34**) and he seems to have intended a doorway into it which would have removed the ovens. Alterations made during Phase 4 make it impossible to say whether this was done at that time or later.

Room 4/3i was partitioned from its access staircase, with a box-like timber structure in the SE corner to give headroom over the stairs. The door is 19th century. In the NW corner is a secondary (blocked) fireplace placed diagonally. The window in the N wall was reduced to two lights, probably in connection with the insertion of a flue for the fireplace. A further window of two shallow lights has been inserted into the W wall, with a flat lintel, as opposed to the more normal arched lintel. The S jamb has been squared off to accommodate a garderobe chute which is located in the thickness of the wall here.

Later alterations

During works carried out after 1926 by Nottingham City Council, an opening was cut through the W wall of room 4/3 linking it with a new room beyond lit by a skylight. A yard was roofed over to create it. The opening is 1.38m wide and would have removed the ovens if they had survived Wyatville's works.

Room 4/4 (The Inner Kitchen: Inventory Table: ill. 28) level 0

The room measures 5.48m N/S by 8.20m E/W and the crown of the vault is 3.25m high. In the 1601 inventory this room is called the 'Inner Kitchen'. It now serves as the boiler-room of the museum and is filled with machinery, making it very difficult to take accurate measurements of features such as the fireplace opening. A central section of the floor, originally flagged, has been raised by 15cms by a concrete platform in connection with the installation of the machinery.

The room is roofed by six groined vaults supported by two central pillars with moulded capitals and bases, but the easternmost bay of this vault arrangement is cut by a wall dividing the kitchen from the room next door (4/5). It seems likely that rooms 4/4 and 4/5 were conceived as one large kitchen designed to be roofed with quadripartite vaults supported on a row of four central pillars. However, it was decided to insert a dividing wall in place of the second pillar from the E. This change in plan leaves the vaulting of room 4/4 cut slightly short, while it is right in room 4/5. The decision must have been taken early in construction, however, because the decoration of the base and capital of the pillar in 4/5 differs from those in 4/4.

The dividing wall is 65cms thick, exactly the same thickness as the W wall, supporting the conclusion that it is original, although an afterthought to the original design. It must have been deemed necessary to support a wall directly above which divided the Wardrobe from the Porter's Lodge (rooms 3/3 and 3/2) in the original ground floor arrangement. A further indication that the wall is not secondary is provided by a stone-chamfered doorway at its N end linking the kitchen with room 4/5. It measures 1.94m high by 1.03m wide and is typical of other Tudor doorways in the basement, with a square head, all round chamfering and a square stop on the N side. The S jamb has suffered damage and the stop has been roughly rounded in repair. The slightly rounded rear-arch is also typical of the other Tudor openings in the house.

Room 4/4 is lit by two shallow windows in the N wall, the tops of which are about level with the crown of the vault, which has been cut back to allow light into the room. The easternmost has three lights, its sill angled sharply downwards to convey light into the room. The westernmost has four lights and probably had a similarly angled sill originally but the head of a doorway has been inserted beneath it (see 4/4a below).

In the W wall at the S end are two rear-arches to doorways side by side. The southernmost, 1.88m high by 1.04m wide, leads to the Lobby (4/1). The northernmost has chamfered jambs and an arched heading and leads into the Outermost Kitchen (4/2). It measures 1.02m across, 1.86m to the springing of the arch, and 2.03m to the crown. The wall between the adjoining kitchens is very thick because it houses the flue for the 'Outermost Kitchen' fireplace, so a short passage is formed 1.26m deep.

In the S wall is a large fireplace opening with a chamfered arch. The flue connects with the fireplace in the N wall of the Great Hall above (now blocked) and also served the N Great Chamber before emerging on the roof of the central tower. To the E of the main fireplace a further recess was marked on the 1932 plan. This can be located by tapping, but a modern stove has been built into the space and the wall above filled. On the W side of the main fireplace is a small recess 1.15m square with a groin-vaulted ceiling approximately 2.5m high. Its arched opening with chamfered jambs matches the main fireplace and a hole low in the E wall connected it with the latter; it was probably used as a smoking or curing chamber.

Room 4/4a

Towards the W end of the N wall a doorway has been inserted beneath the 4-light window, causing the original sloping sill of the window to be flattened out. The doorway leads to room 4/4a which occupies space under the N terrace. It was built by Wyatville when the original terrace was replaced and there is no evidence that the room had a Tudor forerunner. It is roofed by a barrel vault running N/S and has a 1-light window in the N wall. It was probably always designed for storage and is now used as a solid fuel store.

Room 4/5 (The Larder: Inventory Table) level 0

This room measures 5.31m N/S by 5.34m E/W and the crown of the vault is 3.85m high. Referred to as 'the Larder' in the inventory of 1601, it might have been converted to a scullery later. At the time of the survey the room was used as a lumber store, making access difficult, so some measurements are approximate. Against the S wall there appear to be two stone sinks approximately 1m high. The position of these features is compatible with the location of a culvert added to the western sewer system, probably during Phase 3 (see below). At the W end of the S wall, at a height of approximately 1.35m, a stone shelf 1.70m long has been built into the corner. Its W end is built into the W wall and the E end is supported by a stone corbel. A similar shelf 1.40m wide occupies the centre of the E wall supported on two corbels.

The room is roofed by four quadripartite vaults supported on one central pillar and is lit by a 3-light window high in the E end of the N wall, where the vault has been cut backwards and upwards to let light in. The floor is flagged. The larder was connected with the inner kitchen by a doorway at the N end of its W wall. It is rebated to take the door and the N jamb of the rear-arch is built into the wall while the S jamb is chamfered.

A doorway opposite, at the N end of the E wall, led to the wine cellar (4/7) via a passageway (4/6i). This passage was approached by four steps ceiled by a rising barrel vault. At the top step the passage is now blocked. The 1932 plan shows this passageway extended by a flimsy partition wall through room 4/5 to reach the doorway to the inner kitchen. No trace of such a wall remains. If it was drawn accurately, it was thin, like other secondary walls, and is most unlikely to have belonged to the original plan.

At the S end of the E wall four stone steps led to a second doorway flush with the wall, now blocked. The steps abut the S wall, where a gully 0.19m wide has been cut into them to act as a drain. The steps radiate 0.27m outwards on the N side with squared corners. The blocked doorway is 1.86m high x 0.86m wide, has a square heading, quirked top corners, is chamfered all round and led to the Saucery (4/6).

Room 4/6 (The Saucery: Inventory Table) level: + 0.94m.

The room is L-shaped, with a maximum N/S dimension of 4.15m and a minimum of 3.67m. It measures 5.37m E/W. Referred to as 'the Sawcery' in the 1601 inventory, 4/6 was originally accessible from the Larder (room 4/5) by a blocked doorway at the S end of the W wall (discussed above). The rear-arch, still visible in room 4/6, is typical of the Tudor doorways throughout the building. The roof consists of a barrel vault running N/S which is intersected by another running E/W.

At the E end of the N wall is a Tudor doorway, rebated to open into the room. Two Tudor pivots survive on the E jamb and a metal catch attachment on the W, but there is no door. A 2-light mullioned window in the N wall (now blocked) allowed borrowed light into the room from passage 4/6i. Along the S wall three arched recesses have been cut into the sandstone core to a depth of 0.72m at an uncertain date.

Passageway 4/6i level: + 0.70m.

A short passageway ran between the Wine Cellar (4/7) and the Larder (4/5), with a doorway in the south wall to the Saucery (4/6). It is 1.54m wide x 5.37m long and has a flagged stone floor. There is a blocked 4-light window high in the N wall, and a blocked mullioned window in the S wall which provided borrowed light for the Saucery (room 4/6, see above). The ceiling consists of exposed joists running N/S with floorboards running E/W visible above. This represents the floor of the N state staircase, replaced by Wyatville. All the rooms surrounding this short corridor are vaulted and this passage must also have previously been barrel-vaulted to support the stone Tudor staircase above.

At the E end of passage 4/6i is an original Tudor doorway into the wine cellar. It is square-headed and chamfered on the W side, with flat jambs and a shallow rear-arch rebated for a door on the E. It is 2.20m high by 1m wide and has a very heavy plank door reinforced with iron bars, probably dating from the 19th century. The doorway into the Larder at the W end of the passage is blocked (see below).

The thickness of the wall dividing room 4/6 and 4/6i from the wine cellar is in excess of 1m. It will be noted that load-bearing walls in the basement are often excessively thick; in this case the east wall of the north state staircase was carried above.

Later alterations to rooms 4/5, 4/6, 4/6i

Both doorways into the E wall of the Larder (room 4/5) have been blocked, so that the Saucery (4/6 and the adjoining passage (4/6i)) have become, as it were, a single chamber accessible only from the wine cellar (4/7). In room 4/6 a series of four modern brick bins has been built along the centre of the room in an E/W direction for the storage of wine bottles. Similar bins have been built against the blocked doorway at the W end of passage 4/6i and the easternmost of the arched recesses in the S wall of room 4/6 also has a modern central brick division matching these. An extremely heavy door has been fitted to secure the area and all sources of natural light have been blocked out from it. In view of the adjoining wine cellar and the fittings put in, it seems that 4/6 and 4/6i were adapted as a 'strong-room' for the storage of the most prized vintages. Since its creation had cut off access from the kitchens to the E, this might explain the rather extreme measures taken by Wyatville to provide an alternative basement access to the wine cellar (see below). Otherwise, the wine cellar could have been reached only from the exterior or the floor above.

Room 4/7 (Wine Cellar) level + 0.70m.

This can be identified partly by its own character, and partly by the inventory of 10th December, 1596, which clearly identifies the NE corner chamber as 'the chamber over the wine cellar' (Mi I 8/i). It is now used as a masons' workshop.

The cellar measures 9.40m N/S by 5.45m E/W and is roofed by a large barrel vault running NS to a maximum height of 3.80m. It has a flagged stone floor with a central gully dividing into a Y shape to N and S. There is a shallow 3-light window high in the N wall, and a 3-light and a 1-light window in the E wall. The tops of the last two are level with the crown of the vault, which has been cut back to form subsidiary barrel vaults at right angles to the main vault in order to admit the light.

Originally the S wall was not pierced at the E end by the corridor which now exists (this is discussed below). It should be noted that the S wall is excessively thick, approximately 1.75m, but since it supported only a dividing wall above (between the N painted chamber 3/10 and its inner chamber 3/11), without even a flue, it is difficult to account for such thickness at this point.

Slightly S of centre in the W wall a square-headed doorway measuring 2.36m high by 1m wide led to passageway 4/6i and the larder and kitchens beyond. The stone jambs are flat to the E, chamfered to the W, and the lintel is also chamfered. In the NE corner of 4/7 a short flight of five steps leads to room 4/8 in the NE tower.

Later alterations

It seems that the function of the wine cellar remained unaltered until the Hall was taken over by Nottingham City Council, when it ceased to be a wine store and became a masons' workshop.

At an uncertain date, a doorway was inserted into the E wall beneath the 3-light window. It leads by a descending staircase to an underground system of passages used as cellars and cisterns, called the 'Caves'. The character of the doorway, which is wide and perfectly plain, is not consistent with its belonging to the first build of the house and original wall fabric has been roughly hacked through to make the opening and not made good. The underground system was cut out of the rock, then lined in places with brick and is virtually impossible to date accurately but probably belongs to Phase 2. This is discussed in more detail below.

As part of Wyatville's reorganisation, the wine cellar was linked with the E wing of the basement by a corridor which is entered through the S wall (see below).

During the 19th century an area of the SW corner measuring 4.70m x 5.00m was divided off by brick walls and filled with brick-built bins. A wide opening in the N end rises the full height of the chamber. It seems that these alterations are contemporary with those to 4/6 and 4/6i and that less valuable wine bottles were stored in this part of the cellar.

Room 4/8 level:+1.30m.

This room forms the basement of the NE tower and stands at ground level on the N side of the house. It is roofed by a barrel vault running N/S and is lit by a 3-light window in the N wall. The floor is stone flagged. A short flight of 5 stone steps rises diagonally from the NE corner of the wine cellar into room 4/8 and there is no sign of there ever having been a doorway to separate these two rooms. On the W wall is a large doorway to the exterior, 2.20m high by 1.20m wide (**ill. 29**). The opening cuts through the main barrel vault of the room, forming a small barrel vault of its own at right angles. The width of the doorway is doubtless to facilitate the moving of wine barrels which would be rolled down a ramp over the stone steps and into the cellar beyond.

The SE corner of the room is walled off and houses a staircase leading to the ground floor. Four stone steps protrude into the room from the base of this partitioned staircase. On the S side they directly abut the wall and on the N side they radiate, with a square corner, to abut the W wall of the staircase partition. A further step reaches the threshold of the staircase which is barred off by a strong studded door.

In the SE corner, behind the staircase, is a closet entered by an arched opening in the partition wall. Inside here, in the E wall of the tower, is an arched recess which marks the position of a garderobe chute, now blocked. This might have been used as a slop-out directly to the drains.

Later alterations

Brick bins were installed, probably during the 19th century, and a modern lavatory has been installed in the NE corner.

Staircase 4/8S

The purpose of this stair was to convey wine from the cellar to the head of the Great Hall. It consists of a straight flight of four steps, followed by five winders to make a turn through 180 degrees, after which eight further straight steps gain the ground floor room of the SE tower. The steps have been refaced in concrete, but are probably stone beneath.

Corridor 4/WSi level: + 0.82m.

The W service staircase was approached from the lobby/servery (4/1) by a short corridor with an arch at its N end which now has a Georgian timber doorframe and fanlight inserted into it. At the S end the corridor ended with a square-headed stone doorway, 1.87m high by 0.92m wide, which is chamfered on the N and rebated for a door on the S side. The southern two-thirds of the corridor is roofed by a barrel vault, but the northern third, in front of the service stairs, has a groined vault. The W wall of the corridor, which forms the base of the staircase, has two arched niches set into it at a height of about 1m. The southernmost measures 0.82m wide by 1.51m high, the northernmost 0.87m wide by 1.51m high and they are both 0.85m deep. They show no signs of originally having doors, although the S one now has doors fitted, and seem to have been setting-down places for dishes *en route* from the servery to the Great Hall.

Room 4/9 and staircase 4/9S

On the S side of the doorway which ended corridor 4/WSi the arrangement of the basement in the Tudor house was fundamentally different from that bequeathed by Wyatville and the picture becomes quite complicated. Originally a small square landing led on to a straight staircase descending towards the W into room 4/9, the Ale Cellar. A flight of about ten steps would have been sufficient to reach floor level, 1.99m below that of the corridor. The roof of the staircase was a narrow barrel vault running at right angles to the main barrel vault of the ale cellar. The joint of these vaults can now be seen in a mezzanine chamber (4/9i) inserted by Wyatville. The staircase was bricked up c.1823 when the whole of room 4/9 was cut horizontally by a mezzanine floor, but the evidence for its existence is discussed in detail below.

Room 4/9 (Ale Cellar: Inventory Table) level: -1.17m.

The floor of room 4/9 is 0.79m below the ground level of the yard outside the W wall, which was enclosed as part of Wyatville's service block extension. However it is likely that it matched the ground level of the original Tudor courtyard which preceded this extension. The chamber was originally large and tall, measuring 12.05m long by 5.75m wide, and roofed by a barrel-vault running N/S which reached a height of approximately 5.6m at the crown. At the N end of the W wall was a doorway to the exterior, now blocked (**ill. 30**). This doorway matches the lobby entrance (4/1) further N (**ill. 27**) and was clearly designed to balance it on the W elevation.

High in the S wall there was a shallow 3-light window. As ground level was low on the W side of the house, the windows on this wall rose to full height. To keep symmetry with the fenestration on the upper floors they showed as 4-light windows on the exterior, but only the two central lights were open on the interior. Their barrel-vaulted tops run at right angles to

Ill. 54: An abortive plan by Wyatville for the western service extension c.1823. By courtesy of the Hallward Library [MiP3 p.3]

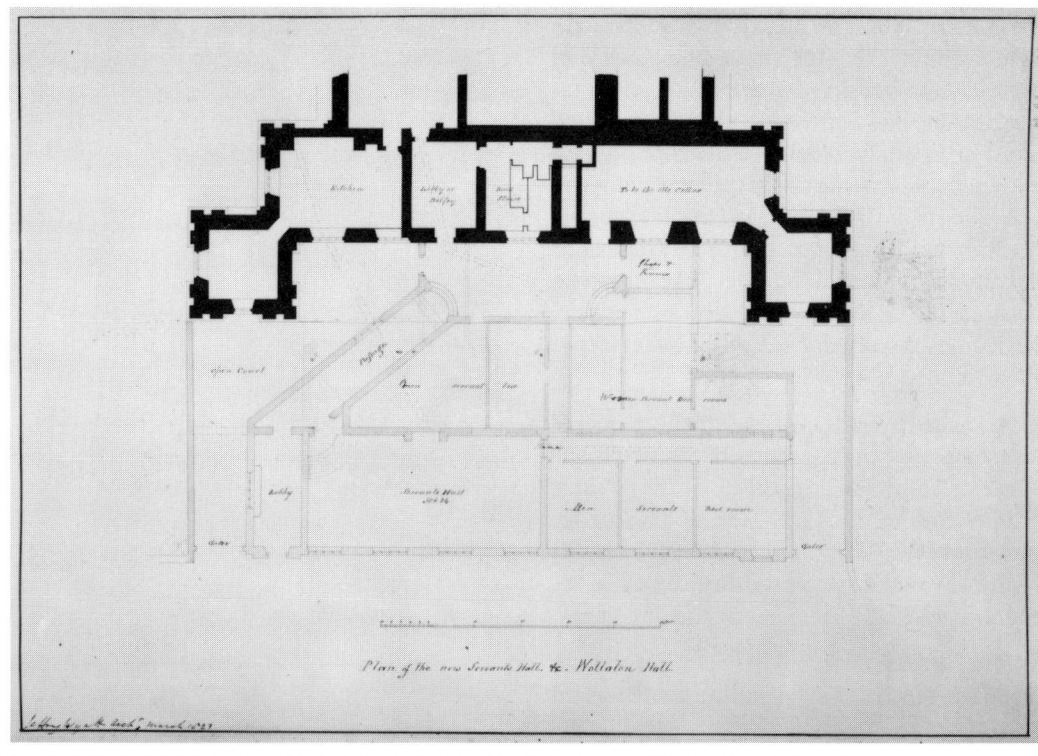

the main cellar vault and are preserved in room 4/9ii (**ill. 33**), where they are still only 2-lights wide, although they have been widened lower down (see below). When the room was used as a cellar it would have been desirable to limit the intensity of the light and this would also help to moderate the temperature.

In the SW corner, set diagonally, is a tall doorway measuring 2.63m high x 1.03m wide which leads into tower room 4/10. It is set back in a short passage 1.32m. long caused by the thickness of the walls meeting here. This is barrel-vaulted at a height of about 3m.

The Cellar Stairs 4/9S

A Tudor ale cellar would normally, though not invariably, have a direct staircase link with the buttery separate from the kitchen stairs. On Smythson's plan (**ill. 5**), which only covers the ground floor, a staircase of eight straight steps with four winders at each end is shown against the W wall of the buttery (3/17). Clearly this staircase cannot have gone up to the S state withdrawing room on the first floor but it is logical that the architect planned a descending staircase from the buttery to provide a direct link with ale cellar. The problem is that it is difficult to see how this staircase could ever have been built as planned. It would have cut through the ceiling of room 4/9 at the very point where the main barrel vault running NS intersects with another, narrower vault running EW, affecting the stability of the whole structure. It would then have cut across and blocked the doorway to the exterior, which is undoubtedly contemporary with the first build. In addition, as shown on Smythson's plan, it would have been too short to reach the floor of room 4/9 from the Buttery. We must therefore presume that, then as now, an architect's plan does not represent in every detail what was actually built. It is possible that Smythson had underestimated the depth which would be reached at this particular point as the basement foundation was excavated from the hillside, and that the original plan for the cellar stair had to be adapted as conditions presented on site. The proposed position of the staircase is now inaccessible, but it probably still survives intact. The evidence is as follows:-

a) An abortive plan by Wyatville of his proposed extension, dated 1823, shows the W side of the house well drawn in heavy black (**ill. 54**). A long narrow feature on the S side of the service staircase runs E/W and, although unlabelled, fits well with other evidence for the position of the stairs.

b) The lower part of room 4/9 is 1.5m short of the measurement of a mezzanine floor inserted above. This discrepancy is caused by the stairs themselves being bricked up, while the upper space of the staircase was utilised at mezzanine level.

c) A narrow barrel vault runs E/W exactly over the position of the lost staircase, whereas the main vault of room 4/9 runs N/S and is much wider.

d) A 3-light window in the W wall, originally 2.25m deep but now partially blocked, was available to light the staircase. On the exterior this window appears as a 4-light but could never have been wider than 3-lights on the interior as it is cut by the joint of the two vaults.

17th century alterations

During Phase 2 a new external ale cellar was built (see **ills 37 and 39**) and the Tudor original (4/9) was converted to a servants' hall. A fireplace was inserted between the two windows in the W wall, probably at this time, and the flue was cut through the superincumbent masonry. It emerges on the leads where its chimney-pot is disguised as part of the balustrade (**ill. 32**).

Wyatville's alterations

Wyatville's sketch plan for his extension (**ill. 34**) labels room 4/9 'Old servants' Hall to

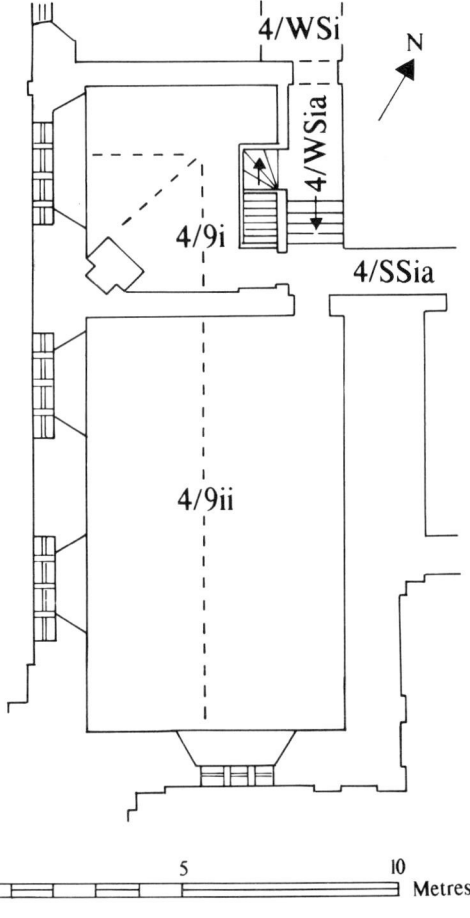

Ill. 55: Plan of mezzanine level floor inserted into the Tudor ale cellar (4/9).

become Bedrooms'. He doubled the available space by inserting a mezzanine floor (**ills 55 and 33**). This served a double purpose as it also provided access at the correct height to drive a corridor through to the S side of the house. This wing had been used solely for accommodation in the Tudor house and had previously been accessible only from the S state staircase.

Room 4/9

The lower part of room 4/9 has become known traditionally as the 'Grooms' Room'. The floor is stone flagged. At the N end the room is cut short by approx. 1.5m by the insertion of a brick wall to block off the original staircase. The ceiling is formed by the floor of the mezzanine suite above at a height of 2.30m. The timber floor-joists run E/W and are supported by a row of five cast iron pillars placed just off-centre along the length of the cellar. The four southernmost pillars are 2m apart but the northernmost also forms the finial post of an inserted timber staircase and is only 1.5m from the next. The second ceiling joist from the N end is not attached to the wall on the W side because it coincides with a window here, so a short cast-iron pillar has been placed on the edge of the window-sill to support it. The joist is cut off abruptly above it. The alterations in this room have clearly been carried out clumsily, with a view to increasing serviceable floor space, but without regard for architectural finish.

The inserted floor cuts across the windows on the W side at the first transom from the bottom. As very little light would have been admitted by these truncated 2-light windows, the embrasures were widened to open them to their full width of four lights. To maximise the amount of light admitted, they were given sharply sloping sills which were cut roughly from the Tudor masonry, then finished in lath and plaster. The jambs are not splayed to the same angle as Tudor examples elsewhere and the N jamb of the S window is very distorted to accommodate the inserted flue.

The external doorway at the N end of the W wall was blocked and its deep recess converted into a cupboard. The original doorway recess measures 1.38m wide x 2.88m high but the cupboard doorway is narrower and is aligned with the S jamb of the Tudor doorway. As a result there is a short stretch of inserted wall on the N side which has a very small square window in it.

Along the N wall is a row of three lead-lined circular sinks dating from the 19th century. The fireplace in the centre of the W wall is blocked and a 19th century iron stove, very rusty, stands in front of it.

Mezzanine floor (ill 55)

The upper part of 4/9 was floored over to correspond with the floor level on the south side of the house (+1.65m). This mezzanine level provided two rooms (4/9i and 4/9ii) and a new means of access to the S wing.

S Wing Access

The thick E wall of room 4/9 was broken through at mezzanine level to link with a newly created corridor (4/SSia) in the S wing. To reach this a new stretch of corridor (4/WSia) had to be created by extending the Tudor corridor (4/WSi) and incorporating the landing of the original cellar staircase (4/9S). As the section of corridor (4/WSia) was achieved by pushing into the roof space of the original ale cellar (4/9), its E side retains the arc of the cellar vault.

To make the best use of available space in the new arrangement, the old staircase was bricked up and abandoned. To meet the S wing at the correct level, the mezzanine floor needed to be 0.82m higher than the Tudor corridor, so five ascending steps were necessary in the corridor extension. Just before these a new timber stair was inserted on the W side of the corridor, which descends into room 4/9. This takes up little space and by flooring over the Tudor original a small but serviceable square room (4/9i) could be created.

Room 4/9i

This chamber measures approximately 4.30m N/S by 4.20m E/W and it overlies the abandoned ale cellar staircase and part of room 4/9. Its E wall has been inserted to divide it from corridor 4/Wsia and on the same side a box-like timber structure intrudes into the room to give extra headroom to the timber staircase from 4/WSia into room 4/9.

The S half of 4/9i is roofed by the Ale Cellar barrel-vault running N/S, although the inserted E wall of the room cuts it longitudinally. At the N end of the room, this vault intersects with a narrower one running E/W, which represents the ceiling of the original staircase 4/9S. At the N end of the W wall is a 3-light window, originally 2.25m deep, but now blocked except for the top panes. Although showing 4 lights on the exterior, this window is unlikely to have shown more than 3 on the interior because of the placing of the groin where the two vaults intersect. It might originally have been open to its full height, as it was designed to light the abandoned staircase (4/9S), but the lower panes were blocked by Wyatville's extension.

In the SW corner a fireplace, now blocked, has been placed diagonally across the room to make the insertion of its flue easier. During the museum phase a modern sink has been placed beneath the window at the N end of the W wall and a range of tall cupboards fitted along the N wall.

Room 4/9ii

Room 4/9ii (**ill. 33**) is simply the upper space of the greater part of the Tudor Ale Cellar with a partition wall inserted at the N end to divide it from 4/9i and the corridor extension described above. It measures 8.65m N/S by 4.57m E/W and is ceiled by the cellar barrel vault which reaches a height of 2.95m at its crown.

The windows are set into two deep barrel-vaulted embrasures on the W side which accommodate only the two centre lights of the great 4-light windows which appear on the exterior. Only the top panes remain exposed, the lower sections are blocked and covered with built-in cupboards dating from the museum phase of the building.

Room 4/10 level -1.16m

The basement room of the SW tower (4/10) was entered from the SW corner of room 4/9. A short diagonally placed passage through the thickness of the wall, 1.32m long and vaulted over at a height of about 3m, leads to a square-headed chamfered stone doorway 2.63m high by 1.03m wide. There is a curved rear-arch and the SW side is rebated for a door which opened into 4/10. Three Tudor pivots survive on the S jamb. The passage continues for 0.78m beyond the doorway but its height decreases by about 0.45m. The room measures 4.5m E/W by 4.75m N/S, and was originally very tall, approximately 5.6m high, which might account for the large proportions of the doorway. High in the S wall was a 3-light window which is shown on Wyatville's service extension sketch-plans (**ills 34 and 54**). The stonework of the N and S walls is exposed.

Wyatville's alterations

A muniment room (4/10i) was inserted into the top portion of 4/10. To make this fire-resistant, it was enclosed above and below by brick barrel-vaults. The inserted vault of room 4/10 runs E/W to a maximum height of 3.30m and its haunches are set into the N and S walls. The muniment room vault runs in the opposite direction (N/S) and the E and W walls of room 4/10 were thickened in brick to a depth of approximately 50 cms to carry its thrust.

A doorway 1m wide was cut in the centre of the W wall to connect room 4/10 with the service extension, replacing a 2-light window shown on one of Wyatville's plans (**ill. 54**). As the 3-light window in the S wall is utilised by the muniment room itself, room 4/10 remained unlit and unventilated. The brickwork towards the floor of the W wall has badly deteriorated because of damp, but a blocked brick archway is discernible at the N end. This might represent the preservation of an earlier access to a drain in this position, where a garderobe chute passes from the chambers above to the western sewer system.

The Accommodation Block

The S state staircase (SS) was totally replaced during Wyatville's programme of renovation, but it must have descended to the basement to give access to accommodation provided in the SW corner for the more privileged servants of the household, and vestiges of it can be seen in room 4/11. Under the collective heading 'the yeomen's lodgings', the household inventory of 1601 details the contents of five apartments, each of which was similarly furnished and these can be reconstructed from evidence still extant (rooms 4/12, 4/13, 4/14, 4/17, and 4/18). The fact that access was by a state staircase and that the accommodation was deliberately separated from the service suite is some indication of the status the occupants of these rooms enjoyed. It should also be noted that a fair amount of the original Tudor architectural detail survives here, for example in the form of door surrounds, and that these quarters were finished to a high standard. This is in sharp contrast to Wyatville's later treatment of servants' quarters.

The 'Yeomens' Lodgings': Southern Range (ill. 24)

Corridor 4/SSi level +1.65m

There is no reason to doubt that the original S staircase was similar in design to the W service staircase. At basement level it emerged into a flagged corridor about 11.5m long running E/W. At the E end the corridor could be closed off by a square-headed Tudor doorway with a chamfered surround and stops, which survives. It is rebated for a door on the E side but there is no longer a door. By the W end of the staircase the corridor is spanned by an arch which carried the weight of the dining parlour E wall on the floor above.

Room 4/13 (Yeomens' Lodging: Inventory Table) level +1.65m

Room 4/13 lay at the W end of corridor 4/SSi. The jambs of its doorway survive, although altered, on either side of the corridor. The chamber measured approximately 6.5m N/S by 5.5m E/W, and was lit by a single light window high in the S wall. There might have been a fireplace in the N wall which could have connected with a flue serving the Dining Parlour and Great Hall above. This chamber must have connected on the W side with an inner room, 4/13i, which would otherwise have been inaccessible.

Room 4/13i level +1.65m

This was an unlit inner chamber to 4/13, measuring approximately 3.30m E/W by 3.75m N/S. It was roofed by a barrel-vault running E/W to a maximum height of 3m, whose purpose was to support a staircase above which led from the S end of the screens passage to the S terrace (3/Sa: **ill. 12**).

Room 4/12 (Yeomens' Lodging: Inventory Table) level +1.65m

Room 4/12 lay between 4/13 and the S staircase and measured approximately 4m E/W by 4.3m N/S. Its N wall survives intact (**ill. 26**) and retains the doorway by which it was entered from corridor 4/SSi. Its design is typical of those in the basement; square-headed, with chamfered surround and stops and a curved rear-arch. Its dimensions are 1.89m high x 0.81m wide. On the W side of the doorway is a window which shed borrowed light into the corridor. It has two lights with chamfered mullions. Its overall measurements are 1.24m wide x 0.97m deep and each light measures 0.41m wide by 0.75m deep. The chamber was unheated and would have had a 2-light window at the extreme E end of the S wall. At the N end of the E wall part of the arch of a further doorway is visible at a height of 2.30m, but it has been cut off and blocked by later alterations. This connected with an inner chamber (4/11).

Room 4/11 level + 1.65m

A small inner chamber to room 4/12, 4/11 was created from space under the S staircase and has been much altered (see below). However, evidence of the blocked doorway which connected the two rooms remains, with one Tudor pivot surviving in its N jamb. Later alterations have obscured the lighting arrangements. It could have been lit by a single pane of a four light window diverted into the room, which is an arrangement found elsewhere in the basement, or it might have remained blind like 4/13i.

Wyatville's alterations (ill. 31)

South Staircase

In replacing the staircase, Wyatville retained the supporting E and W walls of the original basement stair, as well as the central well, but moved the N wall further into the corridor. From ground floor level the present staircase curves towards the E to reach a small square landing. Two further steps down toward the N gains access to corridor 4/SSi through a large doorway with a fanlight above.

Much of the space under and behind the re-worked staircase has been utilised (4/SSii). Access to the understair area is by a doorway off the corridor at the W end of the staircase block. This leads to a narrow room (originally 4/11) with two recesses in the W wall. The more southerly of these is the smaller of the two but could not be measured. The northernmost is created out of the blocked connecting doorway with room 4/12. It still has one Tudor pivot *in situ*, but it has been reduced in height and widened, now measuring 1.62m high x 1.14m wide. Wyatville probably inserted the recess to the S and altered the doorway to make a pair. On the E wall is another arched recess. The ceiling slopes toward the S where stairs are accommodated above. The passage then turns E where a flight of Tudor steps has been removed, and a single light window is placed about the middle of the wall. On the N side is a cupboard-like recess 1.02m E/W by 1.41m N/S set between substantial walls. This appears to be retained from the central well space within the Tudor staircase which was used sometimes as cupboards. (These are clearly drawn on Smythson's plan and are found in the W staircase at ground floor level and above.) Beyond this is a further turn N into a rectangular storage space 2.3m E/W by 3.8m N/S. Here a window high in the N wall gives borrowed light onto the small square landing at the bottom of the staircase. At the southern end of the E wall a doorway was inserted to connect with room 4/14, but this is now blocked.

Room 4/12

In room 4/12 the major alteration has been the insertion of a flue and fireplace against the E wall. This was substantially thickened to accommodate, not only a flue to serve this room, but also a new fireplace in the dining parlour above (**ill. 15**). The underside of the new dining parlour hearth is visible in the ceiling. Thickening the wall has blocked the easternmost light of the 2-light window and a cupboard recess has been made in it on the S side of the fireplace.

Corridor 4/SSia

Wyatville broke down the discrimination between the service and accommodation areas in the basement by making them mutually accessible. A mezzanine floor over the Tudor Ale Cellar (4/9) was partly designed to link the W and S wings (see above). Having made an opening through the dividing wall between 4/9 and 4/13i, it was necessary to drive a 1m wide corridor through rooms 4/13i and 4/13 to reach the Tudor corridor (4/SSi) which lay beyond. The dividing wall is structural and very thick (approximately 2m), so an arch was inserted over the breach to carry the superincumbent weight. A similar precaution was taken further E when the wall between rooms 4/13i and 4/13 was breached. (The doorway between these rooms was just to the S of this and had to be blocked.) This wall was also thick (approximately 1.5m) because it had supported the weight of the W wall of the Dining Parlour above. (This, however, was later removed to extend the Dining Parlour: **ill. 15**) A third arch still further E marks the position of the original doorway into room 4/13.

Room 4/13i

Room 4/13i was divided by a partition wall, the N half of the room becoming part of corridor 4/SSia, and the S half incorporated into 4/13ii (see below). At this point the corridor N wall curves towards the ceiling because room 4/13i was barrel-vaulted.

Room 4/13

Room 4/13 was made smaller (approximately 5x5m) as the northern section of the room was added to the corridor (4/SSia). The room was given a partition N wall which has a doorway at the W end and a window at the E end to shed borrowed light into the corridor.

The doorway between rooms 4/13i and 4/13 was blocked and the recess used to make a cupboard. A fireplace was built against the centre of the new N wall. The flue is conveyed across the corridor in an arch, where it links with an original flue serving the Dining Parlour and Great Hall above. Wyatville strengthened the Dining Parlour floor by inserting two new joists into room 4/13. These run N/S and the easternmost is further supported by a cast-iron pillar.

Stairs 4/S13ii

In the Tudor house the garden stairs (3/Sa) led from the S end of the screens passage on the ground floor to the 'garden door' on the S terrace (**ill. 12**). Room 4/13i supported this staircase upon its barrel vault. In 1832 Wyatville complied with the wishes of Lord Middleton in removing this staircase to extend the Dining Parlour (now called the Saloon) westwards. However Lord Middleton wished to retain an exit to the terrace 'under the Saloon', so the 'garden door' was retained, although altered and reduced in height (alteration of the masonry courses can be seen externally). It opens on to a narrow flight of steps (4/13ii), only 75cms wide, into the basement, where the S wall of room 4/13i was broken through so that they might emerge there. High in the W wall of 4/13ii ghost marks of some of the treads of the Tudor 'garden' steps are still visible.

The Yeomen's Lodgings: Eastern Range (ill.24)

Corridor 4/SSii

Three further rooms completed the Yeomen's Lodgings and these were reached from a corridor (4/SSii), 9.75m long, running N/S. It could be closed off from the neighbouring corridor (4/SSi) by a door (see above). 4/SSii is just over 3.00m high and is approximately 1.5m wide, although it narrows where the rock core of the Great Hall foundation forms its western wall. This discrepancy is masked by an arch at this point. Its design is typical of the basement doorways: square-headed with chamfered surround and stops, but it is chamfered on both sides, with no rebate for a door. Its purpose is to carry the weight of the N wall of staircase 3/Sb above (**ill. 12**).

At the N end of the corridor, cut into the rock core, is a closet which was originally a garderobe. Its chute also served garderobes on both floors above (in the 'Painted Chamber' (3/9) and the Long Gallery), and its shaft can be traced in the eastern section of the sewer system.

Room 4/14 (Yeomens' Lodging: Inventory Table) Modern name: The Steward's Room level +1.65m

4/14 lies at the southern end of corridor 4/SSii. It is entered by a square-headed, chamfered doorway with decorative stops which has a curved rear-arch and is rebated for a door opening into the room.

The chamber measures 6.38m E/W, 5.15m N/S and is just over 3m high. It has a 3-light window in each of the S and E walls, each with a sill height of 1.27m. There was a fireplace in the W wall whose flue also served rooms on the floors above ('The Chapel Chamber' (3/7) and the Long Gallery). There are two recessed cupboards with arched tops which might be original, one in the southern end of the W wall and one in the northern end of the E wall.

During the course of the survey some stonework was revealed when 19th century wainscotting and plasterwork was removed from the lower section of the S wall to counteract damp (**ill. 6**). The section of wall, approximately 4.5m long by 1.25m high, contained several fragments of Romanesque masonry, apparently robbed from an early 12th-century church. These included three fragments of a roll-moulded door jamb; two small attached cushion capitals of a type which might have come from clerestory window openings; several pieces of half column in three different sizes of the type which might have been attached to the major piers; there were also several squarish blocks showing diagonal tooling typical of the early 12th century.

Room 4/17 (Yeomens' Lodging: Inventory Table) level +1.60m

At the N end of corridor 4/SSii a doorway in the E wall originally led into an unheated room, 4/17, which is stone flagged. In its Tudor form this chamber measured approximately 4.75m N/S by 3.75m E/W, the ceiling height is 3.07m and it was lit by a central 3-light window in the E wall. A 2-light mullioned window in the W wall, now blocked, measured 0.93m wide by 0.68m high and shed borrowed light into the corridor. A further blocked window in the S wall shed borrowed light into room 4/16.

Room 4/18 (Yeomens' Lodging: Inventory Table) level +1.60m

This room measured approximately 5.40m E/W by 5.60m N/S and lay at the N end of corridor 4/SSii with an original entrance straight from the corridor. The doorway, now blocked, has been plastered over on the corridor side, but survives as a shelved recess inside the room; it is approximately 1.75m high x 0.77m wide and one Tudor pivot remains. The floor is stone flagged and the chamber was lit by a 3-light window in the centre of the E wall.

In the centre of the W wall is a 19th century fireplace which might occupy the place of a Tudor forerunner. Its flue is cut into the rock core at this point and into the central tower higher up, where it also served rooms 3/10 and the Long Gallery. At the southern end of the W wall is a cupboard with a 19th century door which was not accessible for inspection. The 1932 City Engineer's plan records a rectangular recess in this position similar to the one at the N end of corridor 4/SSii. This marks the course of a second garderobe chute which served the 'Painted Chamber' (3/10) and a garderobe on the half roof. It is therefore possible that 4/18 also had a garderobe.

Room 4/16 level +1.55m

The purpose of this barrel-vaulted room was to carry a staircase (3/Sb) above, which led from the ground floor to an exit into the E courtyard. (In this respect it parallels room 4/13i which supported 3/Sa.) 4/16 is entered from corridor 4/SSii by a low doorway, 1.64m high by 82cms wide which is square-headed and chamfered with decorative stops. The room measures approximately 3.50m N/S by 2.50m E/W and was lit by borrowed light from room 4/17. The window in the N wall is 0.77m wide x 62.5cms deep but is now blocked. The vault runs N/S and its crown reaches a height of 2.0m.

Wyatville's Alterations (ill. 31)

Corridor extension

Wyatville linked corridor 4/SSii with the wine cellar (4/7), possibly because he had blocked access to it from the kitchens in order to make a secure wine-store (see above). To achieve the link it was necessary to truncate room 4/17 and drive a corridor between 4/17 and 4/18. The wall which was inserted at the N end of 4/17 is much thinner than the Tudor walls, and the new doorway into the room is placed at its W end. The original Tudor doorway into 4/17 now leads to Wyatville's corridor, and is masked by a Georgian architrave. The Tudor entrance to room 4/18 was blocked and a new doorway placed further east from the inserted corridor.

The floor level of the accommodation complex is 71cms higher than that of the wine cellar, so six steps, two of which make a turn, were placed at the E end of the new section of corridor. A passage 1.20m wide was then driven through the sandstone foundation of room 4/18, to link up with the wine cellar. In order to provide sufficient height for this passage, the eastern section of floor in room 4/18 was raised, forming a platform to window-sill height (0.88m) and covered in timber floorboards, which form the ceiling of the adjoining passage. Where Tudor walls to N and S were cut through, arches were inserted to bear the load.

Room 4/15 (Gardener's Chamber: Inventory Table) level +1.50m

This room, which forms the basement of the SE tower, was originally inaccessible from the interior. (A plain doorway set diagonally in the SE corner of room 4/14, by which it is now entered is secondary.) It can be identified with 'the Gardener's Chamber' of the 1601 household inventory and was entered by an external doorway

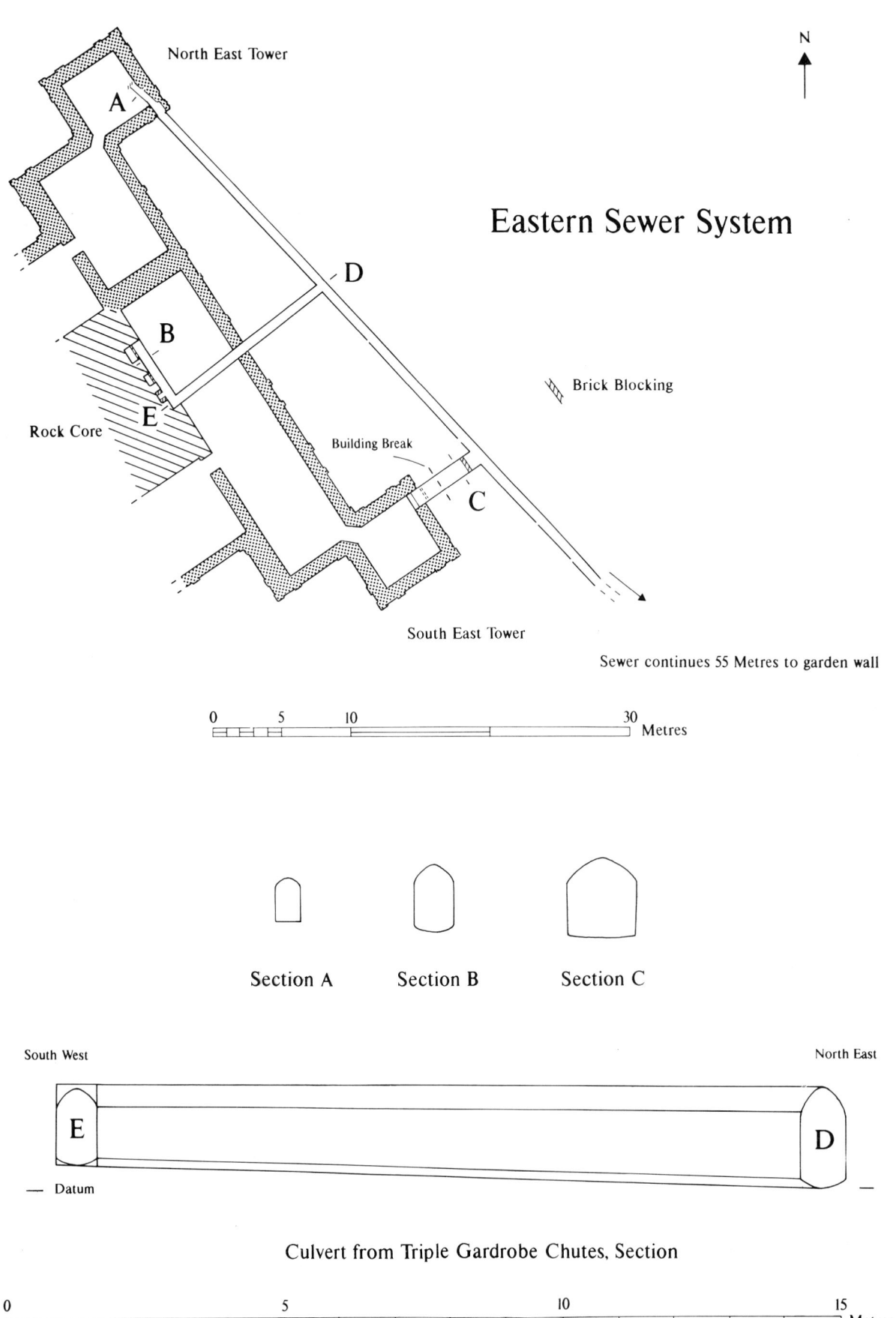

Ill. 56: Plan and sections of the eastern sewer system.

in the W wall, still visible on the exterior, although blocked and plastered over on the interior. The floor level is slightly lower than in room 4/14. The chamber measures 4.66m E/W by 4.50m N/S by 3.13m high and was unheated. A rectangle of masonry measuring 1.50m N/S by 0.77m E/W intrudes into the NE corner. A garderobe shaft is located here and it is possible this chamber had its own sanitation. There is a 3-light window in the S wall with a sill height of 1.27m. Two cupboard recesses, one in the SW corner and one in the centre of the E wall, are of indeterminate date.

Wyatville's Alterations

A fireplace was inserted in the N wall as part of Wyatville's programme of installing heating in all four towers. The stone surround and iron grate are 19th century. The external doorway has been blocked from inside.

Part 3: THE UNDERGROUND WORKS

1. THE TUDOR SEWERS (ill. 37)

Two quite separate sewer systems were built with the house, one serving the east and another the west side. They each comprise a main passage running roughly parallel with the side of the house, connected by culverts to garderobe chutes in the wall thicknesses. The passage then extends far beyond the immediate vicinity of the building, running in a south-easterly direction on the east side and west on the west side.

EASTERN SEWER SYSTEM
(ills 38 and 56)

The main passage is barrel-vaulted and has a steady fall towards the south to take waste away from the house (**ill. 35**). It averages 1.75m in height by 0.88m in width and is constructed of hand-made bricks. The floor is of bricks set lengthways, and it slopes by about 90mm towards a central gully to carry off liquids (**ill. 56, section D**). Two culverts run westwards from it to link up with garderobe chutes which descend through the wall thickness of the house. These passages run under the foundations and must have been built in the early stages of construction, but building breaks can be seen on either side of the culvert walls, so the main passage appears to have been built in a later operation, perhaps as the house was nearing completion. The terraced garden on the south side was largely an artificial creation, part of Smythson's overall plan, and stretches of the sewer might well have been built at natural ground level, or at least at the edge of the excavations of the hill core carried out for the house foundations, and buried later.

The main sewer begins beneath the south-east corner of the north-east tower where a chute, now blocked, descended from the garderobes above. Here the crown of the vault of the main sewer is just below the foundation of the tower wall. It runs south-east for a distance of 44.45m, not quite parallel with the east facade of the house, but veering away from the south-east tower. Over this distance there is a fall of 1.10m, ensuring a shallow but steady slope. At this point the main passage changes angle by 7.5 degrees so that it heads in a more easterly direction (**ill. 37**). It continues south for a further 55m, with a fall of a further 1.27m, before it is truncated by the revetment of the garden terrace. Although the slope is maintained throughout, the fall is too gentle to suggest that the sewer was cleaned by flushing and its height also lends weight to the conclusion that it was cleansed manually.

6m to the north of the change in angle a secondary drain enters the sewer on the west side at springing level of the vault. It measures 0.20m square, has brick sides with a ceiling and floor of stone slabs, and was inserted, probably during Phase 3, to dispose of excess rainwater (see 'surface water drainage', below). A drain from the pond enters the sewer 34.5m from the south end of the main passage. The Tudor work terminates just short of the revetment to the south terrace and the last half metre or so of the passage has been made good when this later wall was built. The break occurs 0.33m and 0.70m from the end on the west and east sides respectively. Beyond the terrace the ground falls away, so it is unlikely that the sewer could have continued much further. There must have been an entrance for maintenance, perhaps then as now in the terrace wall, but there must also have been a massive soakaway situated south of the terrace, where the golf course now starts.

Garderobe chutes

There are in total five chutes in the wall thickness on the east side of the house. Details vary in each case, but in general the chutes are square or oblong shafts which fall quite vertically, with a shallow brick arch forming an opening at one side to connect the shaft with the sewer.

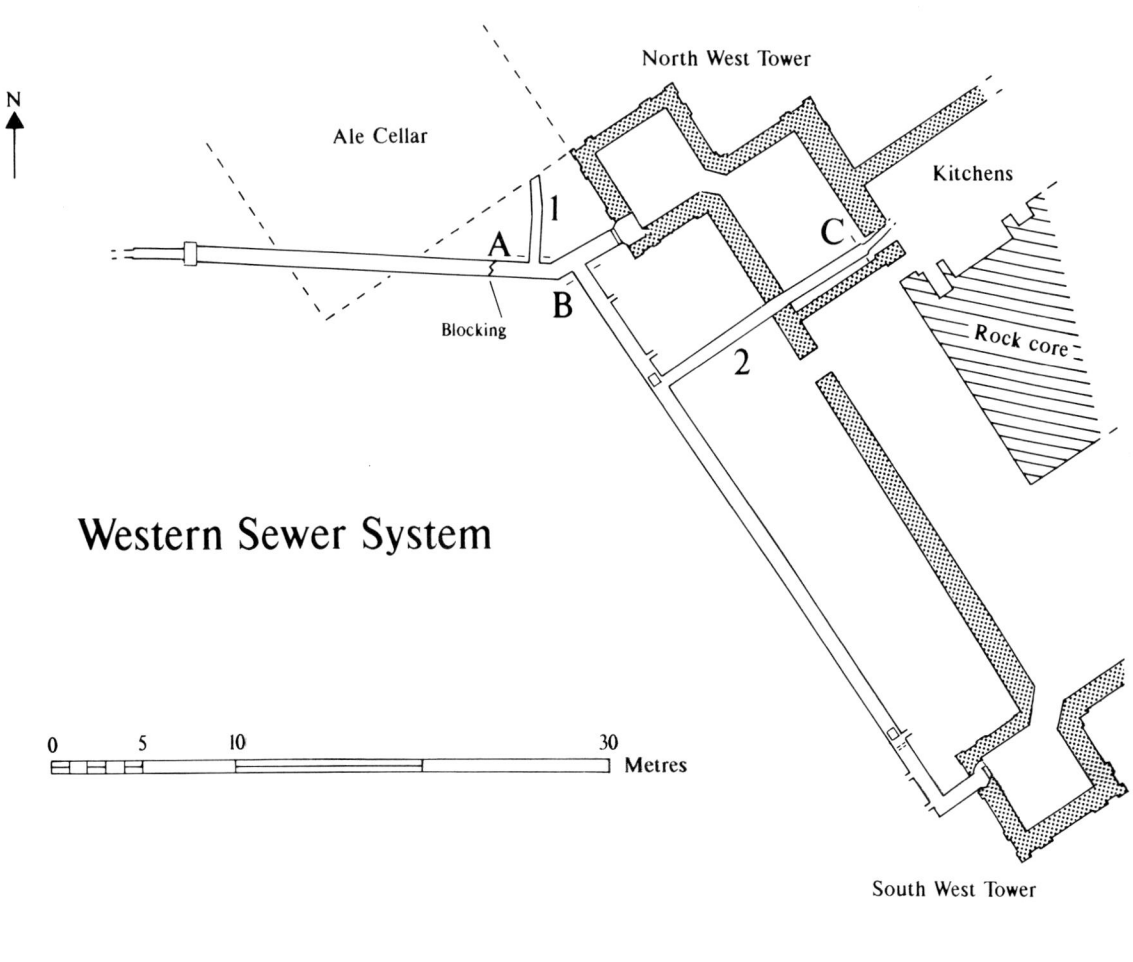
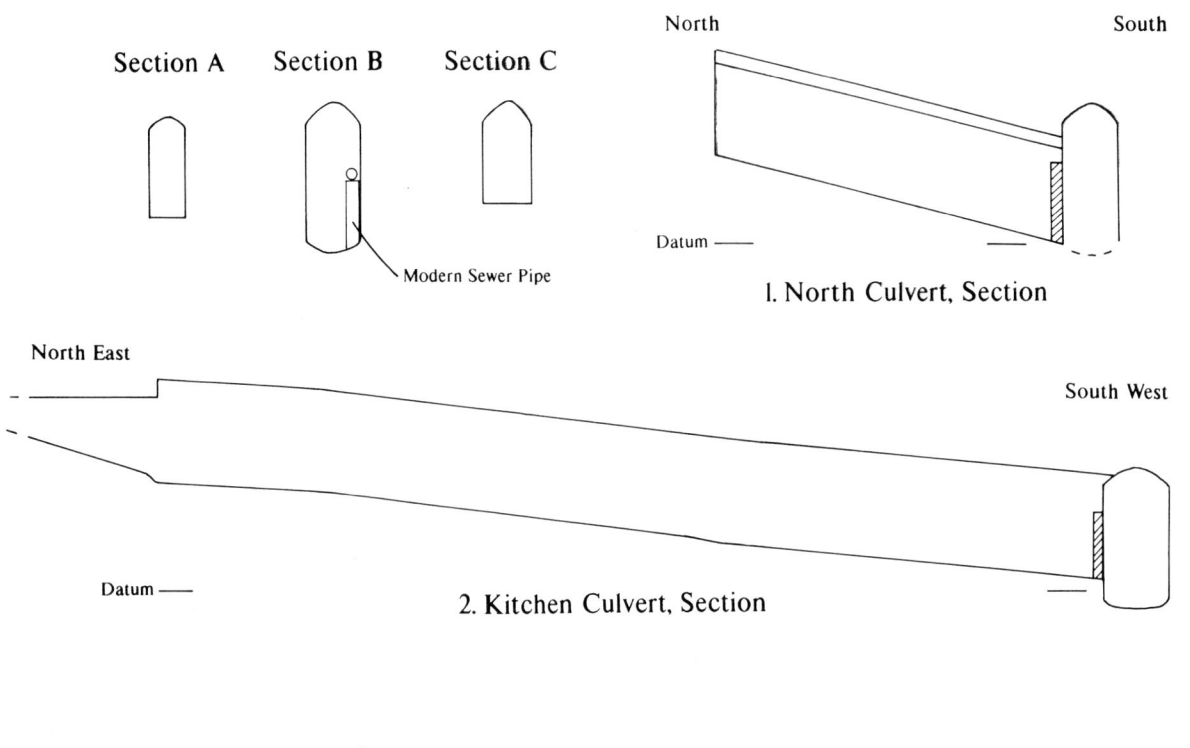

Ill. 57 (opposite):
Plan and sections of the western sewer system.

North-east tower (ill. 56)

The garderobe chute from the north-east tower is situated directly above the north end of the main sewer passage (point A). The shaft is 0.90m square but has been blocked at a height of 1.64m with sandstone slabs.

Later alterations

A second vaulted passage has been added leading from the north-east side of the garderobe chute (point A, section A). It is also brick-vaulted, but is only 0.78m high and narrows from 0.70m to 0.47m in width over a length of 2m before it is blocked. Towards the blocking a break in the east wall, about 0.10m square, is sufficient to reveal that this passage breaks another vaulted brick passage, larger in size and running towards the north-east. In dark and very cramped circumstances with much rubble lying around, only glimpses of this could be seen and it is not known whether it can be associated with the first building phase.

Central Chutes (ill. 56)

At a point 17.5m along the main passage, approximately opposite the centre of the east facade of the house, a culvert 13.55m long (maximum) runs off to the west to link with three further chutes. It turns through 90 degrees towards the north and runs for a further 6.3m, with the openings from the garderobe chutes coming off the west side (point B). This L-shaped culvert is narrower than the main sewer passage (0.75-0.78m), but its construction is similar, with brick barrel vaults forming a groin at the right-angled turn. A building break can be detected near the junction with the main passage. At the blind end the culvert is only 1.22m high for, while the vault height remains constant, the floor falls quite steeply, by 0.58m over a distance of 19.85m, to carry liquid waste towards the main sewer (compare sections B, E and D). The floor also dishes more markedly in the culvert than in the main passage, by 0.15m compared with 0.09m (section E-D). The restricted headroom and steeper fall suggests that the culvert was intended to be flushed out regularly from the chutes, although access was possible if blocking occurred.

The southernmost chute served a garderobe off corridor 4/SSii in the 'yeomens' lodgings' area of the basement as well as 'painted chamber' 3/9 on the ground floor.

The shaft was 1.21m wide by 0.59m deep, but the opening has been narrowed by 0.51m. The central chute served 'painted chamber' 3/10 and probably one of the 'yeomens' lodgings' (4/18) in the basement. It was 1.23m wide by 0.62m deep and its mouth is totally blocked. The northernmost chute served a garderobe off the Long Gallery (2/1) and another on the leads in the central tower wall (1/6). The shaft is 1.24m wide by 0.66m deep and is also blocked.

South-east tower (ills 56 and 38)

15m further south a second culvert runs 4.95m towards the west to join the base of a garderobe chute in the south-east tower. It differs from the central culvert in that it is wider than the main sewer passage (1.22-1.26m: section C), but is similarly constructed. It is 1.65m high at the east end, reducing to 1.42m by the garderobe chute because of the slope on the floor. At almost half way point a building break is clearly visible in both the side walls. 1m from the main passage this culvert is blocked off by a modern wall two bricks thick, although for the purposes of the survey it was accessible with difficulty through a breach.

At the base of the tower the chute enters directly into the roof of the culvert and not to one side, so it differs from the arrangement of the central chutes, but is similar to that of the north-east tower. 0.35m from the west end the culvert vault simply breaks to allow the vertical brick-lined shaft to enter. The shaft is the same width as the culvert (1.22m at this point), is 0.62m deep, and is blocked off at a height of 5.3m. Beneath the level of the culvert vault the base of the chute recedes to a maximum depth of 0.97m and a sloping brick shelf was added to the back wall to deflect falling debris. This is 0.13m deep with a height of 0.20m to 0.30m.

WESTERN SEWER SYSTEM
(ills 39, 57 and 58)

The western system began at the south-west corner of the house and carried waste away towards the north-west. At first it runs more nearly parallel with the side of the house than the eastern system, having short connecting culverts to both the north-west and south-west towers: the relative courses of the two systems can be compared in **ill. 37**. Originally there was no intermediate culvert on the west side. The layout of the basement shows that ground level was naturally lower on the west than on the eastern side of the house and this section of the sewer was probably built within a wide construction trench excavated for the house foundations, and buried later. After the off-shoot to the north-

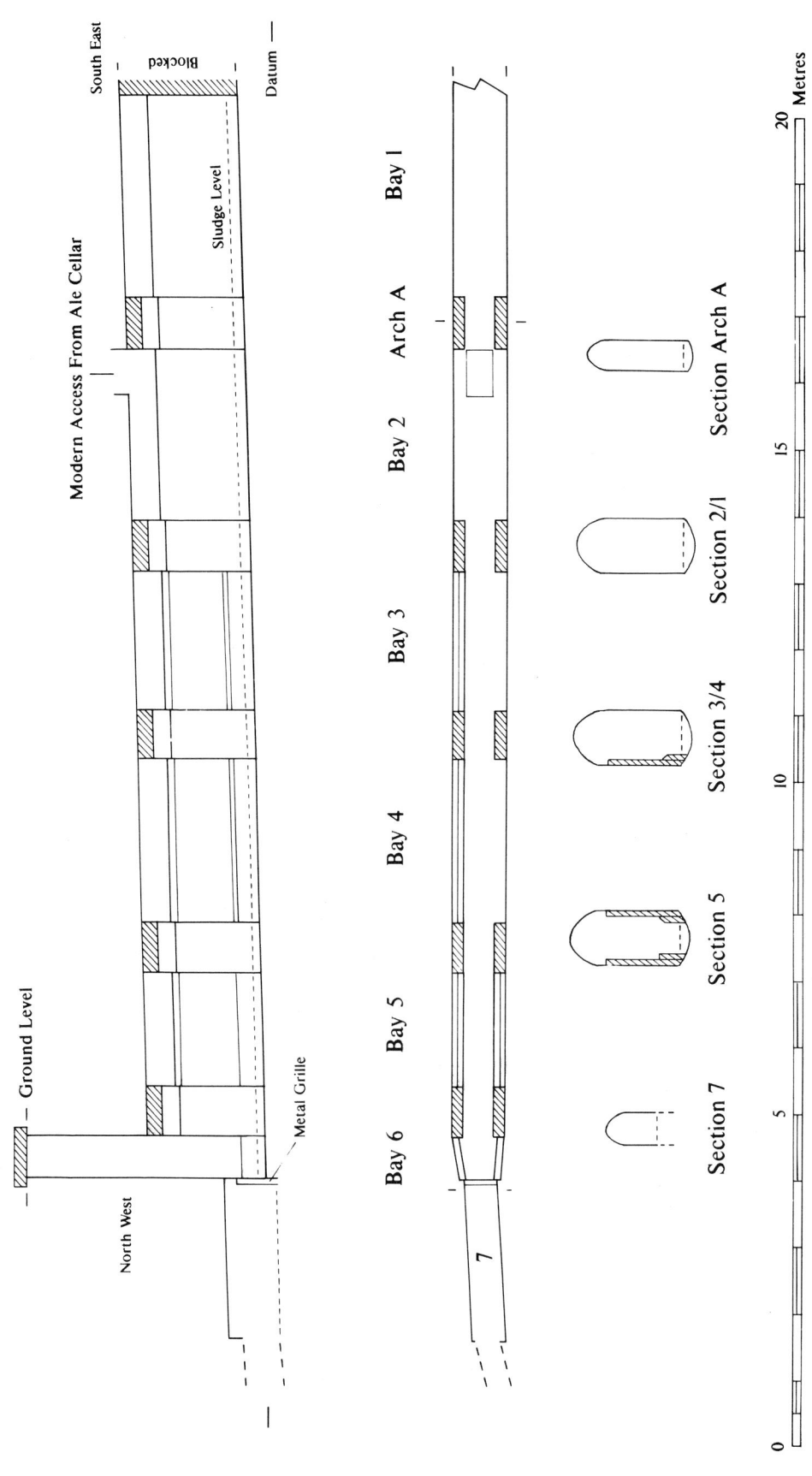

Ill. 58 (opposite): Plan and sections of the western sewer system beneath the subterranean Ale Cellar.

west tower, the main passage veers towards true west. After 19.3m the original work ends abruptly with a later addition and it is impossible to say whether the Tudor sewer ended at this point or has been partly destroyed to make way for the later work. As with the termination of the eastern sewer, however, the land here begins to fall away, so it could not have continued a great deal further. The evidence suggests that the western system also depended on manual cleansing and we can speculate that it ended with a large soakaway.

Two secondary culverts were later added, one from the kitchens and another from the underground Ale Cellar. Overflow channels for surface water drainage were also later additions, one connected to an underground cistern used to store water. The western leg of the main passage was reinforced when the Ale Cellar was built above it during Phase 2 and the main north-south section was similarly reinforced at one point when the service extension was built above it during Phase 3. This section also contains modern cast-iron sewer pipes, still in use.

Main Sewer, north-south section (ill. 57)

The main passage runs north-south almost parallel to the side of the house for a distance of 33.65m and its construction is similar to that of the eastern system, averaging 1.85m in height and 0.82m in width (section B).

South-west tower culvert and garderobe chute (ill. 57)

At the south end the main passage turns through 90 degrees to form a culvert similar in dimensions. There is a groin where the two vaults meet and a clear building break can be seen in the culvert walls, which are 2m long and curve outwards to a width of 1.01m. towards the east end. Here the roof of the culvert ends in an arch where it meets the garderobe chute from the south-west tower. The chute has a maximum width of 1.3m and is blocked above with stone slabs. Another arch at the back of the chute has a springing height of 1.55m but has been largely filled in, obscuring the original depth of the chute base. The blocking consists of a rough mix of brick and re-used stone fragments, including part of a medieval nook-shaft. The rear-arch of the chute has been roughly plastered over and a date of 1707 marked in the plaster whilst still wet. The later work perhaps relates to the chute being taken out of commission, and for this a date of 1707 seems reasonable. Two pipes of very thick lead, 127mm in diameter, intrude towards the south-east corner but are broken off and their purpose is difficult to determine.

North-west tower culvert and garderobe chute (ill. 57)

The north end of the main passage joins the south wall of a culvert from the north-west tower almost at right angles. The culvert measures 0.88m by 1.95m, slightly larger than the north-south passage, with a maximum length of 4m before it changes angle and turns into the western leg of the main sewer. To the east of the junction with the north-south passage, both floor and vault rise steeply (by approximately 0.46m over a distance of 2.34m) towards a chute in the north-west tower. A building break can clearly be seen in the walls. Both roof and floor then level out for a distance of 0.84m just in front of the garderobe chute, although there was so much rubble here that it was difficult to determine floor level accurately. At this point the inner skin of brickwork has been removed from the vault and a rough hole made to allow rainwater to drain into the sewer, exposing some stonework of the tower foundation.

The culvert vault ends with an arch which is secondary, but might have replaced an earlier one. This is now blocked by a modern brick wall 120mm thick. Beyond this the culvert curves outwards into a garderobe chute 1.42m wide with a maximum depth of 1.36m. However it is divided into two, a sophistication which might also occur in the other tower chutes but at a higher level. The first, western, section is 0.75m deep and is blocked by a stone slab at a height of about 3.5m. The second section occupies the last 0.61m and is defined by a further brick arch, this time undoubtedly original, the sides of which cause the chute to narrow to 0.6m. There are socket holes in the sides of this chute, some with fragments of wood *in situ*, which probably provided footing for maintenance purposes. The chute is vaulted over in brick at a height of about 6m. The bricks in the springing of this vault look original, but those in the central section are more modern and it seems likely that in its Tudor form the chute narrowed and then carried on vertically, but has been blocked off.

In the east wall a small, square, secondary drain, 0.27m deep by 0.25m wide, runs off towards the east. The sides are of brick and the floor and ceiling are constructed of stone slabs. Its point of origin cannot be traced but it heads in the general direction of a yard in Wyatville's service extension (outside 4/2, **ill. 31**: see 'surface water drainage', on page 86).

Later additions

1) During Phase 3 a reinforcing arch 0.5m thick was built 4m from the south end of the main north-south passage, designed to support a cross wall inside the service extension (see **ill. 39**)

2) Just to the north of this an off-shoot of the modern sewer pipe runs into the east wall.

3) On the north side of the reinforcing arch the sewer vault has been broken through and the hole blocked with a sandstone slab. A similar feature occurs almost opposite the opening to a secondary culvert from the kitchen (see below), where the blocking slab has been cut by machine, so is relatively modern. The reason for these breaches is not clear but they might represent test holes, possibly made by Wyatville, to establish for certain the relationship of the sewer system to his works above ground.

4) To the south of the reinforcing arch are two small secondary openings in the west wall at the shoulder of the vault. The southernmost is a modern field drain. The northernmost occurs just over 2m from the reinforcing arch. Here a terracotta pipe 220mm in diameter acts as an overflow for an underground brick-lined and shallow-vaulted water cistern which lies to the west of the south-west tower (see 'surface water drainage', below).

5) Two further secondary channels run into the east wall of the sewer, also at the shoulder of the vault. One occurs 2.38m from the north end of the passage and is 0.28m square. It has side walls of brick, which appear to be more modern than those used in the main sewer, with a floor and ceiling of stone slabs. The second occurs 3.04m further south and is 0.25m square. Similar in construction to the first, its ceiling is made of tile. The channels are well placed to have acted as drains for removing rainwater from a yard in Wyatville's service extension (outside 4/2: **ill. 31**), and probably date from this time (see 'surface water drainage', below).

Surface water drainage (ill. 37)

Beneath the yard at the south end of Wyatville's service extension of c.1823 (**ill. 31**) is a large brick-lined cistern, designed to collect rainwater (**ill. 39**). Entry is by a trapdoor in the floor of the yard, but it was not possible to inspect it as part of the survey as it was full. During the 1980s, however, members of Nottingham City Engineers Department drained and photographed its interior and found the remains of a wooden bucket in the bottom. They concluded that it was fed by a feeder channel which enters the east wall of the cistern at its south end. The channel runs underground in front of the south facade of the house, where it was located by the engineers by excavation, and is fed by lead down-pipes from the house gutters.[1] It also runs off into the eastern sewer system (see above). A large circular drainage channel at the north end of the east wall of the cistern, towards the top, carried any overflow into the western sewer (see above). Although at present it is impossible to date the cistern, its connections with the sewers are certainly secondary. Its siting, neatly within Wyatville's yard, suggests that it belongs to Phase 3.

Three other channels might be dated to the same period by their apparent association (although not certainly proven) with the drainage of another yard at the north end of Wyatville's service extension. Two of these discharged into the main north-south passage of the western sewer and the third into the base of the garderobe chute in the north-west tower (see above). Their construction is very similar to that which carries rainwater into the eastern sewer from the channel in front of the south facade.

Main Sewer, western section
(ills 39 and 58)

The western section of the main sewer runs due west for a distance of 19.3m from its junction with the north-west tower culvert. It is divided in two by a modern brick wall towards its east end, but both sections are accessible independently. Unlike the other stretches of sewer, which are relatively clean, the floor is silted with mud to a depth of 0.30-0.40m. Its construction is comparable with other sections of the main passage and its dimensions, 0.8m wide by 1.84m high, are also similar (**ill. 58**, section 2/1). It falls steadily towards the west by 0.75m. Here the Tudor work ends abruptly where a modern ventilation shaft sunk from the ground surface intrudes into the vault. Beyond this the passage continues in vaulted brick for a further 2.5m but is considerably diminished in size (0.5m wide by just over 1m high: **ill. 58**, section 7). At this point it is barred by a metal grille, possibly meant to inhibit the passage of solid matter. After this short section it reduces even further to a square channel, approx. 50cms wide by 85cms deep, with brick sides and stone capping more typical of later work. Part of a similar channel was excavated running east of and adjacent to the 18th century stable block by Nottingham City Engineers Department during their investigation of the Wollaton drains.[2] It is possible that the addition to the western sewer was added when the stables were built in 1774.

[1, and 2] *I am indebted to Mr. P. Coveney of the Nottingham City Engineers Department for this information.*

Later Additions

Even today the walls of the western sewer bulge outwards in places but the westernmost section of the structure must have shown particular signs of weakness. It was reinforced by the addition of five substantial brick ribs which are not keyed into the original brickwork, shown in plan, section and profile in **ill. 58**. This was probably done when the Ale Cellar was built above during Phase 2, a date supported by a sherd of butterpot dating from the late 17th or early 18th century which was recovered from one of these ribs, where it had been used as a spacer between two voussoirs. The westernmost bay formed by the reinforcing ribs (bay 5) was further strengthened by thickening both side walls, also in brick (section 5). The next two bays to the east (bays 4 and 3) were similarly thickened on the north side only (section 3/4). A modern break in the vault in bay 2 has been made to provide access to this section when the passage was blocked further to the east.

Secondary Culverts

1. North Culvert (1 on ill. 57)

A secondary culvert has been added to the north side of the main passage (western section) 0.76m beyond its junction with the north-west tower culvert. It is also barrel-vaulted in brick, but rough joints around the entry and a slight difference in the character of the bricks show that it is a later intrusion. The mouth, which is partially blocked by a modern brick wall, is raised 13cms above the floor of the main sewer, a feature which does not occur in any of the culverts belonging to the original build, and two courses of the Tudor brick wall are visible beneath the opening. The culvert measures 0.49m wide by 1.13m high and the dished floor is made of bricks running lengthways, in imitation of the Tudor work. It reaches a maximum length of 4.74m before it is blocked off by a later brick wall and there is a steep fall of 1.1m towards the mouth. It diminishes in height (to 1.09m) towards the blocking at the north end, and curves markedly towards the east. On plan this curve brings it in line with the orientation of the Ale Cellar, which has a small blocked archway visible at floor level in one of the chambers adjoining the south side (elevation 3, **ill. 60**: see below). It seems likely, therefore, that the culvert was added as a drain to the Ale Cellar and is contemporary with its build. It was not possible to extract a sample of the culvert bricks for Dr. Firman to compare with one taken from the Ale Cellar, and he was unable to inspect them at first hand because of the extremely difficult access and general conditions prevailing in the sewer system.

2. Kitchen Culvert (2 on ill. 57)

Another secondary culvert joins the east side of the main passage (north-south section) 7.14m south of its junction with the north-west tower culvert. As with the north culvert, there is a rough joint around its mouth, which is partially blocked by a modern brick wall. The opening is set into the wall 0.27m above the floor of the main passage, where four courses of the Tudor wall show below it. In the culvert itself the mortar is squeezed through the joints without being pointed off and both bricks and mortar differ from those used in the original work. They are, however, similar to those used in the reinforcing arch towards the south end of the main passage, which might indicate a Phase 3 date.

The first stretch of the passage is of barrel-vaulted brick construction, 2.19m long, and is 0.69m wide by 1.32m high. The floor differs from the other passages in the sewer system in that the bricks are set sideways. After 6.7m the passage bends very slightly towards the south and the floor rises more steeply (see section, **ill. 57**), with headroom diminishing slightly by 6cms. The culvert then becomes square in profile. The side walls narrow abruptly to 0.45m, showing brick jambs on either side, with a D-shaped sandstone lintel above, which reduces the height to 1m. From here the passage becomes progressively more inaccessible and contains much rubble. The ceiling is made of stone slabs, a feature found in smaller channels already attributed to Phase 3 (see above), and remains flat, but the floor rises and the culvert narrows further, by 50mm over 1.5m. After only 1m the height is reduced by 0.2m, but further measurements were impossible because of the amount of rubble in the restricted space. It was, however, possible to see that the passage curves towards the north and is blocked off. On plan it appears to head in the direction of the inner kitchen (4/4) or beyond. There is a shallow stone sink in the larder (4/5).

2. SUBTERRANEAN ALE CELLAR (ills 37, 40, 59, 60, 61)

The Ale Cellar lies beneath the ground to the north-west of the house (see **ill. 37**). The incorporation of circular ventilation shafts in the roof, all now blocked, combined with an absence of windows, indicate that the structure was always designed to be subterranean. Only the south wall and a short southern section of the west wall show above ground. The south wall formed a facade looking on to the west service courtyard from which five doorways opened into it (**ill. 39**). Otherwise only a short section of the west wall (south end) appeared above ground and the only window, an occulus now blocked, can still be seen here on the exterior. A flight of steps which radiate at the bottom still abut this wall beside the occulus. The steps appear, albeit very roughly drawn, on Wyatville's sketch plan of c.1823 for his service extension (**ill. 34**). The cellar, therefore, pre-dates this building, which buts against most of its south facade, causing three of the original doorways to be blocked.

The cellar consists of a series of barrel-vaulted chambers interconnected by round-headed archways (**ill. 40**). It was originally constructed of two types of brick, one of them bull-nosed to create smooth corners on arches and jambs. The floors are of bricks laid sideways, but they are covered in silt and rubbish. Because of the plain, utilitarian nature of the cellar it is difficult to ascribe a date to it on stylistic grounds. The fabric and character of the brick is not unlike that used in the Tudor building (see Appendix III), suggesting an earlier rather than a later date. In view of the long period of disuse of the house after Percival Willoughby's death, Thomas and Cassandra Willoughby are most likely to have converted the Tudor ale cellar (4/9) into a servants' hall (Phase 2: late 17th or early 18th century), thereby creating the need for a new cellar and it may well belong to this phase.

The cellar is quite large, occupying an area of roughly 300 sq.m (**ill. 59**). The floor level falls towards the back (north) by 0.64m (see section no. 2, **ill. 61**). There are nine chambers which were inter-connecting (numbered 1, 2, 3, 4, 6, 7, 8, 9, 10 on **ill. 59**) and one which was originally separate (number 5: chamber 13 is a later addition). No two rooms are exactly the same size, although they fall roughly into two categories: small and squarish (1-7) and long (8-10). Elevation drawings of each chamber, recording width and height, can be found in **ills 60 and 61**. The chambers are connected by open archways (eg. elevation 8b, **ill. 60**: arches are also marked A on other elevations). The jambs of the openings are made of bull-nosed bricks so that they are rounded and there were never any doors attached to them. Each chamber is barrel-vaulted, the orientation of which is marked by dotted lines on **ill. 59**. Each archway has its own vault (shown as dotted ovals), which forms a groin with the neighbouring vaults. There are a total of five circular ventilation shafts, also in brick, and all now blocked. These appear as dotted circles on **ill. 59** and are marked V on elevation 6/7, **ill. 60** and on section drawings 8c and no.2, **ill. 61**). The only conventional window was a small occulus, now blocked, at the south end of the west wall in chamber 1 (elevation 1a, **ill. 60**), for here a stretch of the exterior wall appeared above ground.

Delivery of barrels was apparently made from the surface via a shaft and steep ramp at 12 (**ill. 59**: section no.1, **ill. 61**). A sandpit was situated at the bottom to break the fall of the rolling barrels. From the sandpit, they could be rolled into chamber 10 or through a manoeuvring space (11) into chamber 9. The opening of the chute has been altered in concrete and there is a great deal of coal dust in the area, suggesting that the ramp has been used more recently for the delivery of coal. The chute is now blocked and no one on the Museum staff can remember the cellar ever having been used.

There is a building break visible in the side walls of area 2 (**ill. 59**: section no. 2, **ill. 61**), but as the character of the work is identical on either side, it is unlikely to represent a significantly separate phase. On the north wall of chamber 3 there appears to be a blocked opening to a culvert (elevation 3, **ill. 60**), which might have connected with the north culvert in the western sewer system (see above). There is another on the inner face of the south wall of the cellar towards the east end.

Chambers 1-5 all had entrances from the courtyard, but only that into chamber 2 is still accessible. Chamber 5 was originally only entered from the courtyard, as the openings which now connect it with chamber 4 and the rest of the cellar are secondary. Its vault matches the others, both in character and in the brick type used in its construction. The east wall of chamber 5 aligns almost exactly with the west wall of the north-west tower (**ill. 37**) and its fabric does not match the rest of the cellar, being largely built of ashlar blocks with fine joints (**ill. 62**). It looks as if the wall pre-existed and was incorporated into the cellar, and it might represent the sole surviving fragment of the colonnaded walkway shown on the northern approach to the house on Smythson's platt (**ill. 5**).

Ill. 59 (opposite): Plan of the subterranean Ale Cellar.

4: SURVEY OF THE HOUSE: THE UNDERGROUND WORKS

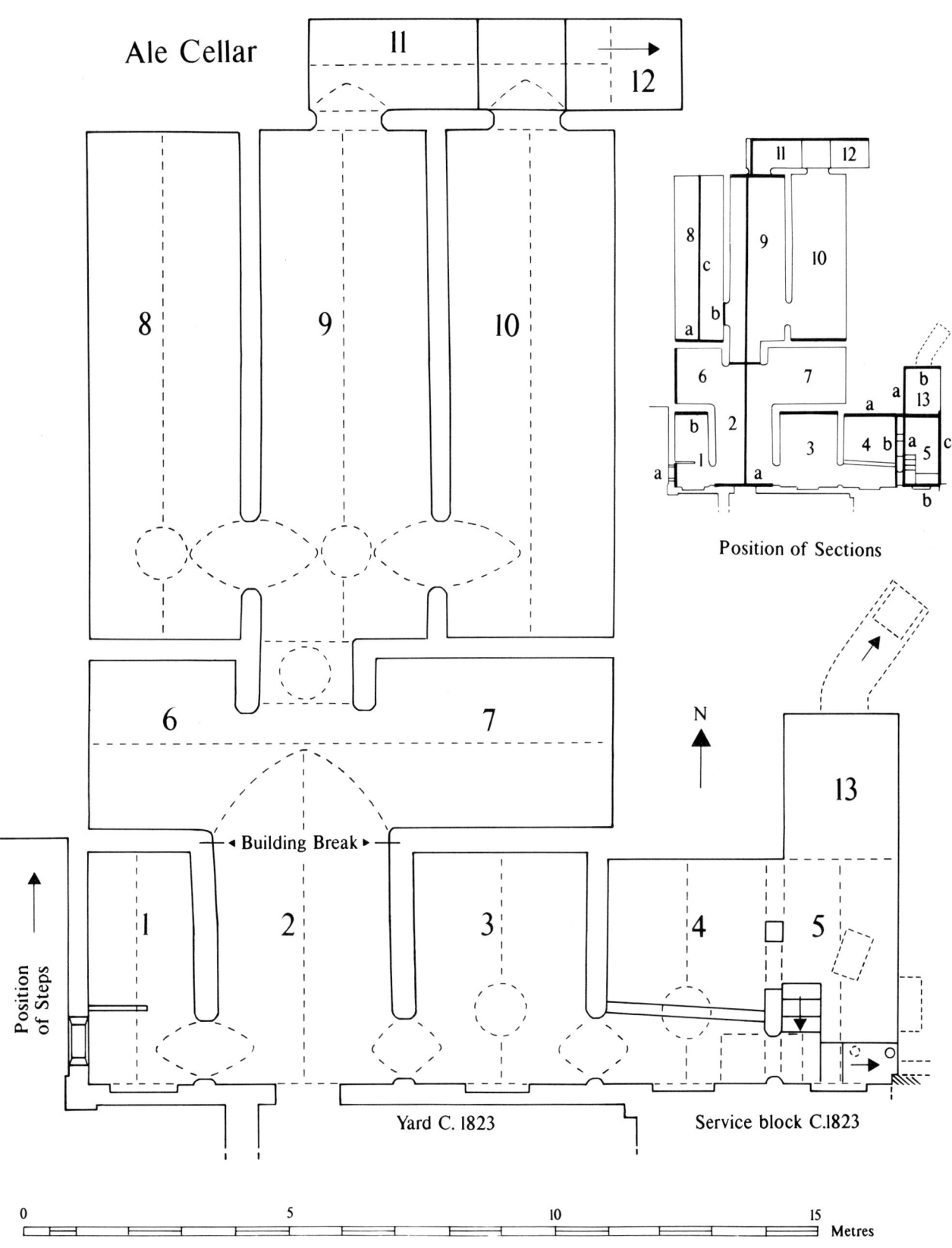

Ill. 60: *Sections and elevations of the subterranean Ale Cellar.*

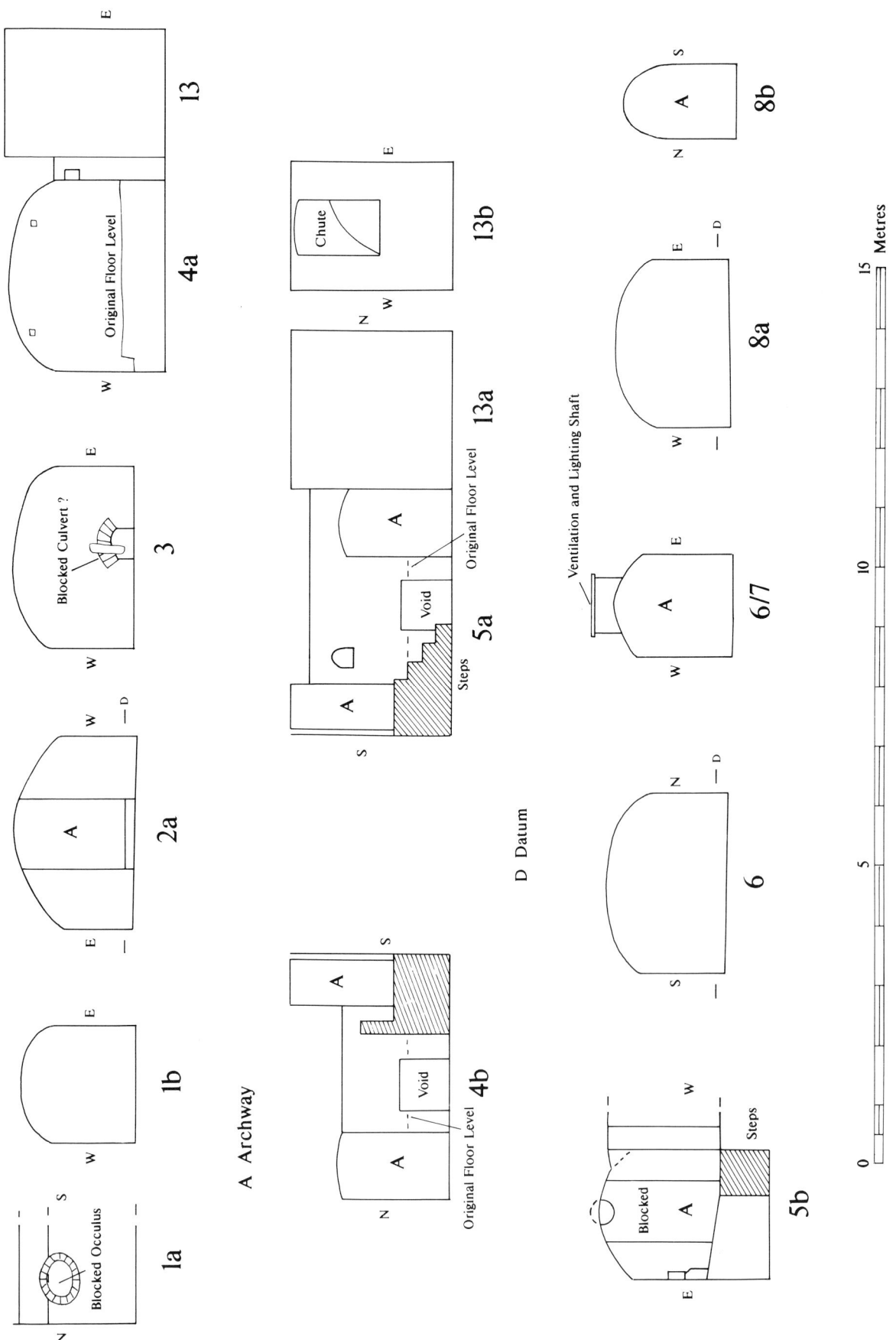

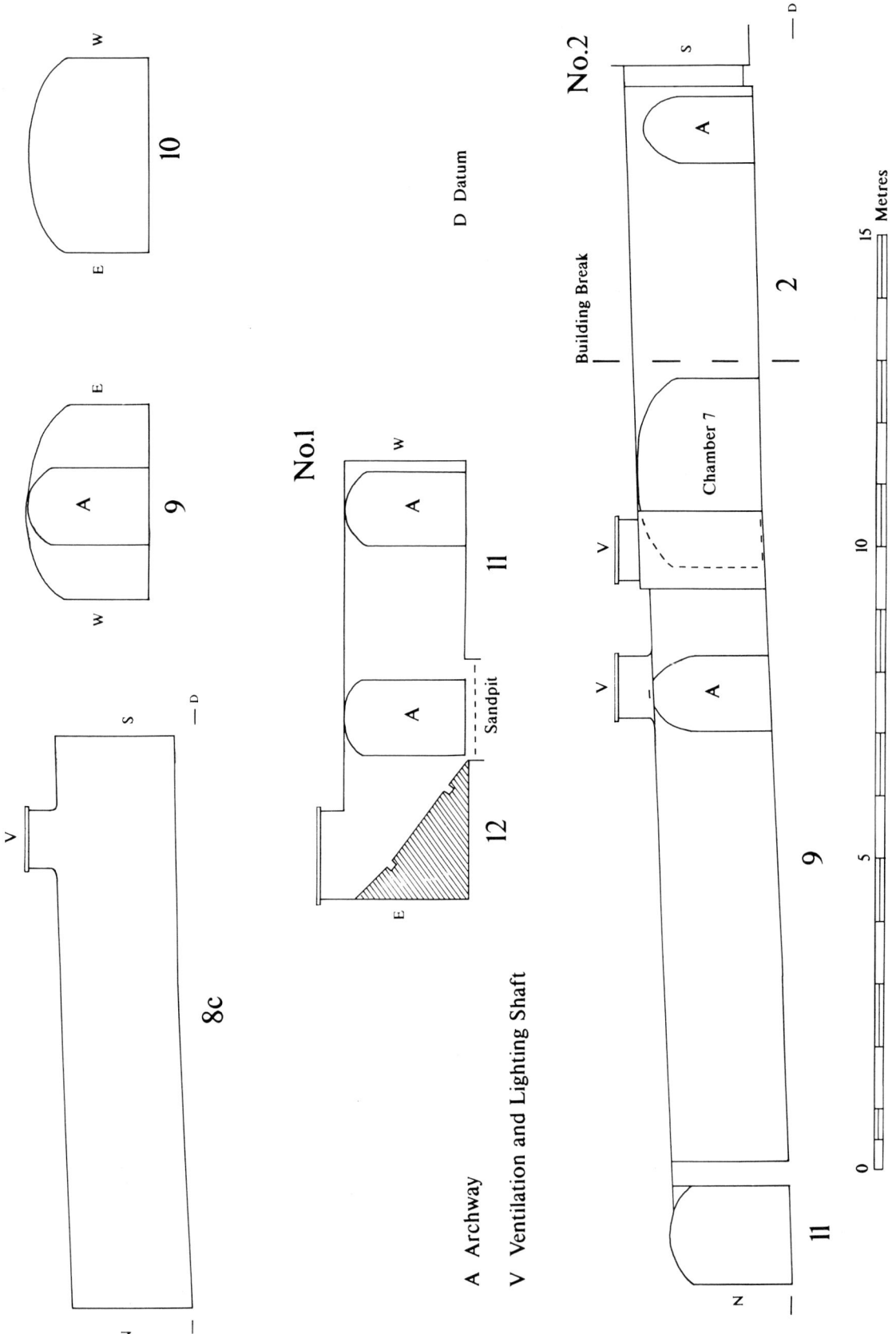

Ill. 61: Sections and elevations of the subterranean Ale Cellar.

Later alterations

Most of the cellar has remained little altered. The east wall of chamber 1 has been roughly refaced in parts with both brick and stone and a short secondary wall sub-divides the room just to the north of the blocked occulus (**ill. 59**). A doorway from the courtyard in the south wall is also blocked.

The most radical alterations are concentrated on chambers 4 and 5. A connecting doorway has been cut between the two rooms at the south end to align with the series of three archways which join other chambers further west. Unlike the others, however, it is square-headed (elevations 4b and 5a, **ill. 60**) and the vaults of the adjoining rooms have had square sections cut out of them to accommodate it. The cut jambs have been faceted to make them appear round in an attempt make them match the other openings in the cellar. The original floor level remains at the south end of the rooms but further north it has been lowered (elevations 4a, 4b and 5a, **ill. 60 and ill. 62**). This no doubt exposed the foundations, so the lower part of the walls have been faced with a different type of brick from that used elsewhere. Although all the bricks used in the cellar are 230mm long, those used in the original build (type 1) are 65mm deep, while those used in the alterations (type 2) are 75mm deep and have a smoother finish. After the floor was lowered, a recess lined with type 2 brick was cut into the east wall of chamber 5 (**ill. 62**). In this room three steps descend from the original floor at the south end to the lower level and in room 4 a low brick wall has been built across at a slight angle to guard against falling into the pit (**ill. 59**). These alterations seem to be connected with the conversion of these chambers into a coal store. An additional chamber (13) was added to the north end of chamber 5. It has a flat concrete roof (elevation 13a, **ill. 60**) and walls of type 2 brick. In the north wall there is a large chute for delivering coal, which turns towards the east and is then blocked (elevation 13b, **ill. 60**). Two further openings were cut between rooms 4 and 5, an archway at the north end and a square-headed opening further south. The latter occurs at a low level, with the soffit at about original floor level (marked 'void' on elevations 4b and 5a: **ill. 60**).

The fabric of the cellar should receive immediate attention. It totally lacks ventilation and a great deal of rubbish has collected in it, especially in the rooms nearest the remaining entrance. More alarming is a considerable vertical crack which is appearing in the walls of chamber 2.

The 'Caves' System (ills 37, 38, 44)

North-east of the house is a system of subterranean storage cellars which has become known as the 'caves'. It is basically L-shaped, running first north-east then north-west and has two off-shoots, one of which is a cistern.

The entrance to the 'caves', through the east wall of the wine cellar (4/7, **ill. 31**), is certainly not original to the house, for the wall has been hacked through and not made good, exposing the roughly cut surface of the stone. Access is by a staircase cut out of the natural sandstone, which still forms its walls and ceiling (**ill. 41**). The flight of nineteen irregular steps have been faced in concrete and descend very steeply to avoid the Tudor eastern sewer, which passes only centimetres above it (**ill. 38**). At the bottom of the steps there is a passage averaging 1.5m wide

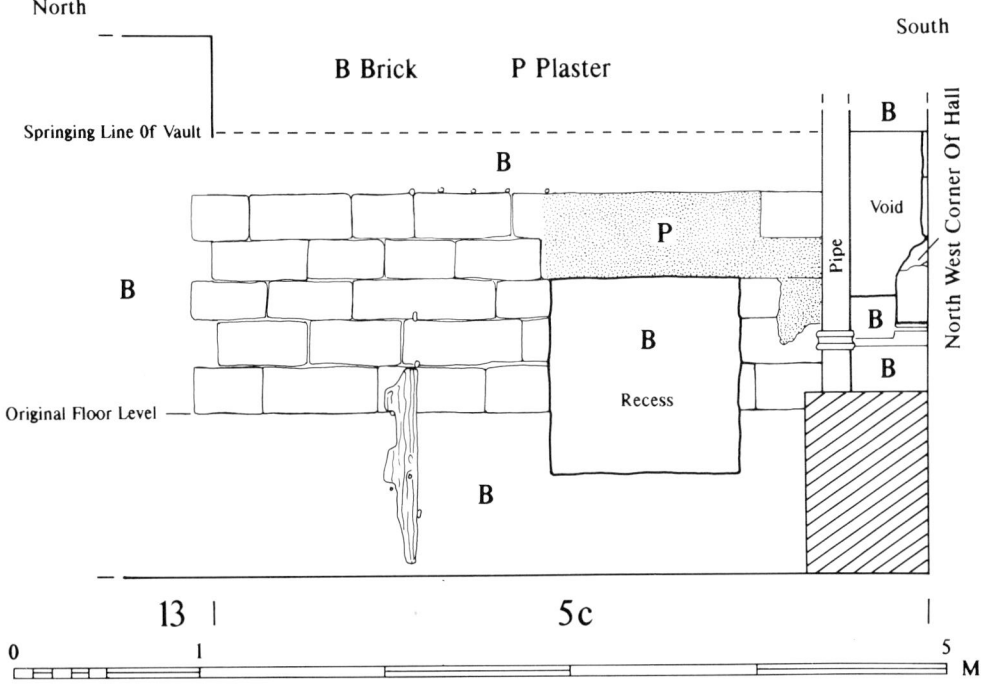

Ill. 62: Elevation of the east wall of the subterranean Ale Cellar.

and 7.5m in length (max.), which changes angle about half way (**ill. 44**). From this point onwards the cellar walls are lined with brick. Three types of brick can be identified, although all are quite similar, and it seems certain that the cellar was originally rock-cut throughout and lined in stages because of rock falls. It is therefore virtually impossible to attribute a date to it except to say that the present entrance, at least, post-dates the house.

The first off-shoot occurs on the south side of the entrance passage and could be quite late in date, for the brick facing on the passage wall has been disturbed to make the doorway, and the chamber has not been brick-faced. It has been roughly hewn from the sandstone and is very irregular in shape. The walls and ceiling are extremely unstable, as the rock is very soft here and frequently falls away, helping to explain the need to face the rest of the complex. It has a row of bins for the storage of wine bottles and there were recesses cut into the walls for the same purpose, which are now badly eroded.

Further east the passage widens on the south side to about 2.6m (section A, **ill. 44**), and there is a spring-fed well in the southern corner (**ill. 45**). After 11.5m it turns north through an angle of 82 degrees, maintaining a similar profile (section B, **ill. 44**). There are brick thralls to carry barrels on either side of this wide, L-shaped passage and a rock-cut gully or drain runs along the outermost edge, underneath the thralls.

After a further 33m the L-shaped passage meets another, running roughly at right-angles. This is rock-cut, unfaced, narrower and much more irregular. After about 15m it is blocked by fallen rock at its extreme west end. Halfway along, an off-shoot to the north is blocked with sand-bags, presumably because it has been considered unsafe at some relatively recent time. On the south side there is an entrance to a rock-cut cistern which is known popularly as 'the Admiral's Bath' (**ill. 42**; section C, **ill. 44**). It fills naturally with water, maintaining a fairly constant level and reaches a maximum depth of 1.3m. A ledge left deliberately along each side makes it possible to reach a further T-shaped passage behind the cistern which normally stays dry, but fills up if the water table is unusually high.

Neither the cistern and its associated passages nor the main L-shaped passage can be dated, but there are notable differences in their general character. The cistern passages are irregular, as if the miners were concerned to follow the natural vein of the rock. They are also narrow and unfaced. The main passage is larger in scale and much more regular. One might expect a right-angled turn, but the angle taken appears to have been designed specifically to achieve a link with the passage leading to the cistern, whilst avoiding interference with its T-shaped off-shoot, as if the cistern and its associated passages had pre-existed. The beginning of the east-west leg of the passage has also been carefully planned to incorporate the spring-fed well set in a square rock-cut recess in the south-west corner (**ills 44, 45**). Any overflow from the spring is carried to the cistern by the open drain or gully along the outer edge of the main L-shaped passage, then in the floor of the rougher passage on the east side of the cistern.

Unless some further documentary evidence comes to light, any attempt at a **chronological sequence** for the 'cave' system can only be tentative. However, the scant evidence which is available suggests the following:-

Phase 1: The Tudor House. Water had to be carried into the house from wells outside, possibly including one now encompassed by the 'caves' complex. The underground 'Admiral's Bath' cistern (and possibly others) was cut to ensure a good supply and was entered from outside the house by one or both of the blocked passages associated with it.

Phase 2: Late 17th or early 18th century? The construction of the subterranean Ale Cellar shows that the possibility of underground workings was present to the owners' minds at this time. The staircase from within the house was cut to provide an indoor access to the well and the L-shaped corridor was designed to link up with the existing water cistern. The wide passage would double as an additional wine cellar. The slightly irregular shape of the L suggests that care was being taken, in what must have been a very difficult surveying exercise, to avoid the southernmost offshoot of the 'Admiral's Bath' whilst still linking up with the passage running north-east from it.

Phase 3: Late 18th or 19th century? The addition of a secure wine storage chamber on the south side of the complex is later still.

APPENDIX I

THE HOUSEHOLD INVENTORIES

The Middleton Collection contains a number of household inventories relating to Wollaton Hall which date from the Tudor and Stuart period, but only five of these list individual rooms.[1] They not only give us a glimpse of the contents of the house, but are a useful tool in its reconstruction. Archaeological evidence has not survived everywhere and in some instances the inventories give us information which has left no other trace. They occasionally confirm inferrences made from other sources. It is not always possible to identify each room with certainty and this is particularly difficult where they have been labelled by the personal names of occupants. Some of the rooms changed name or function over the ten years spanned by the inventories. However, certain rooms are very clearly identifiable and occasionally it is possible to tentatively place others because of their position in the list or by comparing the contents with other inventories. The inventory of 1601 is the fullest and clearest and has been listed first. The others follow in chronological order. The last, of 1609, has not been transcribed in full.[2]

Extracts from the inventories are in normal type and interpretative comments are in italic script.

[1] *A further inventory of 1599 (Mi I 8ii) deals only with the kitchen, and has not been included. Another, of September 1599, gives a list of goods, but mentions no rooms*

[2] *A full transcription of the 1609 inventory can be found in RMC (1911), 485-91*

Mi I 15a/6 Inventory of 8th October 1601

While the 1601 inventory is not the earliest, it lists all kinds of furnishings and includes most of the rooms. It enables us to identify a number of chambers because their locations are often clearly implied by their headings (eg. the east corner chamber at the head of the hall, else the chapel chamber).

At wollaton
die Jovis 8 day
Octo 1601

An Inventarie etc

The tour of the house begins in the hall, covers the east wing of the ground floor from north to south, then carries down the south wing from east to west.

1. The Great Hall (3/5)
In the hall
2 lang table with frames
4 framed formes
2 framed cubbordes
3 lattine candlestick plates
a fire shovell
the north fire iron
the south fire iron
a plaine borded forme
11 holberdes
1 other holberd
a piked pollaxe
an almes tubbe
the seeling

2. The north-east corner chamber (3/12)
The north corner chamber at the head of the hall
a bedstede with tester & valens of reede velvet & clothe of silver
5 greene sta(?) curtines
1 fetherbed & bolster
1 wooll quilt
1 pillowe
2 spanish blankettes
1 greene Ruge
1 matte
2 lethere chayres
1 chayre framd newly covered with lethere
2 lether stooles
1 leuerye locker cubbord
1 little framde table
1 Joyned stoole
1 olde needlwrought quishion
3 trunks
1 little painted flaunders foser
1 little playne boxe
2 windowe curtains of blewcloth
1 fire shouell
1 paire of tonges
1 creeper fire iron
1 paire of bellowes
the seelinge

3. Inner chamber (3/13)
The Inner Chamber
1 bedstede
1 trundle bedstyde
2 fether bedes & ij bolsters
1 matte
1 spanish blankett
1 course blankett
2 olde couerlettes
1 ioyne forme
1 ioyne stoole
1 trunke
3 boxes
1 troiggeuer flaskett
3 chamber pottes

4. 'A little chamber over the last' (3/13i)

This entry implies a mezzanine chamber over the inner chamber, although the present mezzanine chamber in this position looks like Wyatville's work. A similar entry is found relating to space over the SW inner chamber in the 1599 inventory (see below). Both share a common feature in that each is shown with a staircase in Smythson's plan. The mezzanine room was perhaps very low, possibly above window level.

A little Chamber ouer the laste
1 trundle bed
1 flocke bed
1 canvas bolster
1 course blankett
1 read old couerlett
3 shelves

5. The two painted chambers (3/9 and 3/10)

The two painted chambers at the head of the hall
2 bedstides
1 tester & valence of read cloth with armes inbrothered
5 sta curtins of greene & read
2 fetherbedes
1 bolster
2 mattes
1 spanishe blankett
1 read ruge
1 matteres
1 livery clockes cobbord
2 square tables
1 lether chayre
1 ioynde stoole
2 ioynde cheeses
1 foser boxe
1 troiggen hamper
1 troiggen flaskett
1 fire lawndiron
2 fire endirons
1 fire creeperiron
1 seeled portall

6. The south-east corner chamber (3/7)

The East corner chamber at the head of the hall else the chappell chamber
1 bedstyde the tester with valince & iij curtins of read cloth
1 fether bed & bolster
1 wooll quilte
2 spanishe blankettes
2 pillowes
1 blacke Ruge
1 mattresse
1 mate
1 windowe curtine of blewcloth
1 Chaire couered with silke
1 turkeye stoole
1 Chamber potte

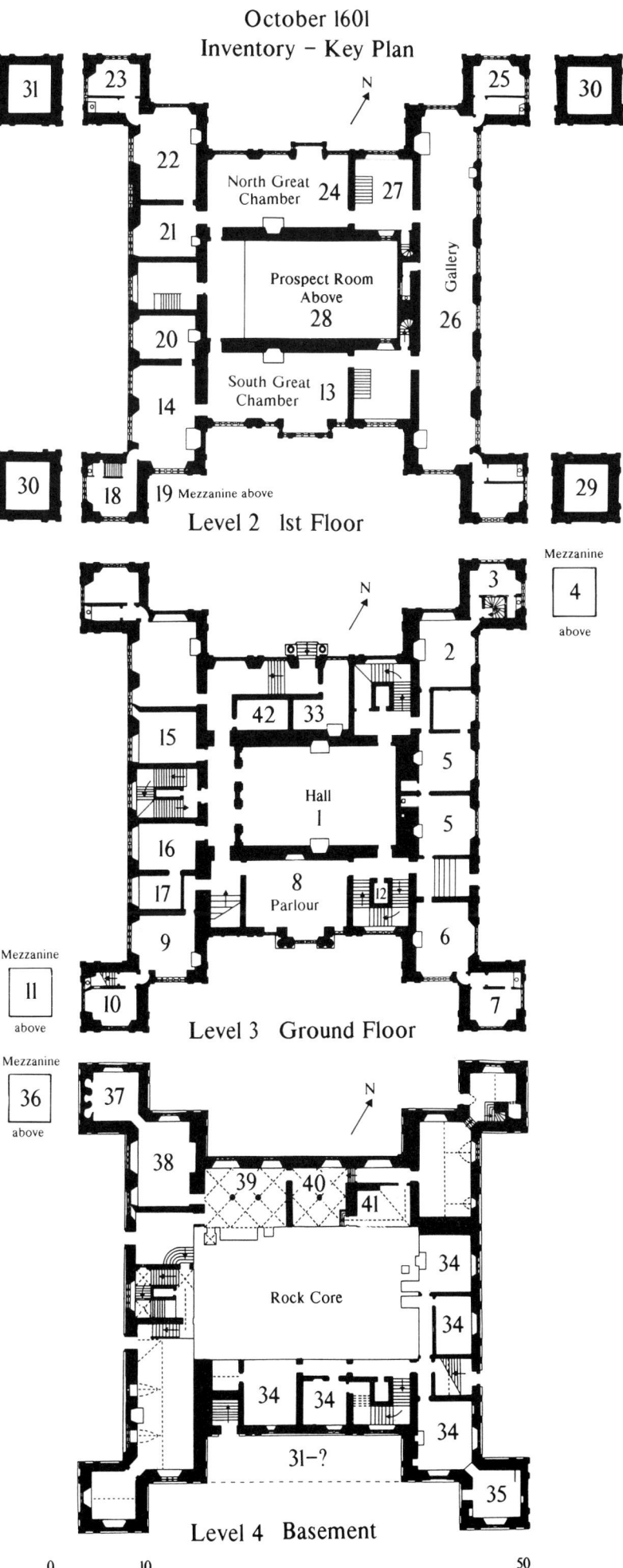

1 paire of pillowes newly couered
1 fire iron grate
1 fire shouell
1 paire of tonges
1 ioynde stoole
1 leuerie table with a dornix carpett
the seeling

7. Inner chamber (3/8)
The Inner chamber
1 bedstide
1 mattresse
1 fetherbed & bolster
1 corse blankett
1 olde spanishe quilte

8. The Dining Parlour (3/6)
The Dyning parlour
1 droowing framd table
1 square table
1 liuery cubbord
3 formes
4 ioynde stooles }
3 ioynde stooles }
1 wood chaire
1 long green carpet
1 shorte green corse <cloth> eras
4 greene cloth quishins
a mappe of Not & Leicer shires
a paire of tonges
a fire shovell
a fire iron gratt
the seeling

9. The south-west corner chamber (3/19)
The southe corner chamber at the foot of the hall
1 bedstide with tester & valence of crymson veluet & cloth of seluer
5 curtins of yellowe taffatie
1 fetherbed & j bolster
1 mattresse
1 matte
1 Wooll quilte
2 pillowes
2 spanyshe blanketes
1 white ruge
1 blewe velvet chaire imbrothere<d>
2 turkye stooles
1 Chamber potte
1 square table
1 turkye carpett
1 windowe curtine of blew cloth
1 paire of tonges
1 fire shovell
1 paire of bellowes
1 fire iron grate
1 mapp of England }
1 mappe of Wiltshire }
1 mapp of warr' & Leic'shire }
a pedigree of the kinges
the seeling

10. Inner chamber (3/20)
The Inner chamber
1 bedstide with woodtester
1 fetherbed with a bolster
1 white ruge

1 spanyshe quilte

11. 'The chamber over the last' (3/20i)
This can be identified as a mezzanine chamber. It is also mentioned in the 1599 inventory.
The chamber over the laste
1 bedstide
1 bolster
1 coverlett
1 matte
The inventory taker then goes to the south state staircase where he notes items in the stair cupboard before going upstairs.

12. 'In a little room at the stair foot of the south great chamber'.
The Smythson plan clearly shows accessible spaces at the base of his staircases and this seems to refer to one of them. It contained a mat and two bedsteads, presumably dismantled. One such cupboard survives in the W staircase.
In a little roome at the staire foote of the sowth great chamber
1 bedstide
1 other bedstide
1 matte
Here the inventory taker makes a note that the next three rooms should be as follows:-
{Place here the pantry}
{the buttrye & the sellere}
{and the butlers chamber}
The document which survives was clearly the rough copy and this direction relates to the fair copy which would have been made from it. The inventory taker wished these service rooms to appear in their logical order, straight after the neighbouring rooms on the ground floor and covering the west wing. However, having been distracted by going back to the stair cupboard which he missed earlier, he seems to have ascended the south staircase, and so he tackles the state rooms next.

13. The south great chamber (2/8)
This inventory reveals more fully than the rest the wealth of furnishings in the best state apartment. Note the collection of maps.
The southe greate chamber
1 drawing table
1 livery cubbord
1 little drawing table
2 long formes
1 shorte forme
1 chaire imbrodered
1 lether chaire blacke
1 read lether chaire
10 turkye stooles
1 stoole covered with silke

6 quishins of tapistre
2 quishins of needlworke
1 latin candlestick plate
1 ioynde stoole
1 paire of bellowes
1 paire of tonges
1 fire shovell
1 fire iron grate
1 iron backe
1 screene
1 mapp of Europe }
1 mappe of the Lowecountris }
The pedigree of Christe }
The mappe of Jerusalem }
The seelinge
a pewter sesterne
a paire of dining tables

14. The south state bed-chamber (2/10)
The 'best chamber' is clearly identified here. Again the rich furnishings should be noted.
The Chamber at the southend of the southe greate chamber alias the best chamber
1 bedstide with tester and head peece and valince of crymsin damaske imbrodered with armes
5 curtines of read taffata
1 matte
1 fetherbed and bolster
1 wooll quilte
2 spanishe blankettes
2 pillowes
1 silke quilte of fleshe coler
1 chamber potte
1 chaire covered with purple velvet
2 stooles the like
1 chaire with needlworke
1 turkye carpet
2 stooles covered with tufted taffata
2 windowe curtins of blew cloth
1 liverye cubborde
5 mappes
1 paire of bellowes
1 paire of tonges
1 fire shovell
1 fire iron grate
the seelinge
The inventory taker may now have taken a break, for he goes down to the ground floor to do the rooms he missed earlier, making another note to remind himself where they should be inserted into the fair copy.

15. The pantry (3/16)
The pantrye } place these before the south greate chamber
1 square table
1 glasse cubbord
1 shorte forme
1 framed table
1 benche
1 shelfe

16. The buttery and cellar (3/17 and 4/9)
The buttrye and sellor
2 binges
1 square table
1 shorte forme
3 wynde stooles
7 seettles to lay beare and wine upon

17. The butler's chamber (3/18)
The butlers chamber
1 bedstid
1 mattresse
1 fetherbed and bolster
1 coverlet
1 other coverlet

He now resumes his tour of the state apartments from the point where he left off earlier, first covering the west wing from south to north, then completing the north and east sides.

18. The Inner chamber to the best chamber (2/11)
The Inner chamber to the best chamber
1 bedstid with a woodtester
1 fetherbed and a bolster
1 corse blankett
1 lether close stoole with a pewter pan

19. 'The chamber over it' (2/11i)
Another mezzanine chamber is implied here. One would expect extra accommodation for personal attendants accompanying important guests.
The Chamber over it
1 bedstid

20. The chamber attached to the south state suite (2/9)
This and the following entry refer to the state withdrawing chambers, although their description seems odd. However they are amply furnished and follow logically in the order of the tour of the house.
The Chamber at the head of the kitchin stayres eastwardes
1 bedstid with an olde tester of tapystrye
1 matte
1 mattrese
1 fetherbed and bolster
1 spaynishe blanket
1 spaynishe quilte
1 pillowe
1 quishin of tapystrye
1 peece of carpett turkye
1 square table
1 woode chaire
1 creepe fire iron
and certen peeces of seeling

21. The chamber attached to the north state suite (2/5)
The chamber at head of kitchen stayres westwarde
1 bedstid
1 matte
1 fether bed and bolster
1 spaynishe blankett
1 pillowe
1 Ruge Cheekered
1 Cannapie with yellowe taffata sarcenet traine
1 square table
1 wood chaire
1 chamber potte
1 fire landiron
the chamber hanginges of dormickes

22. The north state bed-chamber (2/6)
The chamber at the sowth end of the north greate Chamber
1 bedstede wth tester and valance of read and greene velvet
3 sea curtins of divers collors
1 matte
1 mattriss
1 fetherbede and bolster
2 pillowes
2 spaynishe blankettes
1 read Ruge
1 square table
1 wood chaire
1 joynd stoole
1 quishin of greene cloth
1 chamber potte
1 peece of carpett turkye
1 windowe curtine of blewcloth
1 hanging of tapistrye
2 peeces of dormickes viz hanginges
1 fire shovell
1 fire iron grate
1 paire of tongus

23. Inner chamber (2/7)
The inner chamber
1 bedstede
1 matresse
1 fetherbed and bolster
1 ould blankett
1 coverlett
1 olde silke quilte

24. The north great chamber (2/4)
Compared with the S great chamber, the furnishing here seems rather sparse.
The north great chamber
1 drawing table

25. The tower chamber at the north end of the gallery (2/2)
The corner chamber at the north end of the galery
1 bedstide with tester and curtins of tufted canvas
1 matte
1 fetherbed and a bolster
2 pillows
1 spaynish blankett
1 corse blankett
1 silke quilte
1 chaire imbrodered
1 fire iron grate
1 ioynd stoole
the seeling

26. The gallery (2/1)
The galerye
1 presse
3 livery locker cubbordes
1 round table
4 iron bound cheestes
2 wooden cheestes
2 pedigrees of kinges
Sir ffra W pedigree
The arms of the howse in glasse
9 mapps
2 plottes one of Cossett the other of Manbarole
1 fire iron grate

27. At the stair head of the north great chamber (2/NS)
Att the staire head of the north greate chamber
1 shorte table

Having missed only one room (2/3), he proceeds to leads level.

28. The High Hall (1/1)
The High Hall would have been very difficult to furnish, having only narrow newel stairs for access.
The highe chamber over the hall
certen mattes
1 ioynd stoole

29. The south-east turret chamber (1/3)
The east tower chamber upon the leades
1 bedstid
1 tester and valence of buckram
1 trundle bedstid
1 matt
2 mattresses
2 fether bedes
2 bolsters
1 spaynish quilte
1 writing cubborde
2 lether stooles
1 ioynd stoole
1 fire shovell
1 fire iron grate
2 luttes
3 instrumentes with wyer stringes
1 basse vyall

30. The north-east turret chamber (1/2)
The north tower chamber upon the leades
1 bedstide
1 matte
1 fetherbed and bolster
1 woole quilte

1 spaynishe blankett
1 corse blanket
1 ruge cheekered
1 pillowe
1 cnapye of carrell
1 blew cubborde cloth
1 square table
1 quishine of tapistrye
2 ioynd stooles

31. The south-west turret chamber (1/4)
The sowth tower chamber upon the leades
1 bedstide
1 matte
1 fether bed and bolster
1 spaynishe blanket
1 ruge cheekerd
2 windowe curtins of dornicke
1 creepe fire iron
1 fire shovell
1 square table
1 ioynd stoole
1 chamber potte

32. The feather howse
This entry cannot be identified. We might speculate that it was used to re-cycle feather mattresses and that an enclosed space would have been desirable. As the inventory taker was last on the leads, perhaps one of the 'types' on the roof was used. Alternatively, the north-west turret chamber has been omitted, although this humble use of one of the turret chambers seems unlikely.
In the fether howse
1 olde fetherbed
The inventory taker makes one stop on the ground floor before descending to the basement.

33. The porters lodge (3/2)
In the porter lodge
1 bedstid with woode tester
1 fether bed and oblster
1 corse blanket
1 spaynishe quilte
1 ioynd stoole
1 greene quishin
1 creepe fire iron
1 tressele borde
In the basement the inventory taker begins with the accommodation block.

34. The yeomens' lodgings (4/12, 4/13, 4/14, 4/17, 4/18)
The yeomens' lodgings are subdivided into five apartments, each equipped in a standard fashion. The accommodation in the SE section of the basement fits well.
In the yeamons lodginges
1 bedstid
1 fether and bolster
1 corse blankett

1 old white ruge
1 ioynd stoole
1 matte
1 tressell borde

1 bedstide
1 matte
1 fetherbed and bolster
1 old white ruge
1 coverlett
1 ioynd stoole
1 tressell cubborde

1 bedstide
1 matte
1 fetherbed and bolster
1 corse blankett
1 coverlett
2 ioynd stoons [sic]
1 tressell borde

1 bedstide
1 matte
1 fetherbed and bolster
1 corse blankett
1 coverlet
1 tressel borde
As this room has a fire iron, it might be 4/13 or 4/18, either of which could have had fireplaces.
1 bedstide
1 matte
1 fetherbed and bolster
1 spaynish blankett
1 coverlett
1 ioynd stoole
1 creepe fire iron
1 tressell borde

35. The gardener's chamber (4/15)
The basement room of the SE tower had an external doorway into the garden, but no internal access from the house. It is interesting to see which tools he used.
The gardiners chamber
1 bedstide
1 matte
1 still
1 watering pott of brasse
1 paire of garden sheares
1 garden rake
1 spaede
1 garden lyne with a iron prickes
1 hande cutting hooke
2 tressells with a borde
Proceeding to the service area of the basement, the inventory taker seems to begin in the north-west tower and carries on along the north wing.

36. The cook's chamber (4/3i)
This chamber would be a convenient place for the cook to live, but the kitchen boys lay in a house elsewhere (see inventory of 1599)
In the Cookes chamber

1 bedstid
1 fetherbed and bolster
1 corse blankett
1 coverlet

37. The pastry kitchen (4/3)
In the pastrye
pastrye bordes	3
boulting tubb	1

38. The outermost kitchen (4/2)
In the owttermoste kitchen
dresser bordes	4
formes of tressels	2
iron rainge of v barres	1
harth iron barre	1
great iron rackes	2
boyling place harthe iron	1
iron gallow tree	1
iron hookes	6
iron peakes	2
iron fire forke	1
iron coole hamer	1
iron hande branderth	2
chafingdyshale	1
bread grate	1

39. The inner kitchen (4/4)
In the inner kitchen
dresser bordes	2
tressel bordes	2
mustard querns	1p
wood cheeste	1
the boyling beef potte	1
iron rackins with barres	1
harth iron barre	1
iron rackes	2
gryde iron	1
salte tubb	1
greate wood bowle	1
greate wood platter	1

40. The larder (4/5)
In the larder
square table	1
tressell bordes	2
poudering tubb	1
save	1
certen shelues	ij

41. The saucery (4/6)
In the sawcery
Greate wood platters	2
washing tubs	3
littl poudering tubbes	2

The inventory taker seems to have returned to the ground floor where he had left the Wardrobe, surely a nightmare to list, till last. It contained an enormously varied list of items at this date in addition to the expected bedding and soft furnishings.

42. The wardrobe (3/3)
In the wardrope
bedstide	1
matte	1
fetherbedes	2
bolstres	2

fetherbed morre	1	
bolster morre	1	
mattresses	2	
woole quiltes	4	
pillowes	6	
pillowes olde	2	
bolsters	2	
fustian bedtycke with some downe in yt	1	
tester and curtins of chaingable mockadoe	1	
spainyshe greene blankete	1	
coverlettes	2	
spainysh whit blankett	1	
ruge yellowe		
silke read quilte	1	
corse blankett	1	
hanginges of tapistrye	9	
curtins of dornyckes	2	
blewe cloth cubbord clothes	4	
Sumpter clothe of tapistrye	1	
carpett of tapistrye	1	
a little peece of a old ounterpoint		
greene clothe quishine	1	
fustian blankettes	2	
new fustian pillowes	2	
quishins of nedlworke	2	
coche quishin of turkye	1	
read cloth coche quishin imbrodered	1	
longe greene vellvett quisin	1	
longe purple velvet quishin	1	
longe nedleworke quishine	1	
shorte turkye carpettes	2	
longe turkye carpett	1	
longe turkye carpett	1	
short nedleworke carpetes	2	
longe popingsay greene carpet	1	
longe sadgrene carpet	1	
shorte greene cubbordclothe	1	
one other long sadgrene carpet	1	
bedtester of greene velvet with valance all stripped with silver silke curtins reade and greene	1 3	
reade serge stripped with greene silke <eras>it is caled 25.3/4 yeardes		
a peece of yellow and Reade silke curten		
A paire of valence and headpeece of read and yellowe taffata		
Curtens of same	5	
a peece of new dornickes contayneing 6 yerdes		
Mr Tho W his rapier		
chamber pottes	6	
lether close stooles	2	
pewter panns for closse stooles	3	
wood closse stooles	3	
lowe backte chayreframs	2	
little Joynd stooles	3	
drawing table	1	
tables upon tressells	2	
tressells	4	
A bordend lying upon 2 tressells		
iron bounde cheestes	2	
wood platter	1	
a long iron barre for the kitchin to hange potte hookes upon		
stayes of iron with barre the same	3	
iron Running Reckins	2	
Dooble iron pyckes	3	
single iron picke	2	
greate twig baskett	2	
new shuttles	6	
waxe torches	5	
mowse trapps	3	
a little tressell table	1	
lether sumpter bage	1	
a souldiers jacke	1	
a drume	1	
a paire of little dining tables without men		
a tiller bowe with a gaffle		
iron long curtin roddes	2	
a fire lawndiron with a bottome	1	
end irons	2	
a shire shovell	1	
a paire of tonges	1	
a paire of bellowes	1	
earthen perfume pottes	2	
a presse	1	
the seeling		
a skreene twige	1	
a clocke	1	
pewter candlestickes	25	
latten candlestickes	2	
bason and ewer	1	
pewter pottes greate	2	
lesser pewter pottes	1	
bastonynge greate	2	
lether iackes	4	
lether iacke	1	
pewter bassons	2	
pewter saultes with con{tents}	2	

The inventory has the following codicil which is dated over six months earlier than the main part of the inventory.

Edward Allstabroke delivered and shewed to me a note in paper contiayninge the parcells following which note is dated 26 Marche 1601, and therof he sayth his Mres hath a copye

Greate chargers	2
greate dishes	7
of a lesser sorte	9
of a lesser sorte	20
of a lesser sorte	6
butter dishes	10
sawcers	10
pye plates	8
olde dishes	6
burned dishes	5
cullander	1
pottes greate	2
pottes lesse	3
panns	2
Kettle	1
dryping panns	3
iron mortter	1
spittes	14
potthookes	5 paire
brasse ladle	1
beefe forke	1
kitchen knyves	3
frying pann	1

He shewed me a note indented bearing noe date contayning the parcells ffollowinge and therofhe saith his Mre hath the Counterparte

Sheetes	31
table clothes	4
cubbord clothes	8
towells long	3
napkins fine	2 doozen
hallclothes	3
pillowe beares	5
napkins corse	6 doozen

He saith this laste note was made a boute a weeke laste paste

Mi I 9 Inventory of October 12th 1596.

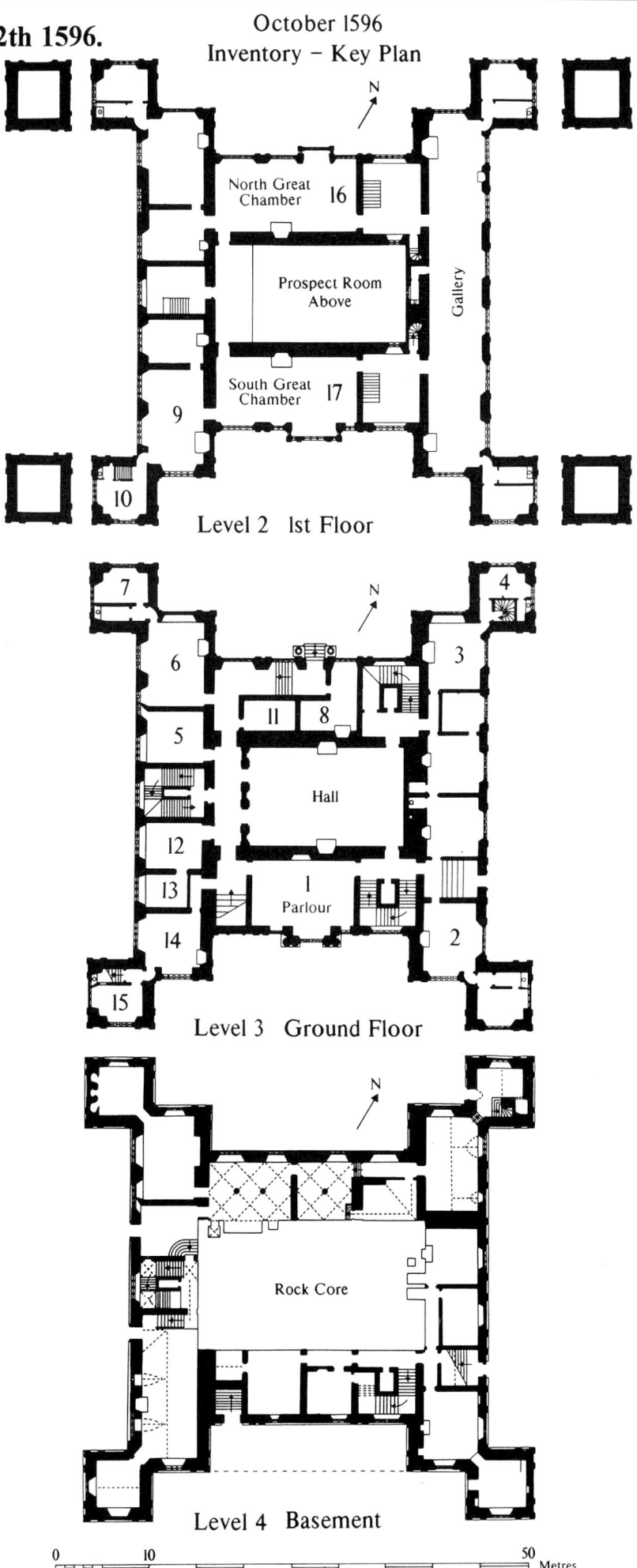

October 1596 Inventory – Key Plan

This inventory was taken in a slightly less logical manner than those of 1601 and December 1596, but it can be followed quite easily. The first 8 rooms were on the ground floor, and were taken in a roughly anti-clockwise direction, although some were omitted. Then two were listed upstairs before ground floor rooms in the south-west corner were taken. Two further rooms upstairs were then added. No rooms in the basement or at leads level were included.

A note of stuffe and beddinge belonginge to wollaton house taken by Smythson October 12 1596

1. The Dining Parlour (3/6)

Although the 1601 inventory only listed furniture in this room, this document is only concerned with bedding. The quantities listed here seem to indicate that members of the household slept in reception rooms.

Inprimis in the Parlor

ffeatherbedds	x
Boulstres	xi
Pillowes	v
Redd Blankett	i
Quiltes	v
Kersie blankettes	viii
Spanish blankettes	iij
Chequered rugges	ij
.... Coverlettes	iiij

2. The south-east corner chamber (3/7)

Identified by the 1601 inventory, its contents show that it was clearly a bed-chamber despite its name. Its inner chamber is omitted from this inventory, but is included in one taken only two months later.

In the Chapell Chamber

ffetherbedds	ij
Boulster	j
Mattresses	ij
Quilt	j
Spanishe blankettes	ij
Redd Rugge	j
Kersie Blankett	j
Coverlett	j
Carpett for a Cubberd	j
Turkey stooles	iij
Little stoole	j
Chayer	j
Quision	j

3. The north-east corner chamber (3/12)

In the North East corner chamber

Mattresses	j	
ffetherbedd	j	
Boulstr	j	
Quilt	j	
Turkey stooles	j	
Litte stoole covered with vevett		j
Quissions	ij	
Spanish blankettes	ij	
Redd Rugg	j	
Pillowes	j	

4. Inner chamber (3/13)

In the Inner chamber to the same

ffetherbedd	j
Boulster	j
Pillowe	j
Carsie blankett	j
Whyte Rugg	j

5. The pantrye (3/16)

Taken to be the pantry itself, this room clearly provided accommodation for the pantry-keeper. Given that the Dining Parlour seems to have been used for sleeping, this is hardly surprising.

In the Pantrye Chamber

ffetherbedd	j
Mattresse	j
Boulster	j
Quilt	j
Pillowe	j
Spanishe blankett	j
Greene quilt lined	j

6. The north-west corner chamber (3/15)

In the North west corner chamber

Mattresse	j
ffetherbedd	j
Quilt	j
Boulster	j
Pillowe	j
Kersie blankettes	ij
Greene blankett	j

7. Inner chamber (3/14)

In the Inner chamber to the same

Mattresse	j
ffetherbedd	j
Bolster	j
Kersie blankett	j
Coverlett	j

8. The Porter's Lodge (3/2)

Like the pantry-keeper, the porter clearly slept at his place of work.

In the Porters Lodge

Mattresses	j
ffetherbedd	j
Boulster	j
Blankett	j
Coverlett	j

9. The south state bed-chamber (2/10)

The best chamber is more clearly identified by the inventories of 1601 and December 1596. The name of the room did not change until 1609.

In the best Chamber

Mattresse	j
ffetherbedd	j
Bolsteres	ij
Pillowes	ij
Spanish blankettes	ij
Chequered Rugge	j
Chayre	j
Turkey stoole	j

10. Inner chamber (2/11)

In the inner Chamber to the same

Mattresse	j
ffetherbedd	j
Boulsteres	ij
Kersie blankett	j
Coverlett	j

11. 'The next chamber to the gate' (3/3)

This seems to be the room which was soon to became the wardrobe. It was very close to the front door.

In the next Chamber to the gate

Mattresse	j
ffetherbedd	j
Boulsteres	ij
Pillowe	j
Spanishe blankett	j
Yeallowe quilt	j

12. The buttery (3/17)

At this date the wardrobe seems to have been the inner room to the buttery.

In the Chamber next the wardrupe

Mattress	j
ffetherbedd	j
Boulster	j
Pillowes	ij
Kersie blankett	j
Chequered Rugg	j

13. The wardrobe (3/18)

This was a general store-room for household stuff. It contained 12 featherbeds and it is feasible that some were carried elsewhere at night, perhaps the hall. It was soon to be moved (to room 3/3), but in 1599 this room was called 'the old wardrobe'.

In the Wardrupe

ffetherbeddes	xij
Boulstres	ix
Pillowes	v
Quishion pillowe	j
Quiltes	x
Spanish blankettes	viij
Little stooles	iiij
Quishions	iiij
Peeces of variues hanginges	vj
Peeces of tapistrie hanginges	xij

14. The south-west corner chamber (3/19)

In the South west chamber

ffetherbeddes	ij
Boulster	j
Blankettes	ij
Pillowes	ij
Quilte	j
Blew Curtaines	ij
Quishions	ij
Stooles	iij
Chayre	j

15. Inner chamber (3/20)

In the Inner Chamber to the same

ffetherbed	j
Mattresse	j
Boulster	j
Blankett	j
Quilte	j

16. The north Great Chamber (2/4)

Because this inventory is mainly concerned with bedding, this and the south great chamber receive scant treatment.

In the great Chamber North

Varioes peeces	iiij

17. The south Great Chamber (2/8)

In the great chamber South

Cayres	ij
Quishions	vj
Buffett stooles	ij
Turkey stoole	j

18-23 inclusive.

The inventory carries on to list bedding outside the house. It demonstrates that many members of the household were not housed within the walls of the main house. Four sets of bedding are given under the names of individuals, giving no indication of where they were housed, but the existence of a *gatehouse and external brewhouse are indicated by the other two entries. These cannot be associated with certainty with those buildings shown on Smythson's platt (**ill. 5**), although it is tempting to interpret them in this way.*

Bedding forthe of the house
Richerd Blacknalle

ffetherbedd	j	mattresse	j
Boulster	j	Pillowe	j
Blanket	j	Coverlettes	j

Edwarde Couchman

ffetherbed	j	Bolster	j
Blanket	j	Coverlett	j
Sheetes	ij		

The keep[er] at the Lodge

ffetherbedd	j	Boulster	j
Blankett	j	Mattresse	j
Coverlett	j	Sheetes	ij

Edward Wylde

ffetherbedd	j	Bolster	j
Blankett	j	Coverlett	j
Sheetes	ij		

ffrancis Warde

ffetherbedd	j	Coverlett	j

In the Brewhouse

ffetherbedd	j	Bolster	j
Coverlett	j		

The following entry suggests this inventory was compared with another, fuller, list which has not survived. Discrepancies and agreements are noted.

The diferences of these two Inventories

Beddes	43
Boulsteres	41
Mattresses	14
Wollebeddes	8
Rugges	7
Coverlettes	24
Spanish blankettes	22
Spanish quiltes	9
Coerse blankettes	24
Covered stooles	11
Quishions	16
Silke Curtaines	0
Pillowes	22
Longe Carpettes	0
Carpett for a cubbord	1
ffustian Blankettes	0
Tapisterie hanginges	22
Cloth Curtaines	2
Cannapies	0
Cayres covered	5
Turkey carpettes	0
Cubborde clothes of blue and greene cloth	0
Coverlettes of Tapisterie	0
Hanginges of darines	6
Olde peeces of darines	4
Saye Curtaines	0
Silke Testeres of beddes	0
Closse stooles	0
ffyer Pannes	0
Tonges	0
Bellowes	0
Candlestick Plates	0
Chaires of wood	0
Tapistrie Tester	0
Silke Quilt	0
Testeres of Redd cloth	0
Curtaines of the same	0
Old peeces of carpettes	0
Chamber pottes	0
Pannes for the closse stooles	0
Litle leatheren cayre	
Pillowe for a stoole	1

Mi I 8i   Inventory of 10th December 1596

This inventory was taken at the entry of Sir Francis' heir, Sir Percival Willoughby, less than a month after Sir Francis's death, which occurred on 16 November 1596. It does not cover all rooms, but makes a logical progression and provides easy identification of the rooms which are included.

An inventorie of beddinge in the new haule at Wollaton taken by Thomas Ware the 10th daie of December 1596. At the entrie of Percyvall Wylloughby.

Starting in the south-west corner, the inventory taker follows a roughly anti-clockwise route around the ground floor rooms.

1. The south-west corner chamber (3/19)
This was adjacent to the postern door to the south terrace and the garden beyond.
The Chamber by the gardain dore
Twoe ffetherbedds
One boulster
One pillowe
One spanish blankett
One kersie blankett
One holland quilte
One chaire and Twoe stooles

2. Inner chamber (3/20)
The inner chamber to the same.
One fetherbed
One boulstere
One pillowe

3. Dining Parlour (3/6)
The dyning parlour
Ffyve fetherbedds
One Mattresse
Ffower boulsters
Thre pillowes
Six Coverletts of dyvers stuff
ffower old thin blanketts, whereof one Bedd
Ffower old quilts
An old greasie boulstere
An old quishion without A cover
A Chare of Wallnuttee

4. South-east corner chamber (3/7)
Identified more clearly by the 1601 inventory, but also by entry 6.
The chappell chamber
One fetherbedd
One mattresse
One boulstere
One Spanish blankett
One Wollbed
One kersie blankett
One blew frish (flemish) Rugge
One Turkie chaire
One Turkie stoole
Twoe buffett stooles
ffower quishions

5. Inner chamber (3/8)
The inner chamber to the same
One fetherbedd
One mattresse
One boulstere
One pillowe
One kersie blankett
One coverlett

6. Painted chamber (3/9)
Note that this chamber had no inner chamber.
The painted chamber next the chappell chamber.
One fetherbedd
One Mattresse
One boulster
One pillowe
One kersie blankett
One redd blankett
One grene quilte

7. Painted chamber (3/10)
Thother painted chamber
One fetherbedd
One mattresse
Twoe boulsters
One pillowe
Twoe spanish blanketts
One Chequered rugge
One Canopie
One blew window curtaine
One Turkie stoole
One little buffet stoole

8. Inner chamber (3/11)
The inner chamber to the same
One fetherbedd
One mattresse
One boulstere
One kersie blankett
Twoe Coverletts

9. The north-east corner chamber (3/12)
The chamber over the wyne seller
One fetherbedd
One bouster
One mattres
Twoe pillowes
Thre Spanish blanketts
One Redd Rugge
One Redd quilt
Twoe Turkie Stooles
ffower pecs of hangings of Arras
One cupbord cloth of nedleworke
Twoe blew windowe Curtaines
One little nedleworke quishion
One stoole covered with velvett

10. Inner chamber (3/13)
The inner chamber to the same
One fetherbedd
One boulstere
Twoe kersie blanketts
One Spanishe blankett
One whyte frish (flemish) Rugge

11. The north-west corner chamber (3/15)
This is the only chamber with an inner chamber near the hall (front) door.
The chamber by the hall dore
One fetherbedd, One mattresse
One wollbedd, Twoe boulsters
One pillowe, Two kersie blanketts
One grene coverlett
Twoe Joyned Chaires
ffower stooles
ffower Quisions

12. Inner chamber (3/14)
The inner chamber to the same
One fetherbedd
One boulster
One pillowe
One matteres
One kersie blankett
One Coverlett

13. The porter's lodge (3/2)
The porter's lodge
Twoe fetherbedds
Twoe boulsters
Twoe kersie blanketts
Twoe Coverletts

14. The wardrobe (3/3)
In the space of two months the wardrobe has been moved.
The wardrobe
Twelve fetherbedds
Eight boulsters

ffower pillowes
One quishion without A Cover
ffower wollbedds
Seaven spanish blanketts
Six pecs *(pieces)* of Dormix for hangings
Eightene pecs *(pieces)* of hangings, some of Arras & some of Tapistrie
Eightene curtains of blew cloth
Twoe great quishions
ffower covered stooles
A little grene spanish curtaine
A Drum

Having omitted only the service rooms behind the screens, (3/16, 3/17 and 3/18), the inventory taker proceedes upstairs.

15. The chamber by the north state suite *(2/5)*

The chamber on the left hand the kitchin staires
One fetherbedd
One boulster
One pillowe
Thre kersie blanketts
One chequered Rugg
One olde chaire

16. The chamber by the south state suite *(2/9)*

The chamber on the right hand the kitchin staires
One fetherbedd
Twoe boulsters
One matteres
One pillowe
Twoe Spanish blanketts
One yellowe quilt
One bedd tester emdrodered with the Armes of the Wylluyhbyes

17. The south state bed-chamber *(2/10)*

The best Chamber
One fetherbedd
One mattress
Two boulsters
One pillowe
Two Spanish blanketts
One chequered Rugg
Two covered stooles
One embrodered Chaire

18. Inner chamber *(2/11)*

The Inner chamber to the same.
One fetherbedd
One mattres
Twoe boulsters
One kersie blankett
One coverlett
One ioyned stoole

19. South Great Chamber *(2/8)*

This would have been used for state dining.
The dyninge chamber on the South side
Twoe chaires

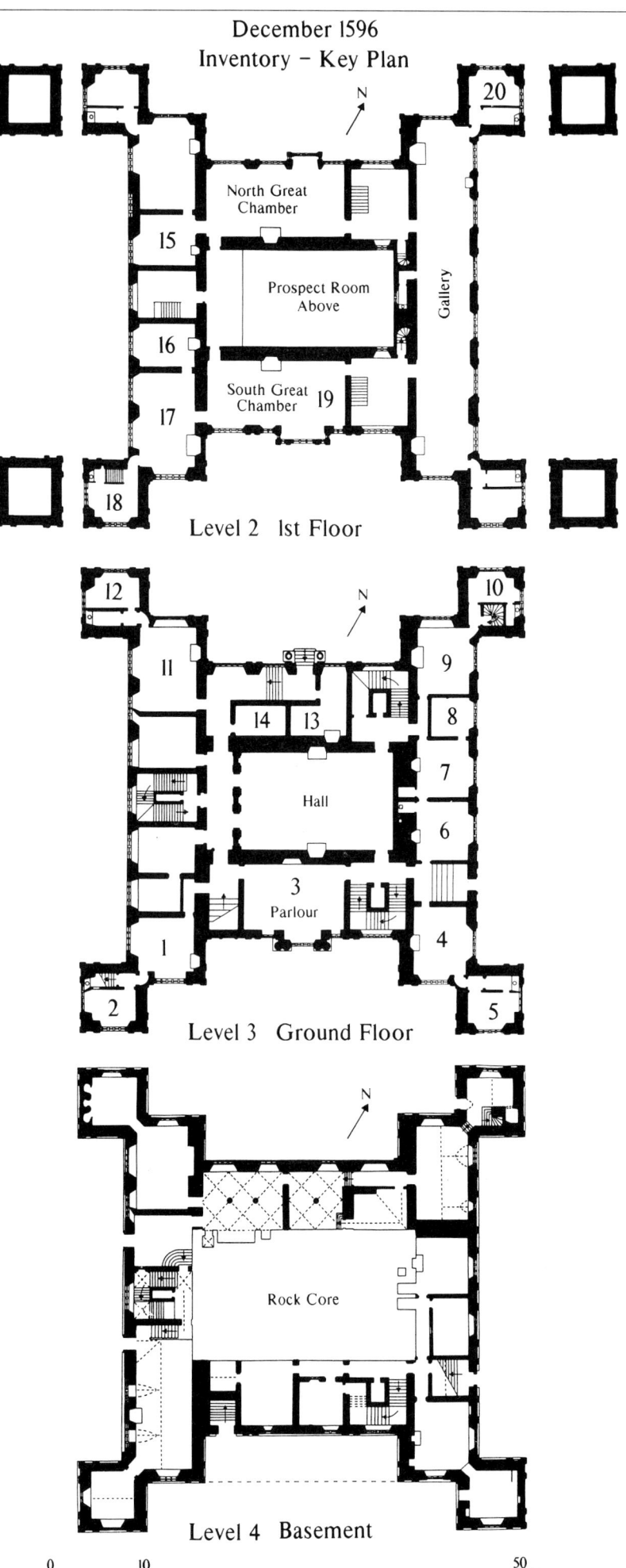

9. North state stair head
The 1601 inventory also mentions the space at the head of the N state staircase. The same item of furniture (one short table) is still there.
At the Gallary dore

10. The gallery (2/1)
In the Gallary

11. The north tower chamber off the gallery (2/2)
In the Gallary Chamber upon the North

12. The south tower chamber off the gallery (2/3)
N.B. By the true compass point, this is to the east.
In the Gallary chamber upon the East

13. The south state stairhead
At the East Gallary doore

14. The south-east turret chamber (1/3)
In the East Turret

15. ?
In the chamber under ye same chamber
This one presents a problem. There is no sign of a mezzanine chamber within the south-east turret chamber, yet it has been included in the tour of the leads. There is a mezzanine chamber above the east gallery tower chamber, but this is Georgian. In any case such a room would have been mentioned in association with the gallery room. Logically, it ought to be the W turret, which is otherwise the only turret chamber to be omitted.

16. North-east turret chamber (1/2)
In the North Turret

17. South-west turret chamber (2/4)
In the Sowthe Tower

18. Dining parlour (3/6)
In the parlour

19. South-west corner chamber (3/19)
The name commemorates the visit of the Duke of York in 1604
In the Dukes chamber

20. Inner chamber (3/20)
In the Inner chamber

21. The north-west corner chamber (3/15)
In the west Chambers next ye gates

22. Inner chamber (3/14)
In the Inner Chamber

23. Pantry (3/16)
In the pantry chamber

24. The north-east corner chamber (3/12)
In my Mr Bed Chamber

25. Inner chamber (3/13)
In the Inner Chamber

26. (3/10 or 3/7)
This is difficult to place because of the personal name attached to it, but is likely to be one of the bed-chambers on the east side. It has an inner chamber, so can only be one of the painted chambers (3/10) or the chapel chamber (3/7). Mrs Sturle (Strelley) was a married daughter of Sir Percival and Lady Bridget.[3]
In Mrs Sturles Chamber

27. Inner chamber (3/11 or 3/8)
In the Inner Chamber

28. The wardrobe (3/3)
In the wardroppe

29. An outbuilding
A small quantity of bedding was delivered.
Delivered to the dairy house

30. ?
This cannot be identified. It contained only one mattress.
In Will Gore's chamber

31. The cook's chamber (4/3i)
In the Cookes chamber

32. The porter's lodge (3/2)
In the porters Lodge

33. ?
This cannot be identified.
In Margrites chamber

[3] She was married in 1606, but probably widowed fairly soon afterwards. Chandos (ed. Wood 1958), 58 and note 1

Table of Inventories

room	12 Oct 1596	10 Dec 1596	7 Oct 1599	8 Oct 1601	24 Sept 1607
1/1				The high chamber over the hall [28]	
1/2				The N tower chamber upon the leads [30]	In the N turret [16]
1/3				The E tower chamber upon the leads [29]	In the E turret [14]
1/4				The S tower chamber upon the leads [31]	The South tower [17]
2/1			The gallery [27]	The gallery [26]	The gallery [10]
2/2		The chamber in the N end of the gallery [20]		The corner chamber at the N end of the gallery [25]	The gallery chamber upon the N [11]
2/3					The gallery chamber upon the E [12]
2/4	The great chamber north [16]		The north great chamber [6]	The north great chamber [24]	In the great chamber next to the Queen's chamber [8]
2/5		The chamber on the left hand of the kitchen stairs [15]	<one of the> two little chambers at the kitchen stair head [3]	The chamber at the head of the kitchen stairs westward [21]	The chamber next to the Queen's chamber [6]
2/6				The chamber at the S end of the N great chamber [22]	The Queen's chamber [5]
2/7				The inner chamber [23]	The inner chamber next to the Queen's chamber [7]
2/8	In the great chamber south [17]	The dining chamber on the south side [19]	The south great chamber [7]	The south great chamber [13]	The great chamber next the garden [1]
2/9		The chamber on the right hand of the kitchen stairs [16]	<one of the> two little chambers at the kitchen stair head [3]	The chamber at the head of the kitchen stairs eastwards [20]	The chamber next the prince's chamber [4]
2/10	The best chamber [9]	The best chamber [17]	The best chamber [1]	The chamber at the S end of the S great chamber alias the best chamber [14]	The prince's chamber [2]
2/11	The inner chamber to the same [10]	The inner chamber to the same [18]	The inner chamber to the same [2]	The inner chamber to the best chamber [18]	The inner chamber [3]
2/11i				The chamber over it (i.e. 2/11) [19]	
NS				At the stair head of the N great chamber [27]	At the gallery door [9]
SS				In a little room at the stair foot of the S great chamber [12]	At the E gallery door [13]
3/2	The Porter's Lodge [8]	The Porter's Lodge [13]	The Porter's Lodge [19]	The Porter's Lodge [33]	The Porter's Lodge [32]
3/3	The chamber next to the gate [11]	The Wardrobe [14]		The Wardrobe [42]	The Wardrobe [28]
3/5				The hall [1]	
3/6	The Dining Parlour [1]	The Dining Parlour [3]	The Gentlewomen's chamber (?) [25]	The Dining Parlour [8]	The Parlour [18]
3/7	The Chapel chamber [2]	The Chapel chamber [4]	The Chapel chamber [8]	The east corner chamber at the head of the hall else the Chapel chamber [6]	Mrs Sturles chamber (?) [26]
3/8		The inner chamber to the same [5]	The inner <sic> to the same [9]	Inner chamber [7]	Inner chamber to Mrs Sturles chamber (?) [27]
3/9		The painted chamber next the chapel chamber [6]	The painted chamber [10]	The two painted chambers [5]	
3/10		The other painted chamber [7]	In my old L<adi>e chamber [11]	The two painted chambers [5]	Mrs Sturles chamber (?) [26]
3/11		The inner chamber to the same [8]			Inner chamber to Mrs Sturles chamber (?) [27]
3/12	The NE corner chamber [3]	The chamber over the wine cellar [9]	My Mr chamber [26]	The N corner chamber at the head of the hall [2]	My Mr bed chamber [24]
3/13	The inner chamber to the same [4]	The inner chamber to the same [10]		The inner chamber [3]	The inner chamber [25]

APPENDICES 111

Table of inventories

room	12 Oct 1596	10 Dec 1596	7 Oct 1599	8 Oct 1601	23 Sept 1609
3/13i				A little chamber over the last [4]	
3/14	The inner chamber to the same (i.e. 3/15) [7]	The inner chamber to the same (i.e. 3/15) [12]	The inner chamber to the same (i.e. 3/15) [24]		The inner chamber (to 3/15) [22]
3/15	The North west corner chamber [6]	The chamber by the hall door [11]	The chamber next the Porter's lodge [23]		The west chamber next the gate [21]
3/16	The Pantry chamber [5]			The Pantry [15]	The Pantry chamber [23]
3/17	The chamber next the wardrobe [12]			The buttery and cellar [16]	
3/18	The warderobe [13]		The old warderobe [4]	The butler's chamber [17]	
3/18i			The inner chamber to the same [5]		
3/19	The southwest chamber [14]	The chamber by the garden door [1]	The garden chamber [12]	The south corner chamber at the foot of the Hall [9]	The Duke's chamber [19]
3/20	The inner chamber to the same [15]	The inner chamber to the same [2]	The two inner chambers to the same [13]	The inner chamber [10]	The inner chamber [20]
3/20i				The chamber over the last [11]	
4/2				The outermost kitchen [38]	
4/3				The pastry [37]	
4/3i			The cook's chamber [14]	The cook's chamber [36]	The cook's chamber [31]
4/4				The inner kitchen [39]	
4/5				The larder [40]	
4/6				The saucery [41]	
4/9				The buttery and cellar [16]	
4/12 4/13 4/14 4/17 4/18		Quelp<'s chamber>	The Taylor's chamber [15] Daniel Farrand's chamber [16] Edward Maidcock's chamber [17] The next chamber to it [18]	The yeomen's lodgings [34]	Will Gore's chamber [30] Margrite's chamber [33]
4/15				The gardener's chamber [35]	
outbuildings	The Lodge [20] The Brewhouse [23]		The little chamber in the garden [28] The maids' chamber [29] The warrener's lodge [30] The house where the kitchen boys lieth [31]	The feather house [31]	The dairyhouse [29]
other chambers outside	Richard Blacknall [18] Edward Couchman [19] Edward Wible [21] Francis Ward [22]	Mr Blacknall Edward Cockeman Edward Wyble Francis Ward			

Numbers in brackets represent the position of the room in the appropriate original inventory

APPENDIX II

A Geophysical Survey on the NW or Entrance Front

by Dr P Strange — **Department of Electrical Engineering, University of Nottingham**

Introduction

Robert Smythson's original design for Wollaton Hall proposed a scheme of outbuildings, courtyards and gardens in the form of a regular square, three units by three units in size, with the Hall occupying the central area (**ill. 5**). Whether this arrangement was in fact executed is not certain. Documentary references suggest that it was, but later landscaping, buildings, gardens and paths now overlie much of the area of the proposed outbuildings. A Geophysical survey offers a practical alternative to excavation for locating wall foundations or destruction material from the original structures. Unfortunately, on this side of the building only the potential site of the gate and the possible

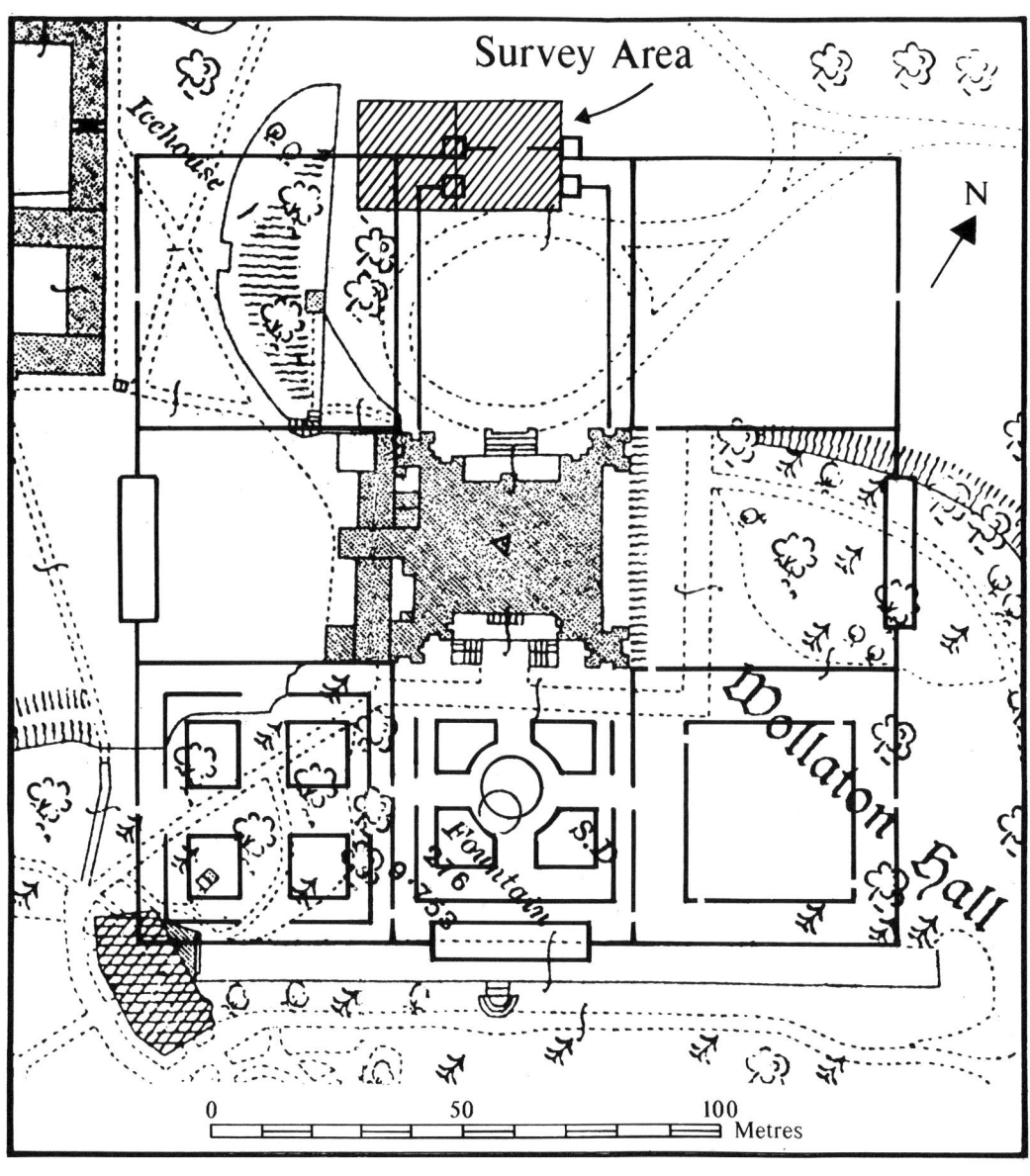

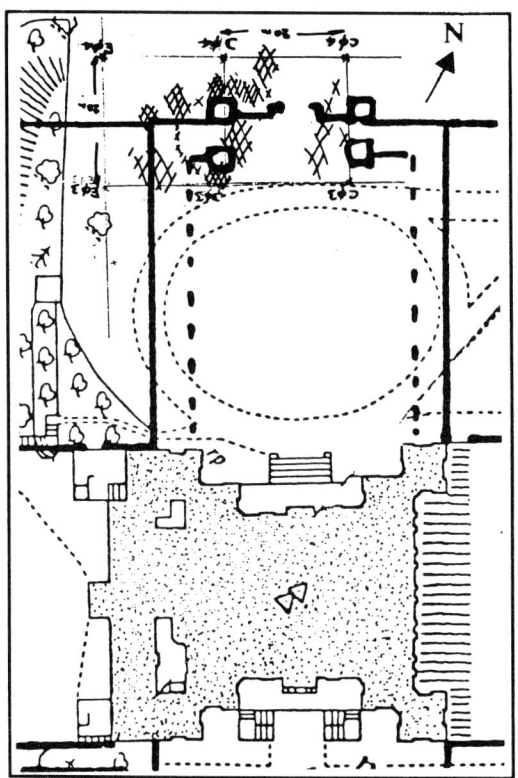

building in the SW outer courtyard wall is unencumbered by tarmac and later disturbances. The survey carried out in July and November 1990 therefore concentrated on the anticipated area of the entrance gateway.

The Survey

Resistivity readings were made over two 20 by 20 metre squares, laid out as shown in **ill. 63**, with the hope of locating the gate piers and parts of the flanking walls of the entrance courtyard. Using a split-dipole arrangement, measurements were made at one-metre intervals over this area to produce 800 measurements in all; these are shown in **ill. 64**, after processing.

Conclusions

The results of the survey are superimposed on the ground plan of Smythson's design as **ill. 65**. It is possible that the two blocks of high resistivity reading may indicate the position of the two SW gate piers and destruction material from them spreading northwards down the slope. A large trench has clearly been cut at some time to the north of them, and there are signs of other disturbance to the ground to the south. It was clear that considerable debris was scattered over much of the area under consideration. In the very dry conditions in July areas of burned grass showed up the positions of rubble, crossed by areas of green grass indicating that the area had been disturbed by recent trenching through this material. In view of these disturbances the survey in this area must be regarded as inconclusive, but it certainly does not contradict the evidence of the design plan.

Ill. 63 (left): General plan showing the location of the geophysical survey. Drawing by P. Strange.

Ill. 64 (below): Processed results of the geophysical survey. Drawing by P. Strange.

Ill. 65 (above): Interpretative sketch of the geophysical survey. Drawing by P. Strange.

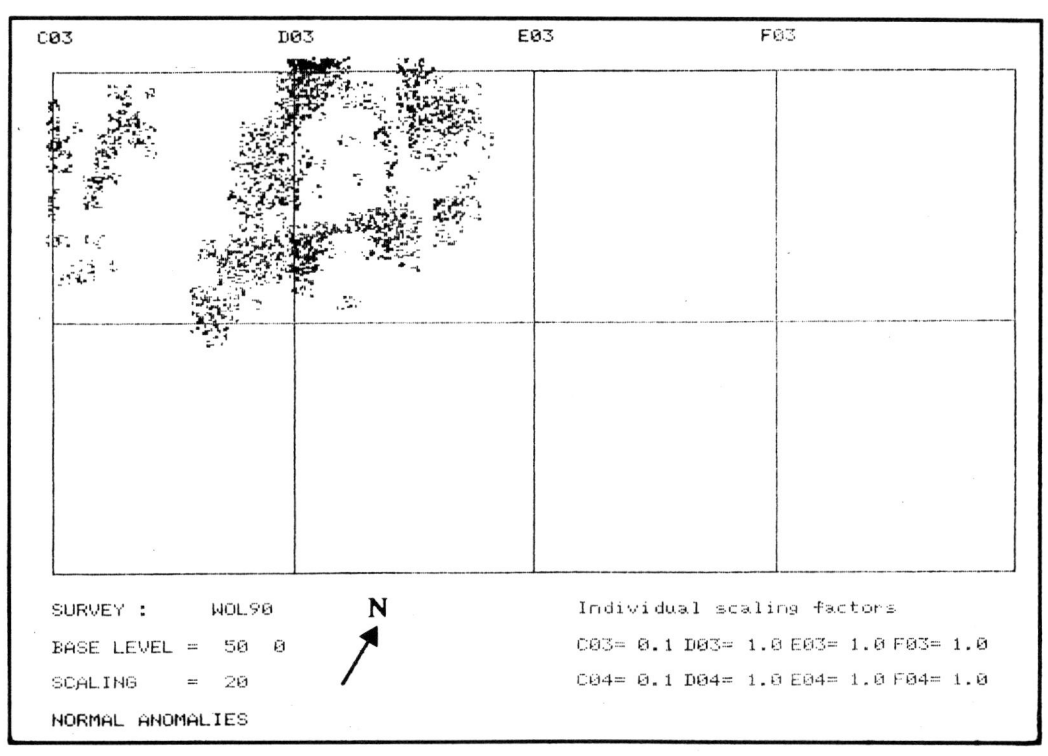

APPENDIX III

Notes on Wollaton Hall Bricks

by Dr. R. Firman *Department of Archaeology, University of Nottingham,*

Dr. R. Firman was able to examine some of the bricks in the external Ale Cellar and in room 3/18i *in situ*. A sample of the same type of brick [which was lying on the cellar floor] was subsequently removed for analysis in the laboratory

Bricks examined included a few in an original rear-arch in room 3/18i, where they happened to be exposed (the Hall is now thought to be essentially a brick building faced with Ancaster Limestone), and in external cellars of uncertain age. Subsequently, later bricks in garden walls, in paving and in the walls of the Industrial Museum and adjacent buildings, were studied for comparative purposes.

The broad conclusions of these investigations are:-

i) In so far as they could be examined adequately (by touch *in situ*, with rare glimpses of the internal fabric and no opportunity to study faces other than headers and stretchers) bricks in the hall and the older (type 1) bricks in the cellars do appear to be the same size and have similar fabrics.

ii) Bricks of a similar size and fabric do not appear to be present elsewhere either in the grounds or ancillary buildings, although there are both larger and smaller bricks with similar fine-grained fabrics to those in the cellars.

iii) The later bricks in the cellars (type 2) appear to be identical to those used for paving in front of the toilets and along the west front. (NB these bricks are characterised by a possible tally or identification mark, apparently inscribed with a stick along the length of the upper face, the like of which neither my wife nor I have ever seen before. Possibly they were so inscribed before they were fired so that they could be easily distinguished, when the kiln was opened, from bricks made with another sort of clay).

iv) Both the early and later bricks in the cellars and those in the hall appear to be made from Coal Measures clay, as were most of the bricks used for paving in the grounds. All other bricks in garden walls and ancillary buildings seem likely to be made from Keuper Marl (now termed Mercia Mudstones) which from the mid-17th century onwards was extensively exploited at Mapperley but was available nearer to hand (eg. in the University Park).

v) The similarity of the bricks in the house and the early cellar bricks (i.e. most of them) strongly supports the view that the cellars are earlier in date rather than later. The lack of any comparable later bricks elsewhere (item ii) above further supports this thesis. There are, however, two features which suggest that they are not Elizabethan:-

a) the fabric of the cellar bricks is utterly different from the stony, heterogeneous, boulder clay bricks which typify most Tudor bricks up to c.1550 in the East Midlands (e.g. Kirby Muxloe, Bradgate, Holme Pierrepont, Edwalton church tower, Kneesall, Hodsock etc.). Nor do they resemble the fine grained but very plastic bricks of, say Gainsborough.

b) The cellars are very elegantly made of essentially only two brick types, namely, a conventional 'brick-shaped' brick and a quarter round bullnose variety for quoins. This latter was not much used, if at all, for pre-Reformation brickwork, chamfered or more elaborate mouldings being preferred. The simplicity of the cellars contrasts very much with the elaborate early to mid-16th century brickwork with which I am familiar. It also contrasts with the flamboyance of the architecture of Wollaton as a whole but this is a matter outside my own speciality.